D1084565

Opening the door

International Library of Social Policy

General Editor Kathleen Jones

Professor of Social Administration
University of York

Arbor Scientiae
Arbor Vitae

A catalogue of the books available in the **International Library of Social Policy** and other series of Social Science books published by Routledge & Kegan Paul will be found at the end of this volume.

Opening the door

A study of new policies for the mentally handicapped

Kathleen Jones

with

John Brown, W. J. Cunningham
Julian Roberts and Peter Williams

Routledge & Kegan Paul
London and Boston

First published in 1975
by Routledge & Kegan Paul Ltd
Broadway House, 68–74 Carter Lane,
London EC4V 5EL and
9 Park Street,
Boston, Mass. 02108, USA
Set in Times Roman
and printed in Great Britain by
Willmer Brothers Limited, Birkenhead
© Kathleen Jones 1975

ISBN 0 7100 8139 1

Contents

Preface   xv

1 The policy background   1
  The Mental Health Act, 1959   3
  The Tizard studies   4
  Circular HM (65) 104   6
  The Ely inquiry   6
  Put Away   9
  Labour policy, 1968–70   11
  Conservative policy, 1970–2   11
  The White Paper and after   13

2 The hospitals   16
  Siting and buildings   18
  Staff–patient relationships   20
  'Good' and 'bad' wards   23
  Sanctions and privileges   25
  Patient–patient relations   26
  Patient activities   27
  Pocket money   28
  Patients' food   29
  Patients' clothing   30
  Objectives and ideology   31
  Leadership   34
  Staff relations   37
  Rehabilitation staff   39
  External relations   40
  Conclusion   41

3 Life on the wards: needs and resources   42
  The wards   42
  The patients   47
  The staff   62

4 Nursing attitudes   67

   Principles of the 1971 White Paper   67
   Treatment Orientation Scale   68
   Research literature   69
   Methodology   70
   Age, sex, marital status   71
   Work pattern   72
   Previous experience   74
   Length of service   75
   Qualifications   75
   Nationality   79
   Summary   79
   Statements in the Treatment Orientation Scale   80
   Scores on the Treatment Orientation Scale   81
   Responses to attitude statements   83
   Summary   93

5 Problems of the 'back wards'   96

   Ward 99   97
   The 'back ward' syndrome   104
   The centrality of routine   119
   Conclusion   124

6 Hospital and community   131

   Research design   132
   Family and personal contacts   133
   Neighbourhood contacts   140
   Official contacts   147
   Conclusions   150

7 Community care   154

   The ten-year plans   156
   The training centres   162
   Hostels   167
   Other forms of residential care   178
   Social work services   179
   Relations with the health services   180
   Conclusion   183

8 The idea and the reality   185

The problems of violence   186
The economic formulation   188
The eugenic formulation   188
'Normalisation' as the answer   190
Deviancy theory as the answer   190
A fresh assessment   191
Professional lack of fit   195
A new 'caring profession'   197
The problem of inertia   202

9 Summary and conclusions   205

Recommendations   207

Postscript   213

Appendix 1: a case conference at Maple Grange   217
Appendix 2: time schedule for the project   221
Appendix 3: checklist on hospitals for the mentally
            handicapped as social sub-systems   223
Appendix 4: job description for community
            service organisers   226
Appendix 5: notes on the methodology of the
            attitude survey   228

Notes   243

Index   253

Tables

1.1 Changes in services for the mentally handicapped, proposed in Cmnd 4683, 1971   2

3.1 Annual number of admissions per 100 occupied beds, Gateshire Region and England and Wales, 1968–72   48

3.2 Annual number of departures per 100 occupied beds, Gateshire Region and England and Wales, 1968–72   48

3.3 First admissions, Gateshire Region and England and Wales, 1966–72 (first admission as a percentage of all admissions)   49

3.4 Patients referred to local authority on discharge, by sex and hospital: Gateshire Region, 1971   50

3.5 Census sample: sex and age   51

3.6 Census sample: age groups in comparison with home population (Great Britain)   52

3.7 Census sample: in-patient rates per 100,000 regional population, by age and sex   52

3.8 Census sample: length of stay to date   53

3.9 Incontinence   54

3.10 Physical mobility   54

3.11 Feeding, washing and dressing   55

3.12 Vision, hearing and speech   55

3.13 Ability to read, write and count   56

3.14 Behaviour problems   57

3.15 Ability to wash self, by sex   58

3.16 Ability to dress self, by sex   58

3.17 Aggressive behaviour, by sex   58

3.18 Anxious behaviour, by sex   58

3.19 Patients requiring continuous process care   60

3.20 Nursing staff, by sex and whole-/part-time   63

3.21 Nursing staff, by grade and whole-/part-time   63

3.22 Rehabilitation staff   64

4.1 Ward staff, by ward grade for the total, sample and respondent populations   71

A*

4.2   Ward grade and sex   71
4.3   Ward grade and age   72
4.4   Ward grade and marital status   72
4.5   Day shift, by ward grade, sex and whole-/part-time   73
4.6   Night shift, by ward grade, sex and whole-/part-time   73
4.7   Nursing assistants, by age and day/night shifts   73
4.8   Nursing assistants, by age and whole-/part-time   74
4.9   Hospital mobility, by ward grade   74
4.10 Ward grade, by length of nursing service with the
      mentally handicapped   75
4.11 SENs, by method of enrolment and length of service   76
4.12 SENs, by sex and method of enrolment   76
4.13 Registered nurses, by sex and qualifications   77
4.14 Registered nurses, by RNMS and date of last
      qualification   78
4.15 Registered nurses, by sex and date of last qualification   78
4.16 Ward grade, by country of origin   79
4.17 Scores obtained by the four grades of ward staff on
      the Treatment Orientation Scale   82
6.1   Situation and size of hospitals in community survey   133
6.2   Patients' contacts with families and friends   134
6.3   Visiting, by age groups   135
6.4   Visiting, by length of stay   135
6.5   Patients with homes: distance from home to hospital   136
6.6   Distance from home, by hospital   136
6.7   Percentage of patients receiving visits and going home,
      by hospital   137
6.8   Percentage of patients receiving visits and going
      home, by age   139
6.9   'Parole' patients at each hospital and between urban
      and rural hospitals   142
6.10 Patients going into the community: urban and rural
      hospitals   142
6.11 Voluntary groups entering hospitals and engaged in
      direct contact with patients   144
6.12 Patients taken on hospital outings and holidays   148
7.1   Planned increase and actual increase in training centre
      places, 1962 and 1972   156
7.2   Planned increase and actual increase in training centre
      places per thousand population, 1962 and 1972   157

7.3 Actual places in training centres, 1972, plans for
1981 and White Paper requirements   158

7.4 Additional places in training centres for hospital-
based patients, 1972, plans for 1981 and White Paper
requirements   158

7.5 Planned increase and actual increase in hostel places,
1962 and 1972   159

7.6 Planned increase and actual increase in number of
hostels, 1962 and 1972   160

7.7 Hostel beds, 1972; plans for 1981 and White Paper
requirements   160

7.8 Boarding out/lodging places, 1972, plans for 1981
and White Paper requirements   161

7.9 Comparison of social skills: trainees and hospital
patients   164

7.10 Hostel residents, by age and sex   169

7.11 Hostel residents and hospital patients: incontinence 170

7.12 Hostel residents and hospital patients: physical mobility 170

7.13 Hostel residents and hospital patients: feeding, washing
and dressing   171

7.14 Hostel residents and hospital patients: vision,
hearing and speech   171

7.15 Hostel residents and hospital patients: reading,
writing and counting   172

7.16 Hostel residents and hospital patients: behaviour
problems   173

7.17 Destination of residents leaving hostels during 1972,
by sex   174

A.1 Total ward grade percentage figures for the Gateshire
Region compared to sample percentage figures   231

A.2 Ward grade, staff working part-time in the total and
sample populations in the Gateshire Region (percentage) 231

A.3 Discriminatory power ranking of attitude statements
in the Treatment Orientation Scale   240

Figures

4.1 Responses of trained and untrained staff to statement 20: 'There is a sharp dividing line between "normal" and "mentally subnormal"'   84

4.2 Responses of trained and untrained staff to statement 11: 'Patients should be sterilised'   85

4.3 Responses of trained and untrained staff to statement 4: 'Promiscuity and mental subnormality go hand in hand'   85

4.4 Responses of trained and untrained staff to statement 5: 'Once a nurse has been trained in mental subnormality, he has all the knowledge he needs for the care of patients'   86

4.5 Responses of trained and untrained staff to statement 10: 'When looking after patients, ability and commonsense are more important than formal training'   87

4.6 Responses of trained and untrained staff to statement 15: 'Kindness is more important than a therapeutic programme for patients'   88

4.7 Responses of trained and untrained staff to statement 3: 'Therapy can achieve little with low-grade patients'   89

4.8 Responses of trained and untrained staff to statement 19: 'Little can be done to help low-grade patients to improve'   90

4.9 Responses of trained and untrained staff to statement 9: 'No one really knows why patients improve'   91

4.10 Responses of trained and untrained staff to statement 17: 'We cannot expect to understand the odd behaviour of patients'   91

4.11 Responses of trained and untrained staff to statement 14: 'The conditions of hospital wards are as good as they can be with the type of patient living there'   92

4.12 Responses of trained and untrained staff to statement 2: 'Doctors in this hospital just don't know what it is like on the ward first thing in the morning'   93

4.13 Responses of trained and untrained staff to statement
      16: 'Mental subnormality often leads to mental illness'   94
5.1   Nurse-patient interaction   111
5.2   The 'back ward' syndrome   120

Preface

Better Services for the Mentally Handicapped,

Better Services for the Mentally Handicapped, a White Paper setting out a plan for development in the next ten or fifteen years, was published in April 1971. It followed a period of unprecedented public concern and agitation about the conditions of mentally handicapped people in hospital. The reports of the committees of inquiry at Ely and Farleigh Hospitals were still very much in the public mind, and had been paralleled by many smaller and more local inquiries into allegations of ill-treatment. Dr Pauline Morris's national survey, *Put Away* (1969), had documented the state of the hospitals in great detail, and had suggested some remedies. The Hospital Advisory Service had been set up under the direction of Dr A. A. Baker, and had toured hospitals for the mentally handicapped, among others, making some very critical comments and recommendations for improvement. R. H. S. Crossman, as Secretary of State for the Social Services in the Wilson Government, had carried out a number of personal visits to hospitals, and had taken a strong interest in reform. A Labour White Paper, based on work by Professor Peter Townsend and other expert advisers, was in draft when the Conservatives won the General Election of 1970.

If the political slant changed, the interest was no less great. Sir Keith Joseph shared his predecessor's concern, and the determination to improve the conditions of the mentally handicapped did not slacken. The White Paper, produced less than a year after the change of government, was the culmination of the process.

These events, which are dealt with more fully in chapter 1, form the background to the present survey. In July 1971, three months after the publication of the White Paper, a Regional Hospital Board (hereafter referred to as the Gateshire Regional Hospital Board) asked the Department of Social Administration and Social Work in the University of York to study services for the mentally handicapped in the light of the new policies, and to recommend action.

Why yet another survey? In the first stage of the work, we were repeatedly asked this question by staff at all levels. Some had worked in hospitals which formed part of Dr Morris's national sample, most had been involved in visits by HAS teams. It was not surprising that they felt that they had had enough good advice; they simply wanted to be left to get on with the job.

There were three reasons why we felt that a fresh study was worth while. First, though there was a good deal of information available about hospitals, and a scattering of studies about the community services, nobody had looked at the two together, as complementary parts of a single system. The guidelines laid down in *Better Services for the Mentally Handicapped* meant that the old antitheses of 'hospital or community' were obsolete; we had to think in terms of both, and in terms of a complex interweaving of services between them. A study which could take as its base the area of a Regional Hospital Board (about one-fourteenth of England and Wales) and look at all the services within its boundaries therefore had a special relevance.

Second, while we greatly admired much of the work which had been done in the 1960s, we felt that there was room for a new approach. Sociologists, reformers and administrators had alike worked *de haut en bas* – formulating new policies and standards, and judging the hospitals and their staffs in the light of them. This was valuable, but we had some sympathy with the often overworked and frustrated staff who had to carry the daily problems of care in the face of continuing public criticism. We thought that there was room for a survey which started from the actual situation as they and their patients experienced it and worked up to what was possible in the way of amelioration, rather than starting from abstract principles and working downwards. This empirical and inductive approach has its limitations; but if it is more modest in scope and intention, it may be more securely based, for it offers real possibilities of change with staff co-operation.

Third, we believed that the process of introducing new social policies does not end with national statements. The Morris team, the committees of inquiry and the HAS teams all, in different contexts, looked at *what was wrong*. The major shortcomings of the services were exposed, and proposals were made for remedying them; but the implementation of such proposals is often uneven and curiously slow. At this stage, it is useful to focus on another set of problems. Social policy is not only made in State departments and in senior common rooms. It is the product of thousands of decisions, large and small, made at different levels by different people up and down the country. The process of the percolation of policy down through

Boards and committees to the level where the service actually meets
the patient involves problems of administration and of societal and
personal attitudes which it is important to study in their own right.
The gap between policy formulation and local implementation can
often be very great. T. S. Eliot expressed this (perhaps in a more
cosmic sense) in *The Hollow Men*:

Between the idea and the reality
Between the motion and the act
Falls the Shadow.

So there were good reasons for 'yet another survey'. We hoped
that our investigations would go some way towards closing the gap
between the idea and reality for the mentally handicapped.

The Regional Board needed the information quickly, as a basis
for policy decisions. Social scientists prefer to work slowly, recruiting a balanced team, developing a body of theory on which to base
hypotheses, setting up their own means of collecting statistical data,
because they do not really trust anyone else's figures; but the social
services will not stand still while we do these things, and there is
always the risk that by the time the data is worked over to our
academic satisfaction, it will be too far out of date to be of any
practical use.

After discussion, the two members of academic staff involved
decided to invite into the team four higher-degree students and a
graduate secretary, who were already on the campus and could
start work in September (within eight weeks of the Board's offer).
With intensive work, we thought that we could produce an interim
report by Christmas 1972, and this was in fact achieved.

Notes on the time schedule are given in Appendix 2. However,
in order to explain the shape of the study, it is necessary to describe
here the four main stages of the project. Stage I involved intensive
seminar work, the collection and circulation of background data
and general policy discussion. Chapter 1 on 'The policy background'
is based on the work of this period. An interim version was published in the *Year Book of Social Policy in Britain, 1971* (ed. K.
Jones, Routledge & Kegan Paul, 1972). Stage II involved members
of the team in continuous daily contact with given groups of hospitals, the 26 hospitals and units of the Region being split between
them. This lasted from three to five months, with a full day's team
discussion once a week, and resulted in the general introduction
to the hospitals in chapter 2.

In Stage III we decided to concentrate on specific problems in areas where recommendations could be made for action in the relatively near future. This pragmatic approach excluded, at least for the time being, a number of interesting and worthwhile areas of more fundamental study, such as the broad question of public attitudes to mental handicap. The eventual choice was limited to five areas: a study of available statistics; a study of nursing attitudes; a study of ward management problems; a study of hospital–community relations; and a study of local authority community care provisions. The team changed direction, each member taking responsibility for one area of study throughout the Region. At this stage, five post-graduate students on the course for the diploma in social administration were added to the team on a two-day-a-week basis and they were able to take on sections of the work as dissertation topics. Reports on these issues form the basis of chapters 3–7.

Finally, there was the task of reducing something like half a million words to a single report, of redrafting, carrying out subsidiary checking investigations, verifying and updating.

It is not often that research of this kind can be carried out on such a highly-organised model. Under the pressure of necessity, we think we have learned something about research organisation as well as the needs of the mentally handicapped. The key factors were team cohesion and a high level of motivation.

In addition to the group named as co-authors, we should like to thank Ajmal Ahmad, Sally Ashman, Pamela Barr, Hilary Follett, John Lewis, Susan Sladden, Sandra Smith and Elizabeth Urben for their contributions both to the survey material and to the frequent team discussions. We also acknowledge with gratitude the assistance of Dr Norman Rea of the Department of Education, Dr John Beddington of the Department of Biology and Dr R. J. Lavers of the Institute of Social and Economic Research, University of York; of Mr Vincent Gorman, Principal Nursing Officer, Northgate Hospital, Morpeth; of Dr Pauline Morris in making available the ward schedules used in *Put Away*; of the medical, nursing and administrative staff of the 26 hospitals and units; of the staff of the 11 local authority Social Services Departments; and above all of the Regional Hospital Board, which not only initiated and financed the survey, but started action on a number of our recommendations before it was overtaken by the process of Health Service reorganisation.

1   The policy background

The proposals of the White Paper on the mentally handicapped,[1] published in June 1971, were both simple and sweeping. In the past, provision for the mentally handicapped had been heavily concentrated on hospital beds. There were some 59,000 beds in England and Wales, many of them in old and isolated buildings originally designed for custodial care, and quite unsuited to modern needs. In the future, hospitals would be primarily used for treatment, not residential care. They would provide for in-patients, day patients and out-patients, and have co-ordinated therapeutic programmes. Psychiatrists would play an increasing role in the provision of genetic counselling, early detection and assessment services, working in a variety of administrative settings such as children's departments in district general hospitals or clinics. Local authorities would take on the responsibility for providing residential care in small units which would be 'homes, not hostels', and also by such means as foster care, group homes and flatlets with social work support. The total cost of this reorganisation would be roughly £120 to £130 millions in capital. Development would be phased over fifteen to twenty years, though in some areas it might be completed in ten.

Detailed planning figures, given in table 5 of the White Paper, show a very great change in the balance of services. Hospital beds for adults would be cut by nearly 50 per cent. Beds for children would be maintained at something nearer their present level, but there would be expanding provision for day patients, both children and adults, amounting to a tenfold increase on present estimated figures. Residential provision 'in local authority, voluntary or privately-owned residential homes' would increase nearly seven-fold, while extra places would be found in foster homes and lodgings. The picture of hospital contraction and community care expansion is shown in Table 1.1.

This represents a net expansion of 16,950 places – and the plan specifically states that it does not take account of population growth or of the increasing longevity of the mentally handicapped, so it is expansion in real terms. In addition to the extended provision of

1

*Table 1.1   Changes in services for the mentally handicapped,
         proposed in Cmnd 4683, 1971*

Type of accommodation	No. of places, 1969	No. proposed	Increase/ decrease
Hospital			
In-patient (adults)	52,100	27,000	−25,100
In-patient (children)	7,400	6,400	−1,000
Day patient (adults)	500	4,900	+4,400
Day patient (children)	200	2,900	+2,700
Community care			
Residential homes (adults)	4,300	29,400	+25,100
Residential homes (children)	1,800	4,900	+3,100
Fostering, etc. (adults)	550	7,400	+6,850
Fostering, etc. (children)	100	1,000	+900

residential and day places, there would also be an expansion in
services: about a 30 per cent increase in educational services for
children of school age and an increase of over 40,000 vacancies in
training centres for adults.

The 1971 scheme fits well into post-Seebohm thinking. Local
authority Social Services Departments have been made responsible
for a very large development in residential care at a time when the
scattered residential provision of the past – old people's homes,
homes for the physically disabled, approved schools, children's
homes and hostels for the mentally ill and mentally handicapped –
is being co-ordinated into one system. The importance of this work
in terms of money and staffing is such that many authorities have
appointed an Assistant Director (Residential Services) to carry out
the task. The teaching of all mentally handicapped children, whether
in their own homes, in community homes, or in hospital, is already
in the hands of local authority Education Departments, who took
over responsibility for education services in hospitals on 1 April
1971. The health services are to give up doing things which are not
really part of their brief, and to concentrate on their own proper
tasks – hospital accommodation for those who need constant nursing services because of the severity of handicap, and clinical treatment on an in-patient, day patient and out-patient basis. Specialists
are to move into closer contact with general medicine, and the whole
clinical team into community medicine. These trends conform also

to the patterns of management proposed for the reorganised National Health Service.[2]

The intention is that the mentally handicapped will no longer be treated in a segregated, second-class service, but will take an increasing part in the general provision of social, educational and health services for the whole population. Lines of demarcation which have hampered developments in the past are to be removed, developments which are in accord with current social and administrative thinking are to take place and the promise of more money should be an earnest of good intentions. All we need now is goodwill, co-operation and clear priorities.

So much for the official picture; but civil servants do not write in a vacuum, and in order to evaluate the solutions proposed to the problems of the mentally handicapped, it is necessary to summarise fourteen years of controversy. (Or perhaps 'controversy' is too strong a word. We have controversies about social insurance or housing, but in the study of mental handicap, not enough people care about the problem to engender heat. One expert speaks, and there is a long silence. Then another says something rather different, and there is another long silence. So it goes on.)

The Mental Health Act, 1959

The first pronouncement in the series came from the Royal Commission on Mental Illness and Mental Deficiency, 1954-7,[3] whose report formed the basis for the Mental Health Act. The Royal Commission spoke of 'a reorientation of the mental health services towards community care and away from hospital care except where the special facilities of the hospital service are needed'. Mental illness and what was retitled 'severe subnormality'[4] were to be known collectively as 'mental disorder'. Some people objected to this on semantic grounds, pointing out that 'dis-order' implied a prior state of order, which was patently not the case with the mentally handicapped, but the joint term was convenient and came into use.

The new provisions for the treatment of both the mentally ill and the mentally handicapped involved the abolition of existing forms of certification and the reclassification of most patients as of informal status. This was particularly satisfying to the National Council for Civil Liberties, whose pamphlet *50,000 Outside the Law* was widely current in the 1950s.[5] Mental Health Review Tribunals were set up to hear appeals against detention in the case of the minority now compulsorily detained. Local authorities were to provide an extension of residential and day training facilities. While the clinical differences between mental illness and mental handicap were well established, it was contended at the time by the responsible civil servants that administratively they might well be treated as one set of problems; mentally handicapped and mentally ill could share the same training centres, the same hostels, perhaps the same hospitals. Experience has not borne out this suggestion, and the present trend is to treat the two separately once more. They remain, however, yoked together by the Mental Health Act. The difficulty of integrative social action, in this or any other field of social policy, is that it does not protect the rights of minority groups, and the mentally handicapped, being a smaller and more static group than the mentally ill, have sometimes been overlooked as a result.

The Tizard studies

One of the most powerful influences on thinking about mental handicap was (and still is) the work of Professor Tizard and his colleagues at the Medical Research Council Social Psychiatry Unit at the Maudsley Hospital. *The Social Problem of Mental Deficiency* (O'Connor and Tizard, Pergamon, 1956) had already had an influence on the thinking of the Royal Commission. *The Mentally Handicapped and their Families* (Tizard and Grad, Oxford University Press, 1961) provoked some serious thinking about the circumstances in which mentally handicapped children could be kept in their own homes, and what produced a breakdown in family care. Tizard's *Community Services for the Mentally Handicapped* (Oxford University Press, 1964) was a major publication containing four studies: a study of the prevalence of mental handicap in London and Middlesex, in which he contrasted 'ascertained prevalence' (the numbers of mentally handicapped who actually received services) with 'administrative prevalence' (the numbers who ought to receive services in a fully developed public health, education and welfare service); a study of family problems, summarised from the previous book; a study of educationally subnormal children; and the Brooklands study, which reported on the work of an experimental unit where imbecile children were treated on the principles developed in residential nurseries for children rather than on medical and nursing lines. In the early days, there were difficulties:[6]

... we were harassed by a multitude of problems that arose in

part because of the nature of the new venture and ... because of the lack of opportunity to make adequate preparation.
The staff were uncertain of how to behave in their new roles; the children were for the most part profoundly disturbed by their transfer from a familiar environment in which they had spent the greater part of their lives (for nearly all the children admitted to the hospital are under the age of five years); and much time and energy had to be spent in preparing equipment and in makeshift arrangements while we waited for equipment to arrive.

After a time, however, the success of the scheme was evident. It became clear that many of the children's problems arose from previous emotional deprivation and lack of one-to-one relationships, and there were 'marked and significant' changes in intelligence and language ability:[7]

> They became able to play socially and constructively at a level approaching that of their mental age. Emotionally they became much less maladjusted. ... They developed strong attachments to members of staff and to other children ... in all these respects, the behaviour of the children at Brooklands was in striking contrast to their earlier behaviour in the parent hospital, and to the behaviour of their peers who remained in the hospital.

These findings, later elaborated in King, Raynes and Tizard, *Patterns of Residential Care* (Routledge & Kegan Paul, 1971) were to have a profound effect on the training of nurses for the mentally handicapped. 'Normalisation' became the watchword as it became increasingly recognised that some at least of the problems of the mentally handicapped in hospital were of the hospitals' making. The publication of Russell Barton's *Institutional Neurosis* (Williams & Wilkins, Baltimore, 1958) and Goffman's *Asylums* (Doubleday, New York, 1961) had made a similar point, but without the specific empirical backing in the field of mental handicap which Tizard was able to give it.

Community Services for the Mentally Handicapped ends with a brief but well-argued case for 'an alternative form of administrative provision' based on a proposal for the integrated care of the mentally handicapped and their families in an area with a population of 100,000. This uses the argument, later to be echoed in the 1971

White Paper, that medical services for the mentally handicapped should 'form part of the general medical services of the community'. The distinction between institutional and community care should be minimised. Patients at home and in institutions, whether run by the Hospital Service or by local authorities, should share the same diagnostic and treatment services, the same schools and day centres, the same sheltered workshops and training centres. Though there might be administrative distinctions involved in where patients lived, they should not limit the facilities to which they had access. Considerable emphasis was laid on a diagnostic and counselling service, on day care, and on small family-type units.

Circular HM (65) 104

In 1965 a government circular was issued to Regional Hospital Boards, Hospital Management Committees and Boards of Governors of teaching hospitals, to give some official guidance. It reminded its readers of the recommendations of the Royal Commission of 1954–7 concerning the shift to community care, and urged the provision of adequate facilities for investigation and assessment. It provided a list of types of patients suited for in-patient admission, and of criteria for discharge. It spoke at length about the development of community teams, the importance of day care, making full use of services designed for the general population, and the evils of regimentation. However, the tone was vague ('adequate facilities must be provided ... special attention needs to be given to ... facilities should be available') and there were no precise targets or detailed statistical proposals.

The Ely inquiry

In July 1967 stimulus to action came from another quarter. The *News of the World* received from a correspondent serious allegations concerning the treatment of patients in Ely Hospital, near Cardiff. They very properly forwarded these to the Minister of Health, and published an article based on them on 20 August. An official inquiry was set up, and a report subsequently issued.[8] The hospital itself, built as a Poor Law industrial school for orphans and later a workhouse, was of 'grim and unalluring appearance'. In recent years it had, like many buildings of its kind, too solid to knock down and too expensive to replace, received the chintz-and-cream-paint treatment, so that it was pleasant enough inside, though of an unyieldingly institutional character. It was not overcrowded. It was not, as far as can be made out, seriously understaffed. Allegations of cruel treatment of male patients by male staff were carefully investigated, and in some cases held to be justified. An old man of eighty-seven had been struck; a deputy chief male nurse had sworn in referring to another patient. A third patient had been treated with 'undue roughness ... insensitivity ... laxity' and subjected to 'unjustifiably extended seclusion'. There was 'an unduly casual attitude towards death at Ely' coupled with, in some cases, 'unduly low standards of nursing conduct'. In the end, disciplinary action was taken against one male nurse.

Reading the report again three years after publication, one is struck by the acute contrast between the upper middle-class and professional world of the Committee of Inquiry, with its scrupulous sifting of dead evidence and its careful assessment of sometimes dubious informants, and the life on the ward, where patients and staff acted out a grim pattern of interaction. The patients themselves are described dispassionately – 'Addison', deformed, bearing injuries on his face from an accident forty years earlier, doubly incontinent, difficult to manage, often violent or obscene; 'Byron', severely subnormal, epileptic, suffering from psoriasis and epileptic attacks, doubly incontinent, dirty, pestering the other patients; 'Chaucer', severely subnormal, spastic, paraplegic, with faulty articulation. Such multiply disabled people are, by any definition, difficult to nurse. Whether the nursing staff included some people who were by nature coarse and brutal in their behaviour, whether the job made them so, or whether most of us would behave in the same sort of way if subjected to the same sort of work pressures is a matter for discussion rather than snap judgments. But there are some macabre little cameos; for instance, the case of 'Dryden', whose wife asked for his false teeth to be brought. A nurse brought a bowl full of teeth, saying that 'most belonged to dead patients' and 'proceeded to fit them by trial and error'; the case of the boys in Villa 2, where sixty patients were cared for by two staff at any one time. There was repeated testimony to their loss of weight, their filthy and stinking condition, and the appalling conditions of the wards.

And this was the British National Health Service in 1967. The really shocking thing was that, seen in one light, it was no one's fault. The Hospital Management Committee had been trying to get a nurses' training school, but without success. Their plans for the architectural improvement of Villa 2 had been held up for lack of money. They had long been trying to do something about an inefficient laundry system (an efficient one could have coped with the worst manifestations of incontinence). The physician superintendent was 'kindly', but his hands were tied because the traditional role of superintendent had been modified by the concept of tripartite administration, medical, lay and nursing. The chief male nurse was 'basically a good man', but without the training for the job. And all this had happened on the doorstep of a Regional Hospital Board with a strong tradition of research into hospital management and staffing problems. There was a recognition in other parts of the Hospital Service that what could happen at Ely could happen elsewhere, and that it could happen in basically well-run hospitals. There was no criticism at Ely of the female side of the hospital, and the Committee of Inquiry thought that the problems might be specific to particular wards or even particular shifts.

In another sense, it was everybody's fault. In the Committee of Inquiry's immortal phrase, 'nobody was batting for Ely'. Nobody, at any stage or at any level, generated the furious energy necessary to draw the problems of this particular hospital to the attention of the resource-controllers. A group of unambitious, well-intentioned people ambled along their accustomed path while the problems got worse around them. For instance, the junior hospital medical officer 'never failed to examine a patient when asked by a charge nurse' but was slow to use his own initiative: 'He makes no claim to specialist knowledge or experience of mental illness or subnormality, has attended no specialist conferences, reads no specialist literature. He has concerned himself almost exclusively with the organic disorders of his patients.'

The local authority had taken no action to provide community care. The voluntary societies had passed the hospital by – there was no League of Friends to provide extra comforts and prod the officials. Poor buildings, lack of money and untrained staff had resulted in low standards. Some of the staff knew this, but felt powerless to act. Meanwhile the situation had deteriorated on some wards from a custodial equilibrium in the days when staff were readily available and employing authorities could be selective, to a rough and squalid hell when they had to take what staff they could get. The immediate reaction was the scapegoating of one nurse; but something was clearly very wrong with hospitals for the mentally handicapped, and many people looked to Dr Pauline Morris's investigation, then already in progress, to pin-point the problems.

Put Away

The study, *Put Away*, financed by the National Society for Mentally Handicapped Children, was published in 1969.[9] It was based on a national sample of 35 hospitals, each of which was visited by members of the team with lengthy questionnaires. The report strongly confirms the Ely picture – the lack of energy and incentive in a low-prestige service, the failure to provide a coherent pattern of accountability and responsibility, the low standards and the intermittent squalor. Dr Morris is not unsympathetic to staff working in impossible conditions, and expresses their frustrations and dissatisfactions very clearly. In two hospitals, 'Cloverfield' and 'Blackbrick', she traced the progress of Circular HM (65) 104, with depressing results. At Cloverfield, it was welcomed:[10]

> By April, it had been discussed by both the Medical Advisory
> Committee and at a session of the Hospital Management
> Committee itself, at which the medical director maintained that
> it reflected credit upon the Cloverfield group, since there was
> nothing in the circular that was not already part of their hospital
> policy. In other words, it was suggested that there was nothing
> in the circular that was inconsistent with the formal ideology
> of the hospital as perceived by the upper echelons of the
> hierarchy.

Meanwhile the nursing staff tended to reject it as 'unrealistic' because it presupposed a full staff establishment, and showed no understanding of the problems of treating such patients. The social worker did not see it, at least while the research was in progress, and the union officials said they did not know of its existence. Such patterns of mutual congratulation and fragmented communication may be largely defensive.

At Blackbrick, the physician superintendent was enthusiastic about the circular, since he had been involved in its preparation and saw it as a useful instrument for change. There was a certain amount of polite discussion among senior staff, who knew of his involvement, but the majority of staff were not much interested in policy discussion. They tended to concentrate on day-to-day issues rather than on wider aims and problems, and saw policy pronouncements as 'apocalyptic' rather than 'rational'.

Dr Morris's conclusions are blunt. She concludes that much of the difficulty in administering hospitals for the mentally handicapped stems from the fact that, since 1948, we have adopted a clinical model for institutions whose primary purpose is socio-therapeutic. Hospitals tended to run for their own bureaucratic ends, not to serve the individual needs of patients. In future, there should be three levels of care – intensive 'hospital' care for the most severely sub-normal patients requiring constant medical or nursing attention; day care for patients who might live in foster homes, community homes or outlying units of the hospital, travelling in for clinical and social therapy; and local authority care in small community homes for patients not in need of hospital care. Within the hospital, the pre-dominance of medical and nursing ideologies should be challenged by the development of a 'training' branch, the two to be 'function-ally autonomous but of equal status'. The 'training' branch would be responsible for education, work, leisure activities, community relations and such auxiliary services as physiotherapy and speech therapy. There would probably be conflict between the two branches:[11]

> Nevertheless the presence of two complementary but competing systems may represent productive competition, in so far as it may attack and overcome resistance to change. Conflict as manifested at present appears to be largely dysfunctional since blocked channels of communication prevent it resulting in innovation.

In the introduction to the study, Professor Peter Townsend is concerned to set the problems of the mentally handicapped in the widest possible perspective. He makes considerable use of deviancy theory in suggesting that the mentally handicapped are not a distinct and identifiable group; their condition is defined by society, and the definitions are often highly suspect. More recent research has modified the faith in the efficacy of intelligence tests which was current in Cyril Burt's day. We now know that these tests measure only a very limited range of abilities; that results may vary from test to test and certainly from one age to another in the same child; that practice improves performance; and that tests may reflect middle-class Western norms, to the detriment of working-class and immigrant children. 'Human excellence', says Townsend, 'is a social product as well as an individual quality': and conversely, the same might be said of mental handicap. If people are treated as mentally subnormal, they often conform to expectations and appear subnormal. They can be stunted by their environment, particularly in an institutional setting. In fact, there is a continuum from very high intelligence to very low intelligence, and our places on it are not fixed; within limits we can move up or down. Similarly, there are no clear-cut criteria of personal incapacity or social deviancy which can be used to define the mentally handicapped as a group. But the general public, Townsend argues, has an emotional vested interest in continuing to treat the mentally handicapped as a separate and definable group. It cannot admit its closeness to them, because it is afraid of them. 'In particular, there are fears and prejudices about violence and promiscuity which are as difficult as racial fears and prejudices to allay.'[12]

Labour policy, 1968–70

After the events at Ely, R. H. S. Crossman, as Secretary of State for the Social Services, set up a Working Party which was to meet for two years and to make sweeping proposals for improving the services. Members of the Working Party included Professor Townsend, Dr Pauline Morris, Professor Revans and Mr Geoffrey Howe, QC. A number of interim measures were taken following the advice of this group, including the approval of plans for small 'Crossman units' in hospitals for the mentally handicapped, and the setting up of the Hospital Advisory Services under Dr A. A. Baker. A White Paper was drafted, and was reportedly ready for publication by early 1970. However, when the General Election took place in the summer of 1970, neither the Working Party's findings nor the White Paper had actually been published.

Conservative policy, 1970–2

The Conservative Secretary of State, Sir Keith Joseph, took over a growing problem. Reports of abuse and neglect continued to be made in the Press, coupled with allegations of wrongful detention. It was clear that the pressure groups – and with them, a sizeable section of the general public – wanted to get patients out of the large institutions. A typical problem was that of the two Dewsbury women discharged after 44 and 51 years respectively in a hospital for the mentally handicapped. Public indignation was quickly aroused when it was reported that their long period of detention was due to the fact that they were originally unmarried mothers. It dissipated very quickly when people in the service made it clear that they, and thousands of other patients, could have been discharged many years ago if adequate forms of alternative accommodation had existed.[13]

The Farleigh Inquiry, which had been delayed by the institution of criminal proceedings against three male nurses, finally reported in April 1971.[14] Here was the same sort of story which had been told at Ely, but with some additional factors – allegations of open cruelty, the exhumation of patients' bodies, the suspension of a consultant, and eventually heavy prison sentences. The National Association for Mental Health gave its verdict:[15]

[The Farleigh Report] puts under a microscope defects in the management of one hospital which allowed persistent acts of cruelty on helpless patients to go undetected over many months.

We stress that these events might be repeated in many other hospitals for the mentally handicapped where the same conditions of shortage are to be found – that is, in almost all the 200 hospitals for the mentally handicapped in this country.

In Farleigh patients with gross long-term handicaps did not command the spending of scarce capital money. Management failed to act decisively, and failed to recognise the potential danger of concentrating a group of very difficult patients without any proper individual assessment or treatment plan. *These failures can be found elsewhere.*

Meanwhile, teams from the Hospital Advisory Service had begun to tour the hospitals, making rapid assessments of the outstanding causes for concern, and sending detailed reports to Regional Hospital Boards and Hospital Management Committees. Though there was initially some adverse reaction at hospital level on the grounds that a visit of two or three days allowed little time for an appreciation of local conditions, the value of these comparative assessments, coupled with firm recommendations, was soon realised. Issues which had been hanging fire for years began to seem capable of solution.

The appointment of a Health Service Commissioner 'to reinforce the rights of those who use the Health Service' was announced in Parliament on 22 February 1972. Since then, cases of alleged abuse have almost ceased to appear in the Press. It is to be hoped that this is because they no longer occur and not because the Press has lost interest.

The White Paper and after

The publication of *Better Services for the Mentally Handicapped* meant a move forward from the purely negative phase of preoccupation with abuse to a positive phase where new medical and social policy would create a better service. A critique by Professor Peter Townsend[16] perhaps gives some idea of the gap between the Labour solution and the Conservative one. Townsend welcomed the proposal to shift the balance from hospital to community care and to empty half the hospital beds; but he sharply attacked the proposal to leave the hospital beds in a framework dominated by medical and nursing concepts and the apparent decision not to implement Dr Pauline Morris's recommendations for the development of a 'training arm'. The recent recommendations of the Briggs Report suggest that this is still a live issue, though the pace of change may be more gradual than Professor Townsend and Dr Morris would like:[17]

74 A new caring profession for the mentally handicapped
should emerge gradually. In the meantime, in the training of
nurses in the field of mental handicap, increased emphasis
should be placed on the social aspects of care.

While Townsend found the proposals 'tragically disappointing in nature and in scale', many observers welcomed them as reasonably realistic. They basically represent Tizard's thinking, sharpened and given administrative relevance by Dr Albert Kushlick's work in Wessex[18] and concurrent administrative changes. The setting up of local authority Social Services Departments, the unification and reorganisation of the health services and the local government reorganisation of 1974, at least make possible a one-for-one relationship between health and social services at Area Health Authority/County level. If liaison between the two is successfully achieved, it should lead to the kind of service which Tizard envisaged.

It is all possible, but will it happen? One of the most difficult features of the 1971 scheme is that, in proposing a shift from institutional to community care, it also proposes a shift from central government to local government financing.

Local authorities have had power to provide adequate services for the mentally handicapped for a very long time. They were given power to develop systems of voluntary as well as statutory super-vision under the 1913 Act, power to develop occupational and train-ing centres in 1927, power to do almost anything they wished under section 28 of the National Health Service Act, 1946. The Mental Health Act, 1959, spelled out in detail what they should be doing, and the Community Care Plan of 1963 and its subsequent revisions published what they said they were going to do. But often these plans appear to be drawn up without either the means or the will to implement them. Many a local council drags its feet. Providing services for the mentally handicapped wins no votes, and may offend the ratepayers. The mentally handicapped command no power, and their pressure-groups, such as the National Society for the Parents of Mentally Handicapped Children, do not use conflict tactics. In the mind of many a local councillor, their priority ranking is pre-cisely nil. As the battle for reform moves from central to local government, it becomes more diversified, more fragmented, more difficult to command. A national cause may easily degenerate into dozens of local squabbles.

Local authorities, grappling with reorganisation and the many new demands placed on them by central government for social services of one kind or another, have had many other problems to worry about. Directors of Social Services will not necessarily give priority to what must be one of their comparatively minor problems as they face the enormous task of shaping a new service out of the fragmented muddle of the past.

In October 1972 Sir Keith Joseph, delivering the Hargreaves Memorial Lecture at Leeds, gave an appraisal of the situation. 'The tide of money', he reported, 'is beginning to flow'. In real terms (i.e. eliminating the effect of inflation), the central government funds available for services for the mentally handicapped had risen from £7·5 millions in 1970–1 to £9·3 millions in 1972–3. There was no indication of what proportion of these increased funds would find their way to the local authorities, and no indication that they would be earmarked. However, he mentioned the forthcoming review of local authority health and social services, and indicated that this would be checked every year, and the results published. He antici-pated that 'the lobbies will get to work – a healthy process with which councillors have to live'.

Sir Keith gave an unqualified pledge that until services had been built up there would be 'absolutely no question of closing hospitals', but that 'we have every reason to expect that the community services will be transformed'. He recognised the danger of 'hostels that could turn into dumps' and the existing problems of squalor, overcrowding and staff shortage in the hospitals. He ended with a plea for energy and initiative – 'the passion to make the service effective and first class on the ground' and with the promise that he would build into the service 'as many devices for ensuring that co-ordination and drive exist' as possible, in the hope of making 'inertia and indifference unlikely'.[19]

Since the change of government in February 1974, his successor, Mrs Barbara Castle, has had to deal with the report of yet another inquiry – that on patients at South Ockenden Hospital,[20] which she described in the House as 'a deeply disturbing document', adding 'there is certainly no room for complacency'.[21]

Governments change, and the problems and the promises continue. There is no political capital to be made out of the needs of the mentally handicapped, and the goodwill and sincerity of those who try to bring about reform is unquestionable. Yet many of the problems seem to be intractable. We know some of the answers, just as we know some of the answers to the problems of war, pollution and famine; but the trick is in applying them. The following record of one Region in the years 1971–4 may throw light on some of the less publicised difficulties of bringing about change.

2   The hospitals

On 1 April 1974 the Gateshire Regional Hospital Board ceased to exist, and its work was taken over by the Gateshire Regional Health Authority. There was a comparatively minor adjustment of boundaries, and the new RHA took over responsibility, under the National Health Service Reorganisation Act, 1973, for community health services and practitioner services as well as hospitals. Responsibilities for the hospital care of the mentally handicapped were virtually unchanged by the transfer. Responsibility for their care in the community remained, as before, with the Social Services Departments of local authorities. These departments were also subject to reorganisation on 1 April 1974 under the provision of the Local Government Act, 1972.

The administrative framework has therefore altered since our survey was undertaken, but the distribution of responsibility is not greatly altered. For ease of reference, we shall refer to the Regional Hospital Board and the Regional Health Authority as the 'Region' and the Social Services Departments as 'the local authorities', only distinguishing between the framework before and after reorganisation where this affects the sense of the discussion.

When the field work began on 1 October 1971, the Region had some 3,600 mentally handicapped patients accommodated in 26 hospitals and small units. The latter were usually called 'hostels' by the people who ran them, but since this term has been used officially for many years only to describe local authority provision, we have preferred to use the more correct term 'small hospital units'.

In the first three months of the survey, the hospitals were covered systematically, each member of the team taking one or two hospital Groups and working with them throughout the period. We did not use detailed questionnaires, since we were agreed that the way to begin was to go into the hospitals and to learn what the conditions were on the ground. Each research worker had a checklist of areas of interest to be studied.[1] We were agreed on what to look at, but not, at this stage, on how to look at it or what form our conclusions would take. The development of understanding between members

16

of the team was kept in step by regular weekly seminars. These lasted all day, and were devoted to reports and discussion.

Information was gathered by observation and talking to staff at all levels. Activities as diverse as sitting in on management team meetings and attending patients' old-time dancing sessions were covered. On the wards, there was no set procedure which excluded aspects of ward life. Wards were visited in the busy mornings as well as the quiet afternoons, during doctors' rounds and meal times and staff handovers, early in the morning and during the night shift.

All hospitals, large and small, were covered equally. Increasing demands for community care and small institutional units mean that it is fruitful to observe how small hospitals function. At the same time, the fact that the larger hospitals are still with us, and will be with us for an appreciable time, cannot be ignored. It is in the large hospitals that the period of transition is likely to be most exacting, and conditions least stable.

All senior staff, medical, nursing and administrative, and the heads of ancillary departments, were interviewed, and asked for their views both about the working of the system and the impact of change. Where possible, staff were asked to cite concrete examples to support their opinions, and to describe work situations out of their own experience.

The account which follows is a summary of the findings of the Stage II investigation.[2] These are broad first impressions by a group of social scientists (the field team at this stage consisted of a social worker, three sociologists and a social psychologist). From this general picture, it was possible to pick out special areas for study, and these are reported in succeeding chapters.

Hospitals, patients and members of staff are referred to by pseudonyms. Hospitals with more than 300 beds (i.e. large hospitals) have names beginning with 'L', and are designated *Institutions* – Laker Institution, Landale Institution. Those with between 100 and 300 beds (i.e. medium-sized hospitals) have names beginning with 'M', and are designated *Granges* – Marathon Grange, Maundy Grange. Those with less than 100 beds (i.e. small hospitals or hostels) have names beginning with 'S', and are designated *Houses* – Scroll House, Scenic House. (It was sheer coincidence which placed Swan House in the grounds of Mallard Grange.) Patients are given names beginning with 'P', doctors with 'D', nurses with 'N', and so on. Every effort has been made to preserve confidentiality in fulfilment of our guarantee to those who co-operated in the survey.

ag and buildings

popular stereotype of hospitals for the mentally handicapped is of 'large, old institutions with thousands of patients, miles from anywhere'. We, therefore, began by testing this assumption in terms of the factors of size, age and type of buildings, and location.

No hospital in the survey had more than 1,000 beds. The largest had 843 beds and the next three in size had 460, 363 and 335 respectively.[3] These were the only hospitals with more than 300 beds, and we have designated as 'large' institutions which in some other Regions would be regarded as of very modest size. Seven hospitals had between 100 and 300 beds (the 'medium' range) and fifteen had less than 100 beds. However, in terms of how the patients lived, 50 per cent were accommodated in the large hospitals and 33 per cent in the medium hospitals, the 15 small units taking only 17 per cent of patients. The small units varied in size. Only two had the proportions favoured by the White Paper – 25 beds or less. The mean size of the 15 small units was 44·1 beds.

Of the four large institutions, three started from large private houses and have had villas and other accommodation constructed in the grounds. (This is in effect purpose-built accommodation, though the fact that it has grown over the years can mean that the purpose has been lost sight of at times.) The fourth was a workhouse. The medium-sized Granges showed an extraordinary variety of origin – two workhouses, an Inebriates' Home, three residential houses, two with rather splendid antecedents, and a stables. The small Houses included two isolation hospitals, a tuberculosis sanatorium, several Land Army hostels taken over after the Second World War, a vicarage and a children's home. Perhaps this variety illustrates the British talent for adaptation. Perhaps it illustrates the rather tragic pecking order which exists even in the social services – the mentally handicapped often come fairly low down on the list.

Members of the research team drew up plans of the hospitals they visited. The most common pattern for the larger hospitals was the villa-system which was in vogue in the 1930s. In some cases, this must have been achieved by energetic decentralisation in existing premises. The advantages were in social organisation – the villa-system enabled a large population to be broken down into smaller social groups, and the architecture and layout were more acceptable, since paths, trees and shrubs replaced the long stone corridors of the Victorian era. The disadvantages were administrative: Victorian corridors, whatever their aesthetic disadvantages, at least offer protection from wind and rain. Villas do not. Food got cold if it came from a central kitchen, staff got wet and chilled, and there was a tendency for the villa population to get isolated from the wider framework of the hospitals.

Of the four large institutions, two were isolated in the sense that they were 16 miles and 9 miles respectively from the nearest town. Both had poor bus services and were inaccessible by train. The other two were within city boundaries. These represented both extremes: none of the medium or small hospitals was farther out of town, but few were actually in towns. The reports frequently listed factors like 'ten miles out of town with a two-hourly bus service', 'a mile and a half down a side turning – the road peters out', 'fifteen miles to the city and one mile to the infrequent bus service', 'two miles out, and a one-in-five gradient'. Though a proportion of relatives had cars, there seemed no point in blaming relatives for losing touch with patients if there was no way of reaching them. Even where a bus service existed, the cost of fares may have discouraged visitors.

The following report from one of the research team spotlights the lack of signposting and directions common to many hospitals:

There appears to be little local knowledge of the hospital – the only way I found Landale was by ringing the switchboard and asking for directions after tiring of asking people who had not heard of it, or who were no more specific than 'I think it's over there somewhere'. The only sign anywhere to say that this is Landale is half a mile away on the main road, where the approach road is indicated by an inconspicuous sign ... the only indication of the entrance is the international road sign for a hospital on the approach road. There is no porter's lodge, but a large 'tree' of blue and white signs at the end of the drive indicates where the enquiry office can be found – left past the laundry, boiler-house and dining room and then sharp right to the front entrance.

Such obscuring of identity and function probably had its origins in the days when staff were trying to get away from a too-specific terminology. Some hospitals still had local names of the old stigmatising kind – one was known to people in the area as 'the silly farm' and another as 'the colony', and some had a personality which

ıly too distinctive, as is shown by this account of Mallard
e:

physical location can best be described as isolated. At the
top of a steep, precipitous hill in the heart of the moorland,
the hospital is located on rising ground. The heavily weathered
stone façade of the buildings blends perfectly with the austere,
bleak character of the surrounding moors: a location and
forbidding appearance perfectly in keeping with its former
workhouse status.

Several members of the team commented on the paradoxes of the
hospitals' position. Most hospitals had plenty of land, and yet they
were acutely overcrowded. A number were not physically isolated,
but they shared the social isolation of those that were. 'Physical
proximity does not necessarily guarantee social nearness', noted
one research worker.

Ward accommodation contrasted quite sharply with the bleak
exteriors of many of the hospitals. Although many of the buildings
were old, the wards were nearly all in a good state of decoration
with modern furnishing, heating and lighting. It was evident that
a good deal of money had recently been spent on the upgrading of
physical facilities and some informants attributed this directly to
the extra funds made available under the Crossman administration,
and the work of the Hospital Advisory Service.

Staff–patient relationships

Many nursing staff on the wards had made sincere and disciplined
attempts to create genuine relationships with patients, often at considerable cost to themselves. Cases were frequently cited of staff
who invited patients to their own homes, took them out for an
evening, or accompanied them on shopping expeditions or cinema
visits on their free days. These cases were not confined to the young
or the experienced, to the trained or the untrained – some people
seemed to have the gift of supporting such relationships, and others
found it difficult.

There were problems. Nurses found dangers as well as advantages
in live relationships, and some were well aware that they could hurt
as well as heal:

Two nurses took eight patients to the local pub one evening, in
their own cars. It would seem, however, that when there is

this degree of interest the expectations of the nurse rise appropriately, and when the patient fails to live up to the standards expected the nurse is much more likely to be aggressive in his response if the patient does something wrong (as was witnessed on several occasions) than if there were an attitude of apathy to the patient. The more you expect, the less you tolerate.

Other nurses found that they began to make favourites and to differentiate between patients to a degree that was incompatible with their own concepts of professional performance. As in other human groups, people began to take on group roles – one would become the leader, another would play the clown, a third would be the scapegoat.

The team felt that nurses who attempted friendly personal relationships with patients needed a good deal of guidance and support – and more knowledge of human relations than some of them appeared to possess. At the same time, they pinpointed a number of defences commonly employed by nurses against face-to-face interaction with patients, and felt that discussion of these issues might help further to improve the quality of relationships.

The use of routine as a defence   It was noted many times that staff found routine tasks more congenial and less tiring than interacting with the patients:

> On one ward where only 5 of the 24 patients left the ward, the patients just sat aimlessly around the perimeter of the day room. When asked if activities were arranged to occupy the patients the charge nurse said that the staff were not interested. To illustrate this he got the staff to organise a game of hoop-la and skittles. Greeted with the response of one nursing assistant of 'What have I done to deserve this?', the staff soon tired of picking up skittles and hoops and went back to counting socks and sewing on buttons.

> On a children's ward, a new and innovative charge nurse commented bitterly of her staff that 'They'd rather do anything than be with the kids. If I didn't keep on at them, they'd spend all their time doing other things and they wouldn't come near the kids at all'.

The 'colonial' defence   Two research workers commented that the original title of 'colony' for these institutions still had some point. Staff tended to be easy-going and paternalistic as long as they were not challenged in their supremacy, but quick to resent any attempt at genuine equality:

> The belief is often held that patients are 'cunning' and will take advantage of one unless they are kept in their place. In effect the image is that of the patient as a native, a person who is allowed to act like a member of the élite only in so far as he does not think that he is such a member. Provided that this boundary can be drawn clearly and patients show a proper deference to staff, the latter are able to act with affection towards individual patients and to tolerate acts that are by general standards deviant.

The 'public school' defence A variation of this theme was the 'public school' defence, in which social relationships were roughly like those between a prefect and a 'fag'. Staff employed patients to do routine jobs – sometimes the regular tasks of laying tables and stacking plates, sometimes the dirty jobs like changing incontinent patients, and gave them small rewards:

> On nearly every ward each charge nurse has one patient who is his 'lad'. This patient will be a devoted servant who will run little errands or do little jobs for the charge nurse on the ward. In return he will receive an extra cigarette or cup of tea.

The parental defence Another common reaction was the 'parental' defence, in which the nursing staff took the role of mother/father, and the patients were regarded as dependent children. This made possible both the occasional indulgence and the exercise of a considerable authority.

The assumption of parental roles has been encouraged by a number of studies in social psychology which have taken a Freudian position on the paramount importance of experiences in the first five years of life, and the extent to which adults tend to repeat these experiences in different settings in later life. There is much in this analysis which is meaningful, but like most theoretical insights, it has its dangers if applied regardless of context. Mentally handicapped adults are not children and professional staff are not their parents.

It was noted that in most hospitals, the terms used by the nursing staff to refer to patient groups suggested the adoption of the parental

model. The severely subnormal were often called 'the babies'
the 'boy's ward' might contain 50-year-old patients; a ward for
women patients would be divided into 'big girls' and 'little girls'.
This style of nomenclature may call forth in staff the kind of tender-
ness and protectiveness usually reserved for children, but the team
felt that it was unsuitable and somewhat humiliating for handicapped adults, while the element of make-believe did not make for
sound staff–patient relations:

> On one ward in Laker Institution an old lady always had a
> cuddle from the female charge nurse in the morning and in the
> middle of this she would ask all types of simple routine questions
> such as, 'Do you like my dress, hair, etc?' The ritual would
> usually end with the charge nurse giving her a little kiss on the
> cheek. This would no sooner have finished than another patient
> would come up to have her hair combed, even though she
> could do it herself. When questioned on this point, the charge
> nurse smiled and said, 'The poor dears like me doing these
> little things and I enjoy making them happy'.

Good staff–patient interaction – or patronage?

'Good' and 'bad' wards

All four of the defences cited above involve expressions of ambivalence: the conflict of positive emotions (liking, friendship, a desire
to serve) and negative emotions (disgust, exasperation, anger). That
nursing staff should experience conflict is not surprising to anyone
who has watched them at work in a hospital for the mentally handicapped. They are told to behave as though patients are normal
people – 'normalisation' has been the watchword in the service ever
since the publication of the Brooklands study – and yet many
patients are manifestly not 'normal' in their present behaviour, whatever their potential for development. Nurses are expected to have
high standards of cleanliness and hygiene, and yet at the same time
to encourage patient activity. They are expected to reach an almost
superhuman standard of personal discipline, and yet to tolerate the
most deviant acts without showing dislike or disgust; and they are
very much aware from the government inquiries and the consequent
newspaper publicity that if things go badly wrong, it is the ward
staff who will be held responsible and not 'the administration'.

B*

Nursing staff talked in terms of 'good' and 'bad' wards. A 'good' ward was one where patients – probably the least severely handicapped – behaved in a 'normal' way, and the positive emotions required by management were appropriate. Here the conflict was minimal. A 'bad' ward was one where patients – probably the most severely handicapped and certainly the most disturbed – behaved in ways which called forth the negative emotions. This was a matter for considerable concern, because the patients from the 'good' wards were those most likely to be transferred to local authority care, and many older nurses spoke with nostalgia of the days when the hospitals had a larger proportion of 'good' patients who set a tone for the rest. They felt that conditions had deteriorated, and looked to the future with considerable foreboding. Their attitude to community care was unconditionally hostile, because it threatened the security of their jobs and because they did not trust the community services to care adequately for 'their' patients.

The research team came to the conclusion that the 'bad' wards often constituted a special problem. To be transferred to such a ward was often regarded as a mark of official disapproval. These were the patients for whom 'nothing much could be done' and to be relegated to their care was interpreted as a sign of professional and personal failure. The wards were sometimes called 'back wards' – a term which we prefer because it avoids the value-judgment of 'bad wards' and expresses this element of relegation. They tended to develop their own sub-culture, often characterised by an appallingly poor quality of life for patients and staff alike.

Such wards occurred (as at Ely and Farleigh) in otherwise well-run and progressive hospitals, and our preliminary study led us to three main conclusions:

1　The existence of 'back wards' was much more widespread than was generally recognised. While the incidents which gave rise to the Ely and Farleigh investigations were (fortunately) exceptional, the situations which gave rise to them were to be found in at least one ward in many of the large and medium-sized hospitals.

2　'Back wards' were both defined by and functional to the life of the hospital as a whole. They served as a disposal place for patients (and sometimes staff) who impaired the good, progressive image of the other wards.

3　Many senior hospital staff seemed genuinely unaware of the conditions in these wards, and reacted sharply to suggestions that 'things like that could happen in *my* hospital'. Official denial exacerbates an already difficult situation, and increases the isolation ward staff.

Sanctions and privileges

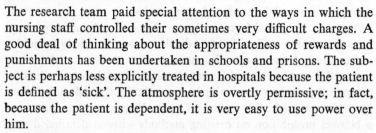

The research team paid special attention to the ways in which the nursing staff controlled their sometimes very difficult charges. A good deal of thinking about the appropriateness of rewards and punishments has been undertaken in schools and prisons. The subject is perhaps less explicitly treated in hospitals because the patient is defined as 'sick'. The atmosphere is overtly permissive; in fact, because the patient is dependent, it is very easy to use power over him.

It should be said at once that we found none of the totally unjustifiable practices which have been alleged in the Farleigh and Ely inquiries. Patients were not beaten or starved or neglected. In one hospital, it was nevertheless quite common for male nurses to control their charges by means of 'a clip round the ear'. We are not able to say whether these were merely token cuffs or real blows. In the same hospital, the consultant twice agreed to the use of the straitjacket during the period of the survey – once for a girl whose offence was kicking a nurse with a bare foot. The use of instruments of restraint was only employed with the express approval of the medical staff, but it was surprising to find that this was still deemed necessary.

Some nurses preferred what are euphemistically called 'psychological methods'. At Maple Grange: 'The main means of control is through verbal sanctions. Patients who violate rules get shouted at and sometimes humiliated in front of their peers.' At Signet House (a women's unit): 'Usually for tantrums of a verbal or physical kind nothing more is needed than a telling off and perhaps sending upstairs till the next meal to produce repentance and floods of tears.'

There were other methods of punishment: the use of side rooms for seclusion, the sending of high-grade patients to low-grade wards (this is classified as 'psychological'), the use of paraldehyde – dropped 'less for ethical reasons than because some patients came to enjoy it and would create difficulties in order to get an injection', or special sentences like being made to scrub a floor.

Another method of control was through the withdrawal of privileges: pocket money might be stopped or outings restricted, patients might be sent to bed instead of staying up to watch television. One research worker made the point that the methods of control seemed largely negative – they were conceived of in terms of punishment for bad behaviour rather than of rewards for good behaviour, and that a move towards the system of giving privileges on trust and then taking them away if the patient failed to keep the agreement, might produce better results.

The use of physical force, bullying, seclusion and the use of drugs by ward nursing staff without medical sanction, is strictly forbidden and certainly frowned upon by nursing directors. Nevertheless these things did happen and this was another example of the lack of communication between senior hospital staff and ward staff. Nurses have always used some means of controlling unruly patients, and a blanket prohibition on existing methods without detailed discussion on what nurses may humanely do instead, can produce very undesirable results.

Patient–patient relations

On the 'back wards', relationships between patients were almost non-existent. On other wards, however, patterns of help and dependency were frequently observed. These were most apparent in wards where able-bodied patients were mixed with the physically handicapped. Ambulant patients regularly wheeled chair-ridden patients about, and gave support to the semi-ambulant. One case was observed in which a blind patient and a deaf patient became friends, supporting and reinforcing each other. Where patients of different levels of social adaptation were mixed, those who were able to do so helped with the washing and dressing of those who were less capable.

The extent to which staff appreciated these relationships varied. Some were sensitive to patients' relationships, and encouraged this kind of interdependency. Provision was made to see that friends ate together, went to classes together, sat next to each other on outings and trips. In the same way, patient enmities were recognised, and the participants kept firmly apart:

> Some patients, for instance, steal food at meals only from
> certain other patients and have to be seated accordingly. On the
> hyperactive ward one of the patients that sleeps in the day room
> must only have certain other patients with him because there
> are some that he becomes aggressive towards. On a very
> crowded ward such relationships are crucial.

Elsewhere, it was reported that 'most patients tend to be loners. Group formation is nebulous, and usually consists of an identification with staff and an attempt to please them'. This frequently took the form of acting out staff–patient relationships, much as small children play 'mothers and fathers':

> In one ward in Lake Institution an elderly female patient looked after 'her children', who were also patients, the latter referring to the former as 'matron'. 'Matron' was thoroughly maternal and took some to the toilet and bathroom. Also, if any of her 'children' were unhappy or disturbed she would spend hours comforting them, or if they were being molested or teased by other patients she would defend them.

Sometimes relationships between two patients became intense, and developed into homosexuality. Charge nurses were sometimes extremely worried about this, and seemed to receive little guidance as to how they should respond.

But many patients were virtually islands, 'each one for himself and himself alone', making no real contact either with staff or fellow-patients, and submitting with apparent docility to the eternal mechanical routine of toileting, washing and feeding.

Patient activities

Though a variety of patient activities were cited in each hospital, the research team were unanimous that 'the same people go to everything'. For a group of patients – perhaps 30 or 40 per cent – life was active and busy. These were the patients who, in the future, may well go out and live in the community. For the others – the ones who will become the bulk of the future hospital population – there was little beyond the ward routine.

Most hospitals had active social programmes: the weekly film, the occasional dance (to which patients from a neighbouring unit may be invited), the summer outing, the Christmas dance. These are traditional activities. Though they too are routinised, they are greatly appreciated. Several hospitals have gone to considerable trouble to find new ways of involving patients with the community, and have worked out special schemes with the League of Friends, the WVS or some other organisation.

Nearly all the hospitals had occupational therapy (OT) or industrial therapy (IT), or both. In most cases, OT was run by the nursing staff, and not by qualified occupational therapists. Many of the activities were at the level of simple handicrafts or tasks, and the distinction between OT and IT was often not very clear:

> The ward has about 35–40 female patients with two members of staff. The patients make trays and glue paper bags. The 'Playgroup' was established three years ago; there are 4 members of staff and 34 of the very severely subnormal ambulant patients (26 female and 8 male) located at one end of the recreation hall, and an attempt is made to occupy the patients with paints and music. It effectively relieves pressure on nursing staff on the ward by transferring the problem elsewhere. When visited, all were seated around tables with crayons; one wandered about, another sat on a radiator with someone else rocking violently back and forth next to it, while another slept under a row of chairs stacked along the side. For the problems these patients present, four nursing staff (one SEN and three nursing assistants) could not hope to even attempt to cope.

On the other hand, some of the IT workshops had reached quite a high standard, and were providing sheltered jobs for patients for something approaching a normal working week. Under the scheme proposed in the White Paper for the pooling of hospital and community facilities such centres might well be designated as training centres.

In the changing social structure of hospitals for the mentally handicapped, very few patients now work to maintain the institution. This is in some ways beneficial – one of the most disturbing aspects of institutional life up to the mid-1960s was the tendency of the system to serve itself, and it certainly encouraged the 'colonial' mentality. Nevertheless, in the days of patient labour, staff and patients were engaged on common enterprises, and the patients were occupied. If patients are not to deteriorate through lack of activity, some better alternative needs to be found.

Pocket money

The amount of pocket money given to patients varied considerably from hospital to hospital. At Meadow Grange patients got somewhere between 15p and 50p, with slightly higher amounts in exceptional cases; the children and the severely subnormal got nothing, but were provided with sweets in lieu. At Maple Grange, 'patients not deemed capable of handling money had it banked for them, and this was drawn out by the charge nurses for special purposes like the purchase of deodorants and special clothes'. At Laker Institution the minimum amount was 25p, and this was given even to the severely subnormal. Patients who were 'well-behaved, hard-working and able to go shopping' might get up to £1.25. At Marathon Grange the range was from 10p to £1.50 a week.

These amounts seemed highly arbitrary, and the system whereby individual members of staff decided the amount and handled the money less than satisfactory. In Laker Institution the procedure was said to be 'unsystematic and subjective', and there would be much to be said for an agreed scale and for some checks on the handling of even quite small funds.

At the same time, where staff are prepared to take time and trouble to supervise patients, they can help them to acquire the ability to handle money, which is one of the most fundamental skills of modern life. At Meadow Grange the nursing director took groups of patients to the shops herself, and at Christmas she arranged special opening hours at Woolworth's so that they could move about freely and choose what they wanted to buy. At Marathon Grange, the League of Friends ran a weekly stall.

The government circular on Patients' Private Monies (HM (71) 90) has led to considerable discussion and to the review of pocket money systems in most hospitals. At Scroll House, where 'opportunities for spending pocket money have been nil, due to isolation and lack of transport', the delivery of a hospital minibus which can be used for shopping trips was fervently awaited.

Patients' food

On the whole, the team thought very highly of the catering arrangements for patients:

The quality of the food is well varied from day to day, and the patients have a choice.

The quality of the food was found to be satisfactory – no complaints were heard.

Wholesome and adequate in amount – breakfast usually includes bacon and tomatoes, and the most popular lunch is fish and chips.

The team felt strongly that, just because there were so few issues over which they could exercise judgment in their daily lives, the patients ought to have some choice in the matter of food, though it was recognised that this added to the problems of serving and involved marginally higher costs.

Two instances were recorded of staff regularly eating food sent up for the patients. This was evidently not uncommon, and was encouraged by the fact that there was no staff dining-room – the staff were expected to eat on the wards.

Patients' clothing

Comments on clothing centred around two issues of ward administration: the difficulty of keeping individual clothing for a large number of people living communally who cannot care for their own clothes, and the difficulty of preserving a reasonable standard, even with considerable expenditure, for incontinent patients whose clothes have to be boiled.

These are perennial problems in psychiatric and geriatric hospitals. The degree of effort taken to deal with them varied considerably, from the hospital in which the patients 'had only grey corduroy battle-dress jackets and pants that fit very badly ... several patients could regularly be seen without shoes, and this did not seem to disturb the staff unduly', to a children's ward on which sister 'washed all the patients' jumpers and dresses herself in the washing machine provided in the half-way house because the laundry would have ruined them'.

Even where money has been made available, there have been some unimaginative purchases: 'Their lack of patient orientation has been manifested by purchasing, for instance, identical sports jackets for all patients in Sistine House, and 20 identical women's overalls for Sinclair House patients, with little regard for variations in size, design and colour.'

It is understood that the Hospital Advisory Service team made strong recommendations about the provision of individual and good quality clothing. These are likely to be resisted in some quarters:

> Mr Norton, for example, talked about the impracticability of
> a new policy that concerned patients' clothing. 'It's all very well
> saying that the lads should have their own clothes, but someone
> like Tony Palmer isn't going to know the difference between

his and someone else's clothes, and how will you get the likes
of Fred Piper to stop keeping their clothes under the pillow
at night?' New policies were rejected because they did not take
into account the individuality of the patients and because
they were 'theoretical' and not grounded in the commonsense
knowledge of what could or could not be done.

The Region has given a lead in the provision of Training Days
on clothing. This may need to be repeated several times before
people like Mr Norton are willing to attend.

Objectives and ideology

How do the hospitals see their own work? It seemed evident from
the team's reports that there was no one clear picture, and that a
period in which everyone knew exactly what a hospital for the
mentally handicapped was and what it did has been succeeded by
one of much uncertainty. Perhaps this is a healthy sign, but the
views expressed were exceedingly conflicting and sometimes con-
tradictory.

At one Group headquarters, responsible for several hospitals for
the mentally handicapped as well as general hospitals, it was simply
assumed that subnormality hospitals were inferior forms of general
hospitals:

> Both the group secretary and the hospital secretary emphasise the
> need to provide, and place no emphasis on the need to discharge.
> This latter point is underlined by frequent references to the
> similarities between geriatric and subnormality hospitals as
> long-stay units. The hospital secretary makes no attempt to
> qualify his ridicule of the concepts of 'normalisation' and
> 'socialisation' (however amorphous and misused these terms may
> be). Where lack of knowledge of the needs of subnormal patients
> and lack of care about their provision occurs, a lack of clear
> thought and confused objectives abound.
>   The control of resources by a faction who tend only to point
> out the need for a 'homely atmosphere' and a faction who tend
> to withhold resources for even this in favour of other hospitals
> in the Group (and specifically the new hospital), has in Group
> No. 4 the effect of confusing and confounding the manifest
> objectives of the other factions. Thus lack of administrative
> action concerning the laundry service, financial pruning of various

food supplies, neglect of grievances and complaints, tended to increase the divergence between the manifest and extant objectives of both the medical and nursing factions.

The idea that all mentally handicapped patients need is 'a homely atmosphere' was propounded in several places by administrators who were clearly under the impression that such an atmosphere could be produced cheaply and easily with a minimum of trained staff, thus releasing resources for acute hospitals. The resultant lack of emphasis on rehabilitation and discharge had expensive results in the longer term:

Efforts to improve the physical environment of the patients and create a 'homely atmosphere' have largely succeeded as this is the only real objective that any of those concerned hold. By the same token, emphasis has been diverted from other potential objectives. With no pressure from any quarter towards patient discharges, there is no move toward individual patient activities outside the hospital. All movement outside the hospital grounds is conducted in groups. The tag of 'long-stay' is thus not challenged and becomes a reality.

In another Group, multidisciplinary discussions had produced some consensus between the hospital secretary, the consultant and the nursing director as to what the hospital's objectives ought to be, and these were elaborated with some sophistication:
1   *Short term*: essentially implementation of the Baker proposals, i.e. adequate and suitable personal clothing for each patient, division of dormitories, review of pocket money and rewards, staff training in previous items, improving catering service to wards, open the two new wards, extend holidays and outings, division of non-dining areas, and development of voluntary services.
2   *Medium term*: upgrading of wards, provision of office accommodation, new OT centre, new recreational centre, staff changing accommodation, full training for Register, extension of engineering and linen store, and provision of broadcast system and residential accommodation for staff.
3   *Long term*: implementation of the June 1971 Command Paper.
In a third Group, it was the nursing director who laid down the objectives in initial lectures to students:
1   A social training ground, where patients can be taught to live happily, usefully and productively.

2   A shelter and place of safety, where all possible steps towards rehabilitation can be taken.

3   A means of providing academic, physical, recreational, occupational and vocational training.

4   A place of control for those needing it.

5   A programme of fundamental research as to the case pathology and prevention of mental retardation where possible.

6   A therapeutic centre, where every effort is made to educate parents, staff and public.

7   A community in the best sense of the word, where the retarded and those who care for them can live and work together to the end that a contribution may be made to the sum total of human happiness.

Over and above this, the hospital should function as a:

i   training school;

ii   provider of out-patient clinics, domiciliary consultations, links with local authorities as ascertainment, investigation, diagnosis, prognosis and placement;

iii   centre for temporary admission.

More than one member of the team drew the classic distinction between the *manifest objectives* (i.e. what the staff explicitly gave as their aims), the *assumed objectives* (i.e. what they really thought they were trying to do) and the *extant objectives* (i.e. what they could actually be observed as doing). A point made repeatedly was that while discharge to the community was a manifest objective – because the White Paper said so – this was neither an assumed nor an extant objective, because staff were almost unanimous that none of the patients under their care were fit for discharge to the community:

It is strongly contended that subnormals cannot live outside, that hospital is the best place for them and they cannot get such facilities anywhere else. It is said that even if they were accommodated in smaller units, like hostels, they would not be able to get the quality of facilities (food, clothing, board and lodging) provided in the bigger hospitals as a result of economies of scale. It is further assumed that these people, even high-grade ones who work on outside jobs, cannot live in the community because they need supervision. Such expressions were often rationalisations of the fear of redundancy among the staff.

A further cause of a gap between the manifest and the assumed

tives was that senior staff were well aware that the fulfilment
he manifest objectives would require a level of financing and
ing which they had never had, and which they doubted that they
would ever be able to achieve. This lent an air of unreality to discussion. The difficulty was solved by concentration on what was
immediate and close at hand rather than on objectives which were
felt to be unattainable in practice. One member of the team put the
matter succinctly:

Assumed objectives
Protecting patients from unkind evaluation by uninformed
outsiders. Providing a controlled life for them so that they have
no worries about managing. Preventing them making fools
of themselves.

Extant objectives
Keeping people who are an embarrassment to society out of
the way.

Sectional and personal objectives
Doing nothing on their shift which can be regarded as slip-shod
or over-zealous by the other shift or which results in minutes
lost from the tea-breaks. I fear, also, getting back to their
families without having expended too much nervous and physical
energy.

Perhaps this is an unduly pessimistic view; but it is unlikely that
people working in hospitals for the mentally handicapped will begin
to work together on a common task until they resolve some of the
confusions and contradictions of the present situation.

Leadership

'Nobody was batting for Ely.' The situation we have outlined is
one in which the gap between official policy and the situation as
it is experienced on the wards is acute, and most of the ward staff
feel that nobody is batting for them, either. Such a situation requires
qualities of inspired leadership. It was seldom forthcoming, though
we report in Appendix 1 an encouraging attempt by a part-time
consultant to provide it on a particular ward.

Official policy since the passing of the Mental Health Act, 1959,
has been for the traditional rule of the physician superintendent to
be superseded by the tripartite system of administration already

introduced into general hospitals.[4] Senior medical, nursing and administrative staff share responsibility for decision-making by consensus. This policy is taken a stage further in the DHSS paper on *Management Arrangements for the Reorganised Health Service* (1972) – commonly known as the Grey Document – which assumes that a similar interdisciplinary consensus can form a working basis for the operation of District Management Teams for whole areas.

Our conclusions in the hospitals for the mentally handicapped were that tripartite administration rarely, if ever, worked, though the forms of failure varied considerably. We cite below some of the situations encountered.

In one Group, a reputedly ineffective hospital secretary had been replaced by one who was only too effective:

> The cordiality and yet ineffectiveness of the previous secretary had frustrated nurses and administration alike, and had certainly caused grievances among the nursing staff. The new hospital secretary had taken a firmer line. Praised by the Group administration, he speaks of the need for a titular head and casts himself in the role. All action for and by the hospital, he contends, should be channelled through him (this even extended to the Chairmanship of the League of Friends) even though he freely admits to an almost complete lack of knowledge of mental handicap or the new ideas about provision for the mentally subnormal. His idea is that it is the central characteristic of the patient, 'inadequacy of intelligence', that is the main constraint against the hospital's achievement of the ideal provision, which demonstrates both his ignorance and his general hospital orientation . . . the Chief Nursing Officer has opted out of the conflict situation.

In another Group, it was the consultant who came out as leader:

> Dr. Dee has sought to centralise control of major decisions in his own hands with the result that the management team which is charged with responsibility for policy within the hospital is little more than a façade.

In a third Group, a power vacuum caused by the virtual withdrawal of the consultant from administrative concerns was filled by the nursing profession:

> The hospital secretary is based at the District hospital 30 miles

ay. He visits Scroll House once every two weeks, at the same
ie taking up provisions and drugs from the Group stores. The
consultant visits from Linsted Institution about once every
3 months. In effect this isolation leaves the nursing officer in
charge with disproportionate power. It also means that she has
to deal with many matters that are not specifically nursing.

In Scenic House, like Scroll House, the nursing officer's
authority is unquestioned. Change can only occur with the
promotion or consent of these nursing officers because on the
one hand few senior staff outside the hospital have any interest
in change, and on the other hand their power over the running
of the hospitals is recognised and treated with respect.

The net result is that nursing, administrative and policy
making leadership are effectively thrown back at the nursing
officers who retain a large amount of autonomy.

These complaints need not necessarily be taken at their face value.
Most senior administrators know that blame is allotted a good deal
more readily than praise, and that it is satisfying to be able to
attach it to a person; but the salient points can be briefly stated:
though the administrative theorists of the National Health Service
required tripartite leadership, doctors, nurses and administrators
in the hospitals surveyed were apparently not yet very good at it.
In a situation where there was no clear structural leadership, such
as that possessed by the old-style physician superintendents, people
did not co-operate in most cases; they resolved the issue through a
power-struggle, and despite the centralised and sometimes despotic
features of the rule of the physician superintendents, there were
many who regretted their passing, if only because they provided
a simple, comprehensible structure within which everyone could
work by agreement and without daily conflict. The following is one
of several reports on the way in which the staff could collude to push
the consultant back into this role:

> While the hospital secretary is someone you turn to to get
> things done, the nursing staff do not expect him to fulfil any
> leadership function. The net result is that ward staff do not
> perceive anyone as laying down practical guidelines and
> objectives that they can follow. The period of transition is a
> period of uncertainty, and the paradoxical element of the
> situation is that this uncertainty reinforces the desire of the
> nursing staff for the medical director to adopt the role of

physician superintendent, the relinquishing of which by the medical director caused the uncertainty in the first place. This desire to return to the old régime on the part of ward staff is perfectly understandable – they knew where they stood and what was expected of them.

Consultants already had a wide spread of clinical responsibility; they have been encouraged in recent years to think of themselves primarily as clinicians and to work increasingly outside the hospitals. Most of them do not have the time to fulfil a physician superintendent's role, even if they had the interest and the temperament; but having abandoned an authoritarian form of organisation, the hospitals appear to have proceeded straight to *laissez-faire* of a most unstructured kind with no more than a passing glance at a balanced democracy. The effects of this lack of control at the centre have been extensively detailed in the Ely and Farleigh reports and need no further elaboration. However, the team reports make it clear that the lack of a clear focus at the centre of the hospitals' administrative life was felt all through their structure. In one hospital, the hospital secretary and the nursing director were both observed to defend themselves against the possibility of having to fill the vacuum:

> The hospital secretary and nursing director both regret the lack of effective leadership from the medical director and the extra work this involves them in. The result is a retreat behind an array of filing cabinets and formalised procedures. For example, everything is put on paper. A request to see the nursing director has to be written down and a reason given, and even if an appointment is refused the request is still filed.

Staff relations

Members of the team were agreed on certain fundamental observations about staff grouping. The chief of these was that the staff relations in urban or suburban hospitals were qualitatively different from those in the isolated rural hospitals. Since this finding has a clear bearing on future hospital planning, we spent some time in analysing findings concerning individual hospitals.

Hospitals in or near towns tended to have much the same staff problem as other hospitals; predictably, a large secondary social group would splinter into small, face-to-face groups characterised by sex, age or professional identity. Grouping was quite often acted out at meal-times, when members of staff took up their accustomed places at table. Expressions of male solidarity or female solidarity were not often encountered, but there were often tensions between younger staff, who wanted change and were confident of the applicability of new ideas, and older staff, who thought that they knew the best way of doing things. To some extent, this situation had been modified by the introduction of management training for more senior staff, and one research worker reported an interesting situation in which 'alternate layers' of nursing staff in terms of seniority contended for innovation or inertia.

In the more isolated hospitals the social organisation of the staff was very different. Staff tended to stand together, without the rifts and tensions which so often characterised social relationships in the town hospitals. We might expect that a degree of unity great enough to transcend barriers of sex, age and professional background could only be achieved at the cost of a unified resistance to the outside world. It is the external enemy who unites the group. And so it proved.

Research workers reported extensive *kinship networks* and *neighbourhood networks* in rural hospitals. The kinship networks resulted directly from the fact that the hospitals were isolated. If charge nurse N or Dr D lived near the hospital, members of his family could be sure of finding a job there, and would have relatively little opportunity of finding one anywhere else. Thus, it was common to find male and female members of two or three generations of one family employed in different parts of the hospital in varying kinds of work. One research worker reported a three-generation family of which eight members out of ten were employed by the hospital in four different types of work – nursing, portering, laundry work and office work.

Neighbourhood networks also resulted from rural isolation. The people who worked at the hospital tended to come from the nearby villages, and to exhibit the strong conservatism which is a feature of English village life. Kinship and neighbourhood networks alike closed ranks to show resistance to change. The member of staff who came in with new ideas was regarded as something of a rolling stone, likely to cause everybody a good deal of trouble and then to move on to another post:

Mr. Nephew's attempts to get patients' teeth cleaned came

under attack on the grounds that it had been tried before and
failed and also because many of the patients are beyond the
point at which their teeth can be saved by such action. Other
nurses place Mr. Nephew in the category of one who is using
Maple Grange as a stepping stone in his own career and who is
not at all interested in the patients' welfare as much as his own
advantage. Parallels are drawn between him and other people
who have come to the hospital with grand plans only to see them
founder on the shoals of hard fact.

Our general conclusion was that, although both urban and rural
hospitals had their staff problems, the urban situation, precisely
because it had some elements of instability and insecurity, might be
much more responsive to change. There are situations in which
fragmentation is better than a resistive unity, and conflict more
desirable than the consensus of inertia.

Rehabilitation staff

Occupational therapists, speech therapists and physiotherapists
played a very small part in the life of the hospitals. The professional
skills available for the care and treatment of patients were almost
exclusively those of doctors and nurses. One worker noted 'the only
other skilled worker available to patients at this hospital is a hair-
dresser'. Physiotherapists visited most units on a sessional basis,
but their services were spread very thinly. One part-time physiotherapist thought that:

> At present physiotherapy is still a nebulous entity to most
> nurses even though its integration with nursing would prove a
> valuable asset to such patients. This lack of understanding on
> the nurses' part prevents them from noticing physical symptoms
> which could be treated. Instead, they see such abnormalities as
> being 'odd' or 'the way Percy has always walked'.

Some members of the nursing profession tended to regard physiotherapists, like occupational therapists, as at best peripheral to the
interests of 'their' patients, and at worst as rivals. To some extent
these professional conflicts may be due to the attitudes of the newcomers, who are insistent on professional status and expertise. There
seems to be little point in a physiotherapist visiting a hospital for
two sessions a week, giving physiotherapy to 20 or 30 patients, and
then departing, leaving a ruffled nursing staff behind her.

There was one speech therapist in the Region. 'Nursing staff', it was reported from Laker Institution, 'do not particularly see the need for one', despite the fact that many patients did not or could not speak. The lack of social work staff was also commented upon. In view of the coming transfer of patients to local authority care, the use of a social worker or community worker to maintain and create links for the patient in the outside world, to form an environment in which the patient can live without undue strain or exploitation, seemed to us vital. Nurses cannot take on, and should not be expected to take on, this complex and vital task.

One hospital in the Region had attempted to implement the proposal put forward by Dr Pauline Morris in *Put Away* for the development of a 'training arm' in the hospital in counterbalance to medical and nursing services. A director of rehabilitation had been appointed. This situation was still new, but seemed to be giving rise, as Dr Morris had predicted, to considerable conflict.

External relations

Two hospitals had a full-time organiser of voluntary services, and other hospitals were increasingly attempting to diversify their contacts. The range and variety of organisations and individuals involved, and of the kinds of relationships engendered, seemed to be very varied. We particularly liked schemes which took patients (individually or in small groups) out of the hospital, rather than concert parties and other devices for entertaining them within the walls.

Visits to the hospital by school-children had helped marginally to reduce the stigma of mental handicap by bringing them face to face with patients, but the team was doubtful whether the children were mature enough to handle the situation in some cases:

> These visits are proudly mentioned by senior staff as an example
> of close links with the local community. But after speaking to
> some of the children it appears that they are just fourth-form
> leavers that the school does not know how to keep occupied.
> There are periodic visits by their form master to make sure
> that they are actually on the ward, but no instruction is given
> by him as to what to expect and the visits are regarded as a
> form of punishment.

We were not clear how much of the activity which went on under the heading of 'voluntary services' was more successful in its public-relations aspects than in its actual effects in reducing the isolation of patients.

Conclusion

In this first and largely impressionistic stage, we attempted to look at the work of hospitals for the mentally handicapped in the Region as a whole. We found much to be said on the credit side – the staff who found a real vocation in their work, with all its frustrations and difficulties, the considerable efforts made to upgrade physical facilities, the generally high standard of catering, the absence, so far as we could discover, of the kinds of extreme ill-treatment and exploitation which have been documented elsewhere.

On the debit side, we tried to isolate the issues which gave us cause for most concern. The chief of these was the unreality of much official policy in relation to the actual ward task. The gap did not occur only between DHSS and the hospitals. It also occurred between senior hospital staff and ward staff. We felt that this arose from two main factors: the policy of integrating hospitals for the mentally handicapped into mixed hospital groups, which meant that decisions were being made and policy enunciated by senior staff who did not know at first hand the work of caring for the mentally handicapped, and the failure of tripartite administration, which often meant no leadership or inappropriate leadership.

'Integration' in the Health Service means several different things. We are attempting at one and the same time to integrate specialisms, such as the care of the mentally handicapped, more closely with general medicine, to integrate the major professions – medicine, nursing, administration – in a multidisciplinary management structure, and to integrate hospital services with community health services. It is inevitable that such fundamental changes should cause anxiety, frustration and some dislocation of services in the short term. The effects of reorganisation will be far-reaching and it may be several years before we are able to evaluate the changes.

3 Life on the wards: needs and resources

In 1972 average daily occupancy of the hospitals for the mentally handicapped in the Gateshire Region was 3,635 mentally handicapped people—about one in fourteen of all the mentally handicapped in hospital in England and Wales. In this chapter, we look at the physical environment in which patients live and staff work, the characteristics of the patient population and some aspects of staffing.

The wards

The buildings and location of the Region's hospitals for the mentally handicapped have been described in chapter 2. A more detailed study of physical conditions on the wards was undertaken, using the questionnaire devised by Dr Pauline Morris.[1]

The overall impression given by the ward returns is that material conditions were generally good. The task of keeping some 3,600 mentally handicapped people clean, warm, fed and well housed is itself a heavy one, and it is clear that a major effort has been made, and made successfully. However, we found room for concern in the use made of the accommodation and in the less tangible aspects of patient care.

Locked and unlocked wards

Of the 104 wards, only 8 were found to be locked. Of these, 7 were wards for children or for severely subnormal patients and the eighth was a hepatitis ward.

The social desirability of unlocked wards is now so strongly accepted by nursing staff that they will occasionally refer to a ward as 'unlocked', even though the door is patently locked at the time.

Patients in bed

We attempted to check whether patients were restrained by being kept in bed in the daytime. We found no cases of patients who had been confined to bed for punishment,[2] or because of shortage of staff. The patients found in bed were of three categories: the elderly, those with minor ailments, or spastics. With a more active policy, some of these patients might have been mobile.

Ward privacy

In some hospitals considerable effort had gone into the attempt to give each patient a secluded bed-space of his own. It is now generally recognised that human beings, like chimpanzees and other animals, need a defined territory which belongs, however temporarily, to them. In about one-third of the wards curtains, room-dividers or small rooms had been used to break up the barrack-like appearance of the ward and to achieve this; but in two-thirds (70 wards out of 104) all or most beds were still arranged in groups or rows without curtains.

It is appreciated that there are advantages for staff in having all patients under full observation, particularly where the ward is understaffed, or the patients need close supervision; but curtains can be pulled back when necessary. They do at least preserve the potential of privacy in a mass environment.

Space between beds

In 45 wards the space between the beds was three feet or more; in a further 41 it was between two and three feet. In the remaining 18 it was less than two feet. In one ward beds were only nine inches apart and, in another, alternate beds were pushed together and touching. The Department of Health and Social Security's standard requires that each patient should have 50 square feet of bed-space. In some cases the required amount of space was available on the ward, but not between the beds.

Bedding

On the whole, beds and bedding were of a good quality. The team looked at bedclothes and tested mattresses where necessary. One ward had hard mattresses, and 21 had bedclothes of rather poor quality. It is not known whether these were for incontinent patients, who are particularly hard on bedding and laundry.

Decorative state of the ward

77 wards were in very good decorative condition; 23 were ready for redecorating; 4 wards were in a flaking, dirty or unpleasant condition.

Flowers, ornaments and pictures; personal possessions

73 wards had been made attractive with flowers, ornaments or pictures (or toys on the children's wards). There are sometimes difficulties – exemplified by a note on the schedule for one ward which read, 'there was one vase, which was removed because a patient started eating the flowers'. But small children do this in their own homes, and teaching them to respect the furnishings is part of socialisation. 31 wards had no flowers or ornaments or pictures.

33 wards had personal possessions – photographs, sweets, transistor radios in the patients' bed-space, i.e. in or on the locker or on the bed itself. 52 had this for less than half the patients, and 19 had none. It was felt that improvement could be made in this respect.

Smell

81 wards had a fresh smell, 18 were found to be 'stuffy' by the investigators and 5 had a strong smell of incontinence. It should be noted that wards were visited during the winter, when the windows are not normally open.

Heating and lighting

Apart from one open fire, which was homely and appropriate in a small hostel, all the accommodation seen was centrally-heated. Lighting was usually central shaded or strip lighting. The latter is clearly regarded as a modern method of lighting, but its effects are peculiarly merciless and institutional – it is not what most people would choose for their own homes and it does not allow for the quiet handling of one or two wakeful patients at night. If the light is on for one patient, it is on for all. There would be much to be said, at least in new or reconditioned accommodation, for shaded bed-lights of the kind which are standard provision in most general hospitals.

Lockers

74 wards had one locker per patient. 30 had less, but these were usually wards for young children or the very severely subnormal. The fact that lockers were provided for each patient did not mean that the patient had a place of his own for private property. One team member described the common practice as 'communal use of private space'.

Window curtains or blinds

90 wards had adequate curtains or blinds, 5 had partial curtaining and 9 were totally uncurtained.

WCs and baths

24 of the wards had locking WCs. 54 had WCs with doors but no locks, 11 had only partitions, 9 were quite open and 6 varied. 38 of the wards had enclosed or screened baths. 57 had open bath accommodation and 9 varied.

This is not merely a matter of a taste for privacy. It is a matter of good nursing practice; mentally handicapped patients need more privacy than other people. Some are grossly disabled, and embarrassed by their disablement. Others are learning to cope with the processes of toileting and bathing. A patient who is learning to control bowels or bladder, or who is physically disabled and learning painfully to wash himself, needs quiet in order to do so. The presence of one helpful nurse would not be resented, but in the words of one member of the research team, 'when it comes to a dozen patients scampering through and cat-calling, it's a different matter'. Fixed partitions present difficulties in the case of physically disabled patients because of lack of room to manœuvre, but there seems no reason why screens should not be employed, as they would be in a general hospital in similar circumstances.

The provision of toilets was often inadequate. On the wards where patients were only partially continent, there were often only seven or eight WCs for 50 or more patients. Adequate toilet training would need something more like one to two patients, and the DHSS Building Note (1969) required one to three.

Where showers were provided, it was noted that in some instances the controls were close to the shower, and it was impossible for a nurse to handle them without getting wet. The possibility of placing controls outside the shower might be explored, though the dangers of unauthorised use by patients are recognised. There ought to be a simple technological answer to this problem, but if there is, no one has yet applied it.

Summary of ward analysis

1 Only 8 wards were found to be kept locked. In each case, there was an adequate reason. However, the distinction between 'locked' and 'unlocked' wards was sometimes something of a fiction – wards might be locked for part of a day and still referred to as 'open' wards.

2 With very few exceptions, patients were kept mobile during the day.

3 70 out of 104 wards had beds arranged in groups or in rows without curtains.

4 18 out of 104 wards had beds less than two feet apart.

5 The decorative condition and furnishings were generally good.

6 31 wards had no flowers or ornaments or pictures. On 71 wards less than half the patients had any personal possessions.

7 Heating and lighting were efficient, but institutional in character.

8 Lockers were provided on most wards, but not all were used for individual storage of property.

9 The provision of baths was often inadequate in type. The provision of WCs was inadequate both in type and in number, in certain instances falling seriously below DHSS standards.

A detailed statistical comparison with the Morris data has not been attempted. Our experience suggested that much of the ward data was of limited validity, partly owing to the numbers of investigators involved and their varying standards, and partly owing to changing circumstances; factors like the arrangement of beds, the number of patients mobile, the display of personal possessions, the use of lockers and the use of side-rooms, could vary from day to day, and certainly from charge nurse to charge nurse. We have, therefore, confined our report to fairly general observations. However, despite the considerable upgrading of wards in the past few years, it is clear that many of the problems noted in the Morris survey still persist. They are primarily failures not of money and supplies, but of imagination. The research team was strongly of the opinion that ward conditions, even good ward conditions, do not provide a suitable living environment for most mentally handicapped patients.

The patients

As in other Regions, the average daily bed occupancy runs somewhat below the average number of beds available. In 1961 the percentage of available beds occupied in hospitals for the mentally handicapped in the Gateshire Region was 96·6, and in 1972 it was 88·9. This suggests some slackening of pressure on beds, probably associated with a higher patient turnover. Generally, high bed occupancy values are associated with long-stay care, since beds are continuously occupied. With a move to shorter or intermittent patterns of care for some patients, beds are likely to remain empty for a few days between the discharge of one patient and the admission of the next.[3] The national bed occupancy rate for the mentally handicapped in 1972 was 92·53, and that for all specialties 82·83.[4]

Between 1966 and 1972 the number of beds available in Gateshire increased by 39, or just over 1 per cent. During the same period the population at risk (i.e. the total population of the Region) rose by over 4 per cent, so that total demand increased and was not met by the supply of fresh beds.

The increased demand was not apparently met by out-patient services. Returns indicated that there were no out-patient facilities at all up to 1964. In 1972 there were 268 out-patient sessions; but these involved only 490 attendances in all, including the registration of 196 new patients, so it looks as though few patients were seen more than twice at most. This skeleton service may have been valuable for some purposes, such as diagnosis or assessment, but it was hardly a substitute for hospital care. We can conclude that either the level of service decreased or that there was a shift from medical to social care.

Admission and discharge policy

Tables 3.1 and 3.2 compare admissions and departures ('departure' = discharges plus deaths) for the Region with the national average.

Several points are notable here:

i Given a fixed stock of beds, or nearly so, and a high percentage occupancy, admissions are a function of departure – patients can only be admitted to beds which have been vacated by other patients.

ii Comparison indicates a slightly faster patient flow for the Gateshire Region than for England and Wales as a whole.

c

Table 3.1   *Annual number of admissions per 100 occupied beds, Gateshire Region and England and Wales, 1968–72*

Year	Gateshire region	England and Wales
1968	21·6	18·7
1969	19·8	17·8
1970	20·2	20·0
1971	16·6	*
1972	25·9	*

* Statistics not available.

Table 3.2   *Annual number of departures per 100 occupied beds, Gateshire Region and England and Wales, 1968–71*

Year	Gateshire region	England and Wales
1968	23·6	21·8
1969	23·6	22·1
1970	24·2	24·8
1971	23·5	28·6
1972	31·1	31·2

Sources (Tables 3.1 and 3.2): Gateshire region: RHB statistics. England and Wales: *Health and Personal Social Service Statistics*, 1973, tables 9.2, 9.9, 9.10.

iii By comparison with other medical specialties, patient flow in hospitals for the mentally handicapped is very low. However, both in the Region and in England and Wales as a whole, about one patient in three moves annually. In the Region this involves a capacity of about 1,300 beds.

iv An examination of the rates of first admissions and multiple admissions gives increasing indications that the 'revolving-door' policy applied to mental hospitals in the 1960s has now reached hospitals for the mentally handicapped (Table 3.3).

At the end of the 1960s only one admission in three in the Gateshire Region was a first admission, and the figure has dropped to about one in seven. Figures for England and Wales have been slower to fall, but exhibit the same trend.

v 'Departure' covers deaths, transfers and discharges. In 1972 deaths in hospitals for the mentally handicapped in the Region amounted to 13·1 per cent of all departures. Figures for England

Table 3.3   First admissions, Gateshire Region and England and
Wales, 1966–72 (first admission as a percentage of all
admissions)

Year	Gateshire region	England and Wales
1968	32·9	43·5
1969	36·3	43·9
1970	19·8	20·1
1971	14·6	18·0
1972	13·2	16·0

Source: DHSS Mental Health Enquiry.

and Wales are not broken down to give an equivalent. Transfers
present a problem from the statistical point of view. Though the
number of transfers from one hospital to another is not large, it
does constitute a movement within the Hospital Service, and it
would be useful to be able to distinguish such cases from discharges
to the community; but since patients returning to the community
may be going to differing degrees of care by the health and welfare
services, the distinction may become increasingly academic.

vi   The question of how patients are referred from one form of
care to another (and whether in fact they are referred at all) is an
interesting one on which no national statistics are as yet available.
Table 3.4, (p. 50) shows referrals for the Gateshire Region 1971.

It can be seen from these tables that the referral rate varies from
92 per cent in male hospital 7 to nil in four hospitals. It is unlikely
that such a large variation is explicable wholly in terms of patient
need. The degree of co-operation and co-ordination between the
hospital and the Social Services Department (or the lack of it) is a
more likely explanation in many cases. Some hospitals are operating
as closed systems, rather than as parts of a wider and continuous
service.[5]

The patient census

Early in 1971 Regional Hospital Boards were asked by the Department of Health and Social Security to carry out a sample census
of mentally handicapped patients in hospital as at midnight on
31 December 1970. The census covered one patient in three by
random sampling.[6] DHSS issued sampling instructions, but did not

stipulate which branch of the Hospital Service should take responsibility for the survey. The most common practice in the Gateshire Region appears to have been for office staff to complete the questions for which recorded information was available, and for ward staff to complete those relating to incapacities and behaviour.

Table 3.4   Patients referred to local authority on discharge, by sex and hospital: Gateshire Region, 1971

	Patients discharged	Patients referred	Percentage referred
Males			
Hospital no. 1	48	—	—
2	55	40	73
3	—	—	—
4	4	—	—
5	—	—	—
6	32	5	16
7	25	23	92
8	38	26	68
9	38	31	82
10	30	6	20
11	10	5	50
12	87	65	75
Total	367	201	55
Females			
Hospital no. 1	76	—	—
2	9	4	44
3	33	11	33
4	40	27	68
5	16	6	37
6	10	7	70
7	44	10	23
8	93	66	71
9	5	—	—
10	3	—	—
Total	329	131	40

Source: Regional returns to Mental Health inquiry. The hospital numbers for males and females do not necessarily correspond, so that the tables cannot be consolidated for both sexes.

The tables which follow are drawn from the census data submitted by the Gateshire Region. Tables in the text are given in percentages. Records were analysed for 865 male patients and 683 female patients (male 55·9 per cent, female 44·1 per cent).

Comparison with the Registrar General's figures for the general population[7] (male 48·5 per cent, female 51·5 per cent) indicates that, unlike hospitals for the mentally ill, where there is an excess of female patients due in the main to the longer life-span of female psycho-geriatric patients, hospitals for the mentally handicapped have a preponderance of males. This is explicable in terms of the comparative youth of the patients, since there is now an excess of males over females in the general population in all age groups up to the age of 45, and most mentally handicapped people do not live to a great age (Table 3.5).

Table 3.5   Census sample: sex and age (N = 1,548)

Age	Male	Female	Total
Under 10	4·5	5·6	5·0
10–19	15·4	12·4	14·1
20–29	18·5	12·6	15·9
30–39	13·1	13·1	13·0
40–49	14·7	15·1	14·9
50–59	14·9	15·4	15·1
60–69	9·1	11·4	10·1
70+	3·2	5·2	4·1
Not known	6·6	9·2	7·8

The table suggests a fairly even age distribution through the middle age groups, but a comparatively small group representing the young and the old. Again, comparison with the figures for the general population makes the point clearer (Table 3.6).

The under-representation of the under-thirties suggests that many mentally handicapped people are cared for at home as long as their parents are able to cope. The death or incapacity of parents in old age may result in hospital admission, since brothers and sisters, with their own family responsibilities at their heaviest in middle life, cannot offer a comparable quality of care. Similar patterns have been observed in relation to patients suffering from schizophrenia[8] and acute epilepsy.[9]

Table 3.6   *Census sample: age groups in comparison with home population (Great Britain) (N = 1,548)*

	Mentally handicapped (sample)	Survey region population	Home population
Under 30	34·9	44·4	45·0
30–60	43·1	36·4	36·5
60+	14·2	19·2	18·5
Not known	7·8	—	—

Sources: Gateshire region population: *Registrar General's Quarterly Returns* No. 490, quarter ended 30 June 1971; home population: *Social Trends*, vol. 1, HMSO, 1970, table 9.

At the other end of the age scale, the mentally handicapped sample has a somewhat shorter expectation of life than the general public; but in view of the popular belief that most mentally handicapped people die young, it is perhaps important to stress that a considerable number now survive into their sixties and seventies.

The differential risk of hospitalisation for males compared with females at different ages is brought out clearly by the following table, which shows the number of in-patients in each age group relative to the mid-year population of the Gateshire region in 1970. While the rates hardly differ in the youngest age group (the rate for females is slightly higher), the excess of males is particularly noticeable for those in their twenties (Table 3.7).

Table 3.7   *Census sample: in-patient rates per 100,000 regional population, by age and sex (N = 1,548)*

Age	Male	Female
Under 10	14	15
10–19	57	38
20–29	72	40
30–39	58	49
40–49	62	52
50–59	69	52
60–69	50	40
70+	31	20
All ages	55	41

Table 3.8 Census sample: length of stay to date (N = 1,548)

Years	Patients (%)
<1	6·7
1–10	32·5
11–20	25·7
21–30	18·8
30+	16·3

Data on length of stay in hospital (since the date of the most recent admission case of those with multiple admissions) is as shown in Table 3.8

Nearly two-thirds of all these patients had been in hospital continuously for more than ten years, and over one-third for more than twenty years. Nineteen had been in hospital continuously since 1919 or earlier – over fifty years. Such patients present formidable and perhaps insoluble problems in rehabilitation. Those legally classified as being of 'informal' status included 843 males and 679 females, only 22 males and 4 females (total under 2 per cent) being formally detained under sections of the Mental Health Act, 1959. This is something of a legal fiction, since patients are not formally detained unless they actively desire to discharge themselves.

Table 3.9 relates to the incapacities of these patients as observed by nursing staff. These observations may vary in objectivity and in accuracy. What is perceived may, in some cases, be a function of the nurses' capacity to nurse rather than of the patient's capacity to conform to social expectations.[10]

Incontinence has always been a problem in hospitals for the mentally handicapped, causing subsidiary problems in the provision of suitable clothing, laundry facilities and arrangements for general hygiene. In certain circumstances, it can seriously affect the management of a ward and the quality of life for those who live and work within it. However, these figures indicate that, though it may be a severe problem, it is not as widespread as is sometimes suggested. Four out of five patients were usually both clean and dry at nights – and more in the daytime. Only 220 (one in seven) were doubly incontinent by both day and night. As might be expected in view of the relatively greater numbers of older females, a slightly higher proportion of females than of males is frequently incontinent, both

Table 3.9   Incontinence (percentages) (N = 1,541)

Wetting nights	Frequently	20·8
	Occasionally	18·9
	Never	60·3
Soiling nights	Frequently	16·2
	Occasionally	14·7
	Never	69·1
Wetting days	Frequently	17·6
	Occasionally	16·5
	Never	65·9
Soiling days	Frequently	15·5
	Occasionally	12·1
	Never	72·4

Note In Tables 3.9–3.18 records for seven patients have been omitted because they were incomplete. The total is therefore 1,541.

Table 3.10   Physical mobility (percentages) (N = 1,541)

Immobile	8·5
Partially mobile	19·3
Fully mobile	72·2

for wetting and soiling by day and night. The differences, however, are not statistically significant.

Table 3.10 relates to physical mobility, another key factor in patient care. Patients described as 'fully mobile' were able to walk unaided on the flat and up stairs. Those described as 'immobile' could not walk at all, even with help. 'Partially mobile' covers the intermediate stages; some could walk unaided on the flat, but needed help to negotiate stairs, some needed help in both cases, and some were totally unable to manage stairs. Again what is noteworthy is that nearly three-quarters of all patients were fully mobile. But almost one patient in ten was virtually bedfast, and this group represents a considerable problem in ward management.

More than four patients in five could feed themselves (Table 3.11), but a higher proportion required help with washing and dressing or had to have these tasks performed for them. It is possible that on short-staffed wards, nurses find it quicker and easier to wash and dress patients than to teach them to wash and dress themselves –

Table 3.11   Feeding, washing and dressing (percentages) (N = 1,541)

Able to feed self	Not at all	10·6
	With help	6·4
	Without help	83·0
Able to wash self	Not at all	26·9
	With help	16·5
	Without help	56·6
Able to dress self	Not at all	22·8
	With help	20·3
	Without help	56·9

particularly where ward routine allows only a limited time before the next item on the programme. The sex differences to be expected in view of the higher ages of female patients were particularly in evidence for washing and dressing. A considerably higher proportion of females than of males were unable to wash and dress themselves, and when the null hypothesis of no association between sex and self-care was tested, the results for both washing and dressing were significant at the 1 per cent level.

Only 4 per cent were blind (Table 3.12), or nearly so, and 4 per cent were deaf, or nearly so. The overwhelming majority scored 'normal' on both counts. A much greater proportion had speech handicaps, 40 per cent being unable to utter more than odd words at most, while a further 2 per cent were said to be able to talk, but did not do so (perhaps for lack of anything to say).

Information on education and employment is difficult to analyse,

Table 3.12   Vision, hearing and speech (percentages) (N = 1,541)

Vision	Blind (or almost)	4·5
	Poor sight	12·3
	Normal	83·2
Hearing	Deaf (or almost)	3·8
	Poor hearing	8·3
	Normal	87·9
Speech	None	18·9
	Odd words only	20·7
	Normal	58·3
	Can talk—does not	2·1

C*

since attendance at a local authority training centre or occupational therapy are listed under 'Education', and industrial therapy and work outside the hospital under 'Employment', and the two sets of items are not related. However, the figures do indicate that only 2 per cent worked outside the hospital and less than 1 per cent attended a local authority training centre. Seven per cent attended the hospital school,[11] and 8 per cent attended school 'elsewhere' – though there is no indication as to whether this means attendance at an outside school or part-time teaching on the ward; 26 per cent helped on the ward, 9 per cent helping 'considerably'; 59 per cent received no education of any kind, and 45 per cent did no work of any kind, not even giving the most limited help on the ward.

Deficiencies in recording, particularly for long-stay patients whose records had been completed many years ago, made it impossible to make an assessment of intelligence. Even where an original estimate had been made at the time of admission, no hospital made a regular reassessment of IQ or mental age. However, nurses' estimates of the patients' capacities, at the time of the survey, in the basic skills of reading, writing and counting were given (Table 3.13).

These figures show very large groups of patients without the fundamental skills for taking part in outside life. Whether or not they are totally incapable of reading, writing and counting, they were certainly incapable at the time of the survey, and would be quite at a loss in a society where it is necessary to be able to read directions, sign one's name and handle money – 59 per cent of all patients could not do any of these things in any degree.

Table 3.13　*Ability to read, write and count (percentages)*
　　　　　　(N = 1,541)

Reads	Nothing	71·3
	Little	15·7
	Newspapers/books	13·0
Writes	Nothing	75·0
	Little	16·0
	Own correspondence	9·0
Counts	Nothing	62·5
	A little	19·7
	Understands money values	17·8

Table 3.14   Behaviour problems (percentages) (N = 1,541)

a	Hits out or attacks others	Marked	9·3
		Lesser	19·4
		No	71·3
b	Tears up papers, magazines	Marked	6·3
	clothing, or damages furniture	Lesser	11·6
		No	82·1
c	Extremely overactive, paces	Marked	10·9
	up and down restlessly	Lesser	11·0
		No	78·1
d	Constantly seeking attention	Marked	9·9
	– will not leave adults	Lesser	15·1
		No	75·0
e	Continuously injuring himself/	Marked	5·5
	herself, e.g. head-banging,	Lesser	6·7
	beating eyes, etc.	No	87·8
f	Anti-social, irresponsible,	Yes	16·3
	given to petty offences	No	83·7

Table 3.14 relates to common behaviour problems involving aggressive, destructive or irresponsible behaviour. The first impression which this table gives is that roughly four out of five patients had no behaviour problems, since between 75 and 85 per cent score 'no' on any one item. If this were the case, a sizeable group of patients should score 'yes' on all items; in fact, only seven patients – less than half of 1 per cent – did so.

The differences between the sexes with regard to behaviour problems were on the whole unremarkable (Tables 3.15–3.18). When the null hypothesis of no association between sex and degree of behaviour problem was rejected, however, the results were of some interest: for both aggressive and anxious behaviour ((a) and (c) in Table 3.14), the chi-square statistic took a value which was significant at the 5 per cent level. While this was attributable to the higher proportion of markedly aggressive females in the case of aggressive behaviour, the result for anxious behaviour was due to a higher proportion of markedly anxious males. Among the mentally handicapped, the conventional stereotypes of 'neurotic female' and 'aggressive male' seem if anything to be reversed; but it may, of

Table 3.15   Ability to wash self, by sex (N = 1,541*)

	Male (%)	Female (%)
Not at all	23·9	30·6
With help	16·4	16·6
Without help	59·7	52·8

$\chi^2 = 9\cdot3$, $P < 0.01$.
* And throughout Tables 3.16–3.18.

Table 3.16   Ability to dress self, by sex

	Male (%)	Female (%)
Not at all	20·0	26·5
With help	22·0	18·0
Without help	58·0	55·5

$\chi^2 = 10\cdot6$, $P < 0\cdot01$.

Table 3.17   Aggressive behaviour, by sex

	Male (%)	Female (%)
Hits out or attacks others		
Marked	7·8	11·2
Lesser	18·8	20·1
No	73·4	68·7

$\chi^2 = 6\cdot3$, $P < 0\cdot05$.

Table 3.18   Anxious behaviour, by sex

	Male (%)	Female (%)
Extremely overactive, etc.		
Marked	12·8	8·5
Lesser	11·4	10·5
No	75·8	81·0

$\chi^2 = 7\cdot9$, $P < 0\cdot05$. Tables 3.15–3.18: 2 D.F.

course, be the case that a higher degree of aggression is expected and tolerated in males and a higher degree of neuroticism in females, so that it is the aggressive female and the neurotic male who stand out from the majority.

The items of this part of the questionnaire seem somewhat uncertain in intent. Is it really a 'behaviour problem' if a patient paces restlessly up and down or seeks attention? These may be perfectly natural reactions to a confined and depersonalised way of life.

If the policy outlined by the 1971 White Paper is to be implemented, we need to know the answers to two questions:

i Does the population of the hospitals for the mentally handicapped consist of two fairly clear-cut groups, one grossly and permanently handicapped, and the other possessed of fairly normal social capacities even in a diminished degree?

ii Are there many among the apparently incapacitated who appear so because of deficiencies in training rather than because of inherent incapacity?

If the answer to both these questions is in the affirmative, then the new policy of running down the hospitals to approximately 50 per cent of present capacity makes very good sense. There are plenty of continent, mobile patients without behaviour problems who can read, write and count, feed, wash and dress themselves, and who have good sight, good hearing and articulate speech. Others may lack these abilities, but can be trained in a small-group setting to develop them.

However, if the answer to both questions is in the negative, i.e. if the disabilities recorded are scattered over almost the whole population and they are inherent rather than institutionally induced, the wisdom of moving 50 per cent of patients to a non-nursing setting is very much more questionable.

The dependency survey

With the help of the Gateshire Region's statistical section, we were able to carry out further work which clarifies this problem. Combining factors in the DHSS questionnaire to make a meaningful picture of dependence involves some selection and some rather arbitrary decisions. The questionnaire allows for considerable incapacity, some incapacity or no incapacity on the following fourteen items:

wetting nights	vision
soiling nights	hearing
wetting days	speech
soiling days	reading
walking	writing
feeding self	counting
washing self	
dressing self	

Clearly these items cannot be equally weighted, since some are interrelated (a doubly incontinent patient would score 4 straight off) and some overlap (if a patient never speaks, he will neither read nor count). Nor can all the possible cross-correlations be attempted, since this would involve 4,780,000 separate items (3^{14}).

Table 3.19   Patients requiring continuous process care ($N = 1,548$)

	Number	Percentage of sample
One severe disability	660	42·6
Severe subnormality and another disability	108	7·0
Three disabilities	223	14·6
Total	991	64·2

A dependency index was constructed on the following lines; it was assumed that the key factor in the hospital's function for such patients was *continuous process care* of a type which local authority homes can seldom provide and families can only provide with very great strain. It was then a matter of looking for factors which necessitated such 24-hour-a-day care. It was decided to include (see Table 3.19):

1   A group with *one* disability (in addition to mental handicap) of such severity that they required continuous process care, irrespective of whether they had other disabilities. These disabilities were:

frequently wetting days
unable to speak
completely immobile

This group totalled 660, leaving 888 of the original sample population of 1,548.

2   A severely subnormal group with an additional disability.

Severely subnormal and sometimes incontinent by day.
Severely subnormal and unable to walk unaided.
Severely subnormal and blind.
Severely subnormal and deaf.

This group totalled 108, leaving 780 of the original sample population.

3   A group scoring in three or more of the following sets of incapacities in addition to mental handicap:

incontinence
immobility
unable to feed or wash or dress
blind or partially sighted
deaf or poor hearing
no speech or odd words only
unable to read or write or count

This group totalled 223, leaving 557 of the original sample population.

On these fairly stringent criteria, 64·2 per cent of the patients require continuous process care. The census includes child patients, for whom a much less rigorous discharge policy is envisaged, and young children, who although comparatively few, are often among the most severely dependent patients. If we assume that *all* patients under the age of fifteen are severely disabled, and subtract them both from the sample number and the number severely dependent, the proportion of severely dependent adults drops to 59·1 per cent.[12] To discharge 50 per cent of all adult patients would mean the transfer to local authorities of at least 9 per cent of the present adult hospital population who are severely disabled and in need of continuous process care. As chapter 7 will show, local authority homes are staffed on the assumption that patients will not require this degree of attention. Many wardens and their staff take full daytime responsibility without intermission, and there is no night shift. If the discharge policy is maintained, local authorities may have to provide some homes with much more intensive staffing than most of them have so far envisaged.

Summary of patient analysis

1   Bed occupancy declined slightly between 1966 and 1971. The population at risk rose by 4 per cent in the same period.

2   Out-patient facilities are increasing, but are still very limited.

3   Approximately 20 patients annually are discharged for every 100 beds; about one patient in five moves annually.

4   The proportion of multiple admissions has risen sharply. By 1971 only one patient in seven was a first admission.

5   There appears to be no established policy concerning referrals to local authority care on discharge.

6   Many patients enter hospital in the middle years of life, often when parental care fails.

7   Two-thirds have been in hospital continuously for more than ten years, and more than one-third for more than twenty years. Since (point 4) most admissions are now readmissions, the population shows little real movement.

8   About 15–20 per cent of patients are seriously incapacitated by incontinence, 28 per cent by limited mobility, 25 per cent by inability to feed, wash and dress themselves even with assistance, and 40 per cent by speech defects.

9   Only 2 per cent work outside the hospital, and less than 1 per cent attend a local authority training centre. Nearly 60 per cent receive no education of any kind, and 45 per cent do no work of any kind.

10   No hospital made a regular reassessment of IQ or mental age.

11   Few can read or write, and only one in six can handle money.

12   About 60 per cent of patients require continuous process care.

The staff

Medical staff

There were only 9 consultant psychiatrists for mentally handicapped patients in the Region, and approximately 6 medical staff in junior grades. One Senior House Officer was full-time, 4 clinical assistants worked on a sessional basis and there were several vacant sessions. The development of out-patient and consultancy work, together with an increasing volume of committee work consequent on the reorganisation of the Health Service, took up increasing amounts of the consultants' available time. Tripartite administration had reduced their direct responsibility for administration, but our impression was that discussion and attempts to reach consensus proved more time-consuming than straightforward decision-making. All were fully stretched, with an increasing scatter of responsibility and clinical attachment. The 26 hospitals and units formed only part of their work and the clinical care of individual patients was in many cases minimal.

Nursing staff

The total number of nursing staff in the hospitals for the mentally handicapped in the Gateshire Region in 1971 was 1,547, or 1:2·3 patients (Tables 3.20 and 3.21). This compares with a ratio for all

Table 3.20   *Nursing staff, by sex and whole-/part-time (N = 1,547)*

	Whole-time (%)	Part-time (%) (whole-time equivalent)	Total (%)
Male	29·6	1·3	30·9
Female	46·7	22·4	69·1
Total	76·3	23·7	100·0

Table 3.21   *Nursing staff, by grade and whole-/part-time (N = 1,547)*

	Whole-time (%)	Part-time (WTE) (%)	Total (%)
Administrative	4·6	—	4·6
Tutors	0·3	—	0·3
Sisters/charge nurses	15·5	1·4	16·9
Staff nurses	4·3	2·4	6·7
Senior enrolled nurses	0·5	0·1	0·6
Enrolled nurses	14·4	6·0	20·4
Student nurses	9·2	—	9·2
Pupil nurses	5·5	0·4	5·9
Nursing assistants	21·9	13·5	35·4
	76·2	23·8	100·0

specialities in England and Wales of 1·21, and of psychiatric nurses in England and Wales of 2·75.[13]

About one-third of all nursing staff were men. Whole-time nurses greatly outnumbered part-timers (WTE), and we were informed that many part-timers worked about two-thirds of a working week, so they did not greatly complicate duty rotas. The shortage of tutors was marked (there were in fact five, of whom four were not qualified tutors), and this was particularly serious in view of the number of staff in training. Most of the senior staff had a psychiatric qualification, but this was more often RMN (appropriate to nursing the mentally ill) than RNMS (appropriate to nursing the mentally handicapped).[14] It is generally much easier for a nurse with RMN to move into nursing the mentally handicapped than for one with RNMS to move into the field of mental illness, since the run-down of mental hospitals has taken place in a period when numbers in hospitals for the mentally handicapped has remained virtually static. One member of the research team was to argue that this was a distinct advantage, since RMNs had a more flexible approach to patient care than nurses who were trained in the field of mental handicap.

As in most hospitals, the bulk of the work of ward nursing is done by enrolled nurses and untrained nursing assistants. The situation in which a fully-trained nurse ceases to nurse soon after qualification and takes to administration has often been commented on, and has been the subject of many training discussions.

Rehabilitation staff

If qualified nursing staff are scarce, qualified staff for rehabilitation are almost non-existent (Table 3.22). The figures in the table are

Table 3.22   Rehabilitation staff

	Whole-time	Part-time (actual number)
Remedial gymnasts	1	—
Occupational therapists	4	3
Speech therapists	1	—
Physiotherapists	3	6
Social workers	3	4

actual numbers for staff in the 26 hospitals for the mentally handicapped. The following points are relevant:

i The workers listed were employed by particular hospital
authorities and in particular hospitals, that is, the one remedial
gymnast and the one speech therapist were not free to work over a
range of hospitals. Most hospitals had no access to these services
at all.

ii In some cases, there were suitably qualified workers in the
Group, but they were not employed in the hospitals for the mentally handicapped. Remedial gymnasts, physiotherapists and social
workers were concentrated in acute general hospitals; occupational
therapists tended to be employed by the large mental hospitals. The
sharing of rehabilitation staff between hospitals even in the same
Group did not seem to occur.

iii In the case of social workers, the 3 full-time staff consisted
of 1 qualified social worker and 2 without any qualification in either
social work or social science. The hospital Groups which contained
hospitals for the mentally handicapped mustered between them at
least 21 qualified social workers, but again these staff were heavily
concentrated in the acute general hospitals.

iv The lack of rehabilitation staff has a clear relevance to the
problems of the patient population.

It is difficult to see how an active process of rehabilitation and
discharge to the community can even be discussed until this dis-
proportion is remedied. To take only one example, the development
of any kind of learning in patients is heavily dependent on the power
of verbal communication. Over 40 per cent of the patients either
cannot speak at all, or speak only a few words. There is only one
speech therapist – in one hospital. The Region has advertised repeatedly for speech therapists, and there is a speech-therapy training school in the Region's geographical area. This is a good example
of social and professional impediments to policy implementation.
To recommend 'more speech therapists' is simple enough; to recruit and keep them is very much more difficult, for a variety of
reasons; salary scales are low, which means that most of them are
young women and there is a rapid turnover due to marriage; there
is a drift to the better employment opportunities of the south; those
who stay in the north go to more prestigious branches of employment; if they go into hospitals for the mentally handicapped, their
skills may not be fully used and appreciated, so that they do not
stay long. We return to this complex of problems in chapter 8.

Summary of staff analysis

1   There are only 9 consultant psychiatrists with responsibility for mentally handicapped patients in the Region. The development of out-patient work and consultancy services must mean a diminution of their services to the 26 hospitals and units.

2   There is a nursing staff of 1,547 (part-timers equated to full-time). Almost all the work of caring for patients is done by nursing personnel.

3   Registered nurses – whether SRN, RMN or RNMS – are employed almost exclusively in administrative posts at ward level or above.

4   Over one-third of nursing personnel – about half the staff actually on the wards – are nursing assistants.

5   About one-third of nursing staff are male.

6   Part-time nurses are almost exclusively female.

7   Social workers, occupational therapists, physiotherapists, speech therapists and remedial gymnasts are virtually non-existent in all but the largest hospitals.

4   Nursing attitudes

In concluding the section on mental subnormality in their first annual report, the Hospital Advisory Group stated:[1]

> It is difficult to convey to those who have no experience of the problems the stress imposed on ward staff. For example, two nurses may be responsible for rousing, dressing and toileting 50 or so severely handicapped patients, most of whom cannot dress themselves without some help, and many are incontinent or become so with minimum waiting. In this situation there may be only two toilets available in the dormitory area. The same ward may have no room for occupational or social therapy, the hospital departments concerned may be too small and none of the patients may leave the ward from one week to the next. These conditions are the fault of management at all levels, not of ward staff, and the latter are understandably resentful of criticism they have sometimes received.

Better Services for the Mentally Handicapped expresses the hope that the nurses will 'improve the quality of their patients' daily life when the means of doing so are put into their hands'.[2] But are the principles and objectives of the policy-makers seen as practicable and attainable by the ward staff? Government documents are necessarily framed in broad general terms. How far are these perceived as realistic by the people in continuous daily contact with the patients?

Principles of the 1971 White Paper

The objectives of the hospital care of the mentally handicapped are carefully defined and a section of the report is set aside to summarise the 'main principles on which current thinking about mental handicap is based'.[3] Fifteen principles are outlined, two examples being:

> Full use should be made of available knowledge which can help to prevent mental handicap or to reduce the severity of its effects.

67

Local authority personal social services for the mentally handicapped should develop as an integral part of the services recently brought together under the Local Authority Social Services Act, 1970.

However, one principle appears to provide the basic philosophy from which such statements of intent are derived. This is the fifth principle (emphasis added):

Each handicapped person needs stimulation, social training and education and purposeful occupation or employment *in order to develop to his maximum capacity* and to exercise all the skills he acquires, *however limited* they may be.

This principle is taken as the foundation on which the White Paper is based and, in measuring the White Paper's relevance for ward staff, we have attempted to operationalise the principle in terms of an attitude scale. This scale is formally defined in the following section.

Treatment Orientation Scale[4]

The Treatment Orientation Scale is a continuum, the two extremes of which are defined in ideal-type constructs of 'optimism' and 'pessimism' towards the treatment of mentally subnormal patients. An 'optimist' is actively oriented towards the needs and situation of mentally handicapped patients. He or she believes that all patients have a potential for development, either manifest or latent, and that every effort should be made to realise this potential. There is an emphasis on the patient as an individual, and a high degree of flexibility in relating to patients.

A 'pessimist' is basically passive in relation to the needs and situation of mentally handicapped patients. A fatalistic attitude is often supported by misconceptions about the nature of mental subnormality. Pessimists see very little point in doing anything other than washing, feeding and providing a protective environment. This produces a custodial approach to the patient. Attempts to improve the level of social functioning of patients are seen as futile, since it is believed that they cannot be helped.

The formulation and definition of the Treatment Orientation Scale in terms of optimism and pessimism towards the treatment of mentally subnormal patients was initially suggested by experiences gained by a member of the team who worked as a nursing assistant on a ward for low-grade patients. Relevant research literature was also consulted. However, little has been written in recent years about staff attitudes and problems. Dr Pauline Morris noted in 1969:[5]

> It is perhaps significant that the majority of writings about hospital provision for the mentally subnormal do not mention the staff in any detail.

Research literature

In view of the interest shown in policy for the mentally handicapped in recent years, one would expect to find in the literature some systematic attempts to measure the attitudes of ward staff, but staff are mentioned only incidentally in the main studies.

In their recent study on residential institutions for mentally handicapped children, King, Raynes and Tizard simply state 'We made no direct study of the attitudes of staff'.[6] The research conducted by Tizard in the Brooklands experiment and by Kushlick in the Wessex Region has indicated the importance of what can best be described as a patient-oriented attitude among staff if the social learning of a patient is to be improved.[7] None the less, what information there is tends at best to be fragmentary and to represent only one grade of ward staff, registered nurses. When Pauline Morris talks about how nurses see their role on the ward, she is talking about sisters and charge nurses who comprise 95 per cent of the sample on which her arguments are based.[8] Similarly, when Maureen Oswin in her section on nurses provides five illustrative examples, only one refers to a nursing assistant while the remaining four relate to sisters and charge nurses.[9]

In spite of this bias, one point recurs throughout the studies – that the ward situation means different things to different people, not only between those working on and off the ward, but also those working on the ward. Pauline Morris applies Parsons' distinction between expressive and instrumental roles to female and male nurses respectively.[10] In a similar vein, Maureen Oswin distinguishes between 'married, unqualified staff' (middle-aged and part-time) and 'unmarried, qualified career nurses'.[11]

Such impressionistic distinctions indicate that different groups of staff approach the ward situation with different expectations. For some there will be a high commitment to helping the patients; for others nursing will be seen as providing a professional training; for others there will be a 'nine to five' attitude to their work which is often found in mass-production industries – their central life interest lies outside their work, which is no more than a means to an end.

Methodology

A. V. Cicourel has stated:[12]

> Questionnaire responses are like the punched holes of an IBM card: the meanings and rules for their creation and interpretation are not to be found in them per se or in aggregates of them, but rather in their differential perceptions and interpretations which produced the researcher's decision in composing them.

To explore such 'differential perceptions and interpretations', we therefore relied primarily on participant observation, followed by a period of three months' informal discussion with staff at all levels. The next stage was to construct a pool of attitude statements relating to the Treatment Orientation Scale. This was presented to respondents in a pilot survey, conducted in two hospitals for the mentally handicapped in a neighbouring Region. After analysis twenty-two statements were selected for the main study.

The final draft of the interview schedule was administered by four interviewers. Ward staff in the hospitals for the mentally handicapped in the Gateshire Region were selected from a sample frame constructed from staff lists for 1 February 1972. These lists were provided by the nursing directors of the hospitals and were organised into four strata:

Registered nurses – sisters, charge nurses and staff nurses.

Enrolled nurses – State Enrolled Nurses.

Nurses in training – student nurses training for the Register and pupil nurses training for enrolment (cadet nurses were excluded).

Nursing assistants – nursing assistants and nursing auxiliaries, aides and orderlies when they were the responsibility of the nursing director and not the domestic supervisor.

A uniform sampling fraction of one in four was applied in each stratum, and selection was by a table of random numbers. Table 4.1 gives the number of staff involved.

The 227 ward staff who were interviewed represent a response rate of 78 per cent. Comparison of the characteristics of the sample population with that of the population from which it is drawn

Table 4.1 Ward staff, by ward grade for the total, sample and respondent populations

Ward grade	Total	Sample	Respondents
Registered	231	58	47
Enrolled	303	76	56
Training	154	39	31
Assistants	479	119	93
Total	1,167	292	227

suggests that the sample is deficient in the representation of part-time female day-staff.[13]

The rest of this section presents the data collected on the characteristics of the sample.

Age, sex, marital status

About one-third of the ward staff in the Region were known to be men.[14] A similar proportion was found in the sample.

Only in the 'registered' ward grade is there a greater number of men than women. Men and women are evenly represented in the training grade. For the remaining two ward grades, men are out-numbered by women – representing about one in three enrolled nurses and one in five nursing assistants. Table 4.3 shows age distribution by ward grade.

There are no substantial differences in the age distribution between men and women for the sample as a whole or within grades. Not

Table 4.2 Ward grade and sex

Ward grade	Male	Female	Total
Registered	26	21	47
Enrolled	18	38	56
Training	15	16	31
Assistant	17	76	93
Total	76	151	227

Table 4.3   Ward grade and age

Ward grade	Under 25	26–35	36–45	46–55	56–65	Total
Registered	6	16	8	11	6	47
Enrolled	1	6	8	27	14	56
Training	20	4	5	2	—	31
Assistant	11	31	22	21	8	93
Total	38	57	43	61	28	227

surprisingly, a greater proportion of staff in the training grade are under 25 years old, but one-quarter of enrolled nurses are in the 56–65 years age category. For the sample as a whole, approximately two out of five staff are over 45 years old.

Table 4.4 indicates that just under one-fifth of the sample are single. The greatest number of single staff, as expected, come in the training group. There are no substantial differences in the proportions of men and women staff who are married.

Work pattern

'Work pattern' is formed by the various combinations of the two variables whole/part-time and night shift/day shift. Tables 4.5 and 4.6 present the results in terms of ward grade and sex.

What is immediately apparent from these tables is that nursing assistants provide the bulk of labour on the day and night shifts,

Table 4.4   Ward grade and marital status

Ward grade	Single	Married	Widowed/ divorced/ separated	Total
Registered	8	39	—	47
Enrolled	7	48	1	56
Training	15	16	—	31
Assistant	12	70	11	93
Total	42	173	12	227

Table 4.5 Day shift, by ward grade, sex and whole-/part-time

Ward grade	Male		Female		
	Whole	Part	Whole	Part	Total
Registered	22	—	14	5	41
Enrolled	12	—	28	1	41
Training	15	—	16	—	31
Assistants	14	1	37	13	65
Total	63	1	95	19	178

Table 4.6 Night shift, by ward grade, sex and whole-/part-time

Ward grade	Male		Female		
	Whole	Part	Whole	Part	Total
Registered	4	—	2	—	6
Enrolled	6	—	5	4	15
Training[15]	—	—	—	—	—
Assistants	2	—	12	14	28
Total	12	—	19	18	49

Table 4.7 Nursing assistants, by age and day/night shifts

Age	Day shift	Night shift	Total
Under 25	10	1	11
26–35	17	14	31
36–45	16	6	22
46–55	16	5	21
56–65	6	2	8
Total	65	28	93

and that the night staff include very few registered nurses. Interesting differences are found in the age distribution between day and night staff and between whole- and part-time staff. Tables 4.7 and 4.8 present the relevant data for the nursing assistant grade.

Table 4.8   Nursing assistants, by age and whole-/part-time

Age	Whole-time	Part-time	Total
Under 25	10	1	11
26–35	15	16	31
36–45	17	5	22
46–55	17	4	21
56–65	6	2	8
Total	65	28	93

From Tables 4.7 and 4.8 it can be seen that over half of the night shift and over half of the part-time staff are in the 26–35 years age group. Indirect evidence that part-time staff could be married women who choose part-time work to fit in with their family commitments, is that all the nursing assistants in this age group are women, married and have families. Nine of the sixteen work on the night shift.

Previous experience

Approximately just under one-fifth of the sample have worked in a subnormality hospital other than the one in which they were working at the time of the interview. There are, however, marked differences between ward grades (Table 4.9).

While nearly half of the registered nurses have worked in more than one hospital for the mentally handicapped, just under one in ten nursing assistants have done so. About the same proportion of

Table 4.9   Hospital mobility, by ward grade

Ward grade	More than one hospital	Ward grade total
Registered	21	47
Enrolled	8	56
Training	4	31
Assistant	7	93
Total	40	227

SENs and nurses in training have worked in more than one hospital – approximately one in nine. There are no substanital differences between men and women for the sample as a whole, or within grades.

Length of service

Over half of the ward staff in the sample have worked in a hospital for the mentally handicapped for less than five years. Just under a quarter of the sample have worked with the mentally subnormal for more than ten years. Table 4.10 shows the breakdown by ward grade.

Table 4.10 Ward grade, by length of nursing service with the mentally handicapped

| Ward grade | Length of service (years) | | | | |
	< 5	6–10	11–15	15 +	Total
Registered	13	12	11	11	47
Enrolled	7	16	12	21	56
Training	30	1	—	—	31
Assistants	80	9	2	2	93
Total	130	38	25	34	227

Not surprisingly, all but one of the nurses in training have less than five years' service. Figures for the SENs and nursing assistants must be seen as complementing one another. 'Enrolment through experience' is a method by which nursing assistants are given formal recognition and reward for their service. It would, therefore, be expected that there would be few nursing assistants with many years' service, for the majority of nursing assistants who would fall in this category would have been offered enrolment. The case is that only 4 of the 59 staff with over ten years' service are nursing assistants, while 23 with this length of service are SENs. However, it is also possible to be enrolled after examination, and the following section looks at the area of qualifications in greater detail.

Qualifications

Just under one-quarter of the SENs have obtained their enrolment after examination, and Table 4.11 indicates how the SENs by the two methods of enrolment compare in terms of length of service.

Although over half the SENs have over ten years' service, less than one in six of these are SENs after examination. There are further differences between the two groups, when they are broken down by sex (Table 4.12).

While approximately one in three SENs through experience are male, this figure drops to approximately one in seven for SENs after examination. Table 4.13 indicates the qualifications for registered nurses broken down by sex.

When the totals for the RNMS and Combined I categories from Table 4.13 are added together, it gives a total of 34 of the 47 registered nurses with a qualification in nursing the mentally handicapped. Therefore, approximately three out of every four registered nurses in the sample have had such a training. Approximately four out of five men have had such a training, compared with three out of five women. Table 4.14 supplements these points as it indicates that, in the sample, the staff who have obtained their last qualification most recently are more likely to hold a qualification in nursing the mentally handicapped.

Table 4.11   SENs, by method of enrolment and length of service

Length of service (years)	SEN by experience	SEN by examination	Total
Under 5	2	5	7
6–10	13	3	16
11–15	11	1	12
Over 15	17	4	21
Total	43	13	56

Table 4.12   SENs, by sex and method of enrolment

Method of enrolment	Male	Female	Total
After examination	2	11	13
Through experience	16	27	43
Total	18	38	56

Table 4.13 Registered nurses, by sex and qualifications

Qualification	Male	Female	Total
RNMS only	14	11	25
RMN only	4	4	8
SRN only	—	2	2
Combined I*	8	1	9
Combined II†	—	2	2
Total	26	20	46‡

* 'Combined I' refers to nurses with more than one qualification including RNMS.
† 'Combined II' refers to nurses with more than one qualification excluding RNMS.
‡ The total comes to 46 and not 47 because one sister, with over 15 years' experience, had no formal qualifications.

Of the 27 who obtained their last qualifications within the past ten years, 25 have RNMS. What is of particular interest in Table 4.14, however, is the low number of nurses working on the wards who qualified six to ten years ago. One possible explanation to account for this could be the implementation of the Salmon structure.

Although the Salmon Committee's recommendations on senior nurse staff structure were published in 1966,[16] they had only been implemented in the Board's hospitals for the mentally handicapped a few months before the survey took place. It could well be that those who obtained their last qualification between six and ten years earlier had been promoted from the ward situation to, for example, the nursing officer (No. 7) position. Not only would they have quite extensive ward experience – at least six years' post-registration plus three years' during training – but it might be felt that they were still young enough to benefit from the management courses that are now available.

This, however, need not necessarily be the only explanation. It may be that there was a decline in the numbers presenting themselves for recruitment to professional training, which had recently been halted by regional unemployment. Or it may be that nurses with between six to ten years' service have moved to other branches of nursing. The questions that such explanations pose need further research to provide detailed answers.

Table 4.14   Registered nurses, by RNMS and date of last qualification

Date of last qualification (years)	Total registered	No. with RNMS*
Under 5	18	16
6–10	9	9
Over 10	19	9
Total	46†	34

* Refers to both staff with RNMS only, and staff with RNMS combined with other nursing qualifications.
† The total of registered nurses comes to 46 and not 47 because one sister, with over 15 years' experience, had no formal qualifications.

Another possible fruitful area for research is suggested when the date of last qualification for registered nurses is broken down by sex (Table 4.15). Only approximately one in five staff who have qualified within the past five years are women. This low number of women compared to men in the sample could be accounted for by one of two factors – either a lower recruitment rate for women, or a higher leaving rate for women. In fact, there is indirect evidence that it could be a combination of these factors.

There are 7 female students under 25 years old,[17] only 2 of whom are married. However, none of the registered women nurses are under 25 years old and all but 2 are married. This could indicate that the low numbers of registered women who have qualified within the last five years and are now working on the wards is because many of those who would be in this category have left nursing to

Table 4.15   Registered nurses, by sex and date of last qualification

Date of last qualification (years)	Male	Female	Total
Under 5	14	4	18
6–10	4	5	9
Over 10	8	11	19
Total	26	20	46

Table 4.16   Ward grade, by country of origin

Ward grade	UK	Other	Total
Registered	44	3	47
Enrolled	55	1	56
Training	28	3	31
Assistant	88	5	93
Total	215	12	227

get married and possibly raise a family. Further, while there are 7 female students under 25 years, there are 9 male students under this age. This could indicate that fewer female students are recruited.

Conclusions are tentative because of the small numbers in the sample. But it is interesting that over half of the registered women in the sample obtained their last qualification *over* ten years ago, while a similar proportion of men obtained their last qualification *within* the past five years.

Nationality

Table 4.16 indicates that there were very few immigrant staff in the sample. All immigrants except the 3 registered staff were female. None had difficulty in speaking or understanding English.

Summary

1   Two-thirds of all staff working on the wards are women, and only in the registered ward grade is there a greater number of men than women.

2   There are no substantial differences in the age distribution between men and women for the sample as a whole or within grades. Approximately two out of five staff are over 45 years old.

3   Four-fifths of all staff in the sample are married.

4   Nursing assistants provide the bulk of labour on both the day and night shifts.

5   Four out of five staff in the sample as a whole have never worked in any other hospital for the mentally handicapped – their experience is limited to one setting.

D

6   Over half of the ward staff have worked in a hospital for the mentally handicapped for less than five years. Just under a quarter of the sample have worked in such a hospital for over ten years. Two out of three staff with over fifteen years service are SENs.

7   Three-quarters of the SENs have obtained their enrolment by experience and not by examination.

8   Approximately three out of every four registered nurses in the sample has a qualification in nursing the mentally handicapped. Staff who have obtained their last qualification most recently are more likely to hold such a qualification – of the 27 who obtained their last qualification within the past ten years 25 have RNMS.

9   Very few registered staff working on the wards have obtained their last qualification six to ten years ago. A possible explanation could be that with the introduction of the Salmon system, such nurses have been promoted to nursing officer grade.

10   Over half of the registered women in the sample have obtained their last qualification *over* ten years ago, while a similar proportion of men obtained their last qualification *within* the past five years. Only approximately one in five registered staff who have qualified within the past five years are women.

Three areas are suggested for further research:

   i   The testing of the hypothesis that part-time staff could be working wives who choose part-time work to fit in with their family commitments.

   ii   The impact of the introduction of the Salmon structure on the availability of qualified staff for ward duty.

   iii   The testing of the hypothesis that there is a lower recruitment and a higher leaving rate for women than for men on RNMS courses.

Statements in the Treatment Orientation Scale

After analysis of a pool of attitude statements presented to respondents in a pilot survey, the following twenty-two statements were selected for the main survey:

1 Over the years the type of patient has become more difficult to care for.
2 Doctors in this hospital just don't know what it is like on the ward first thing in the morning.
3 Therapy can achieve little with low-grade patients.
4 Promiscuity and mental subnormality go hand in hand.

5 Once a nurse has been trained in mental subnormality, he has all the knowledge he needs for the care of patients.

6 Patients in this hospital can respond to care.

7 Nursing experience should be appreciated by doctors.

8 Routine habit-training is essential for patients.

9 No one really knows why patients improve.

10 When looking after patients, ability and commonsense are more important than formal training.

11 Patients should be sterilised.

12 It is best to isolate low-grade patients from those who are not so bad.

13 Patients should not be treated like young children.

14 The conditions of hospital wards are as good as they can be with the type of patient living there.

15 Kindness is more important than a therapeutic programme for patients.

16 Mental subnormality often leads to mental illness.

17 We cannot expect to understand the odd behaviour of patients.

18 Most patients will never know right from wrong.

19 Little can be done to help low-grade patients to improve.

20 There is a sharp dividing line between 'normal' and 'mentally subnormal'.

21 It is not right to expect untrained staff to help patients with therapy.

22 Patients can often lead a life which is just as valuable as anyone else's.

There were five alternative response categories for each statement – 'strongly agree', 'agree', 'uncertain', 'disagree' and 'strongly disagree'. Each response category was allocated a score and two modes of analysis were employed:

i   a score on the Treatment Orientation Scale, i.e. a total score for all twenty-two attitude statements; and

ii   responses to individual statements.

Scores on the Treatment Orientation Scale

Mean scores and standard deviations were calculated for the four grades of ward staff and for the sample as a whole. The data is presented in Table 4.17.

Ranking reflects how optimistic one ward grade is relative to other grades; a low score on the scale, indicating the optimistic pole, is ranked above a high score, indicating the pessimist pole. On this basis registered and training staff can be said to be more optimistic about the treatment of mentally handicapped patients than assistants and enrolled staff. As these figures are suggestive of a difference in responses between trained and untrained staff, scores were calculated for these two categories.

Table 4.17 Scores obtained by the four grades of ward staff on the Treatment Orientation Scale

	Mean	SD	No.	Rank
Registered	57·3	8·5	47	1
Enrolled	67·8	8·2	56	3 =
Training	57·5	7·8	31	2
Assistants	67·8	7·9	93	3 =
Total	64·2	9·5	227	

Originally it had been intended to gauge the effect of training by comparing the responses of enrolled nurses who had taken the SEN examination with those placed on the Roll through experience. However, the small number of nurses who had taken the SEN examination, 13 of the 56 enrolled nurses, made such a procedure impractical. The 'trained' category was therefore constructed by combining the enrolled nurses after examination with registered nurses, and the 'untrained' category constructed by combining the enrolled nurses through experience with the nursing assistants.

As the courses for enrolment and registration differ in curriculum and intellectual demand, it can be argued that it is misleading to place the enrolled nurses after examination and the registered nurses in the same category. Data presented in chapter 3 indicated, however, that the registered nurses are not a homogeneous group. Some are trained in nursing the mentally handicapped, some in general nursing, and some in nursing the mentally ill. A few have more than one training. There is a wide variation in how long ago the qualifications were obtained. Thus, it was decided that enrolled nurses who had taken the SEN examination could legitimately be placed with the registered nurses in the 'trained' category for this limited purpose. Enrolled nurses placed on the Roll through experience were placed in the 'untrained' category along with the nursing assistants for, as indicated previously, enrolment through experience is formal acknowledgment of their service as nursing assistants and not a training as such.[18]

For the purpose of this exercise, nurses in training were excluded. This left a sample of 196 nurses, consisting of 60 trained staff and 136 untrained staff.

In the following analysis, net figures are given in percentages of these two groups, and in the form of bar graphs.

Responses to attitude statements

The social history of mental handicap indicates that, at the beginning of this century, public attitudes were concerned mainly with two areas – the relationship between 'normal' and 'subnormal', and whether the mentally handicapped should be sterilised.[19] Results obtained from this sample show that variations in attitude in these areas still exist among ward staff working with mentally handicapped patients (Figures 4.1 and 4.2).

In the first edition of his textbook *Mental Retardation* (1908), R. F. Tredgold stated emphatically that 'between the lowest normal and the highest ament, a great and impassable gulf is fixed'. Over half a century later, responses to the statement 'There is a sharp dividing line between "normal" and "mentally subnormal" ' indicate that such a view is still common among the ward staff of this sample.

The question of sterilisation is obviously very complex, and advances in genetics and techniques of birth control have added new dimensions to the debate since the Brock Committee's recommendations in favour of sterilisation were quietly ignored by the government of the day in 1934. Although only one statement related explicitly to sterilisation, it was supplemented with a statement relating to the sexual behaviour of patients – 'Promiscuity and mental subnormality go hand in hand'. The results are presented in Figure 4.3.

A surprising aspect of Figure 4.3 is that a quarter of the ward sample were uncertain. One possible interpretation could be that some of the staff were unfamiliar with the term 'promiscuity' and rather than inquire as to its meaning used the 'uncertain' category. However, the term was understood in the pilot survey when respondents were encouraged to query ambiguous and unfamiliar

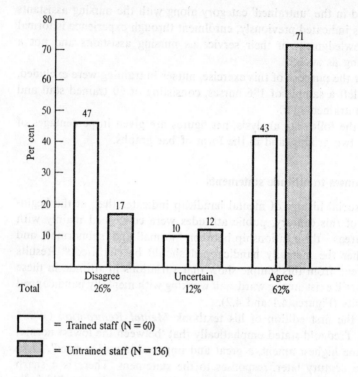

Figure 4.1 Responses of trained and untrained staff to statement 20:
'There is a sharp dividing line between "normal" and "mentally
subnormal"' '

words, and 28 per cent of the trained staff checked the 'uncertain' category.

The narrow percentage difference (7 per cent) between those who agreed and those who disagreed with the statement is interesting in the context of staff who express fears about the sexual behaviour of mentally subnormal patients. An example of staff views is quoted by Pauline Morris:[20]

> These [local authority] hostels should in every case be separated,
> for sexual problems loom high in the lives of these patients:
> homosexuality, child assault, rape, exposure with the men and
> prostitution and some perversion with the women. Ideally the
> men's hostel should be in one town and the women's in a
> neighbouring one. They should be at least two or three miles

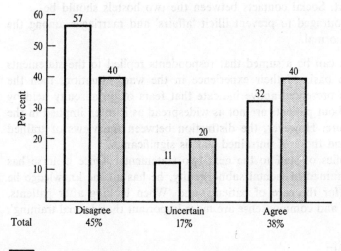

Figure 4.2 Responses of trained and untrained staff to statement 11:
'Patients should be sterilised'

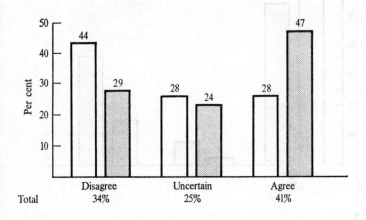

Figure 4.3 Responses of trained and untrained staff to statement 4:
'Promiscuity and mental subnormality go hand in hand'

apart. Social contacts between the two hostels should be discouraged to prevent illicit 'affairs' and marriages among the subnormal.

If it can be assumed that respondents replied to the statements on the basis of their experience in the ward situation, then the figures presented above indicate that fears of promiscuity held by staff about patients are not as widespread as is often implied in the literature. However, the distinction between the views of trained staff and those of untrained staff is significant.

Replies of staff to the next two statements: 'Once a nurse has been trained in mental subnormality, he has all the knowledge he needs for the care of patients' and 'When looking after patients, ability and commonsense are more important than formal training',

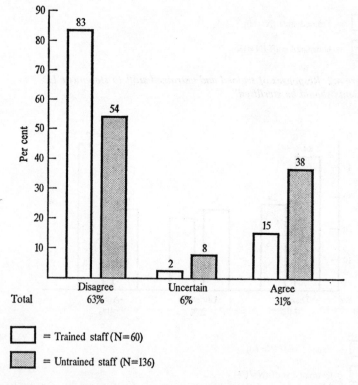

Figure 4.4 Responses of trained and untrained staff to statement 5: 'Once a nurse has been trained in mental subnormality, he has all the knowledge he needs for the care of patients'

suggest that staff of all grades are apt to lay great stress on experience with the mentally handicapped as opposed to training (Figures 4.4 and 4.5).

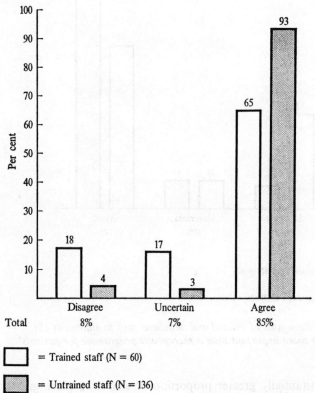

Figure 4.5 *Responses of trained and untrained staff to statement 10: 'When looking after patients, ability and commonsense are more important than formal training'*

In Figure 4.5 the combined percentage figure for trained and untrained staff of 85 per cent for those who agree does not imply that 85 per cent of ward staff think that formal training is not important, only that they attach greater importance to ability and commonsense. Similar reasoning applies to responses to the statement 'Kindness is more important than a therapeutic programme for patients' (Figure 4.6).

D*

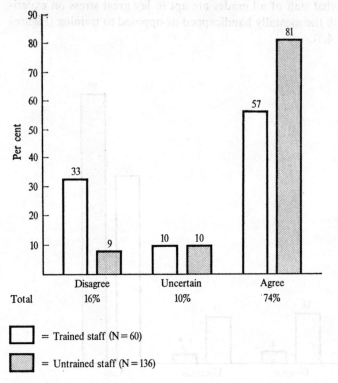

Figure 4.6 Responses of trained and untrained staff to statement 15:
'Kindness is more important than a therapeutic programme for patients'

The substantially greater proportion of staff who place greater emphasis on kindness than on a therapeutic programme for patients is not a rejection of the efficacy of therapeutic techniques. This is illustrated by responses to the related statements 'Therapy can achieve little with low-grade patients' (Figure 4.7) and 'Little can be done to help low-grade patients to improve' (Figure 4.8).

Both Figures 4.7 and 4.8 indicate that untrained staff feel less can be achieved with patients than trained staff. This is further determined by the responses of the two groups of ward staff to the statements 'No one really knows why patients improve' (Figure 4.9) and 'We cannot expect to understand the odd behaviour of patients' (Figure 4.10).

The relative pessimism of untrained staff, apparent in Figures

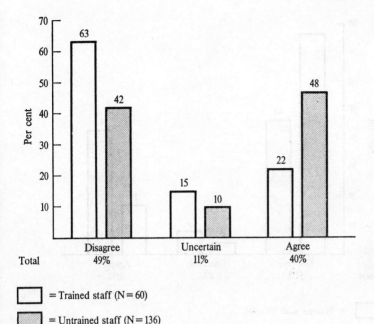

= Trained staff (N = 60)

= Untrained staff (N = 136)

Figure 4.7 Responses of trained and untrained staff to statement 3:
'Therapy can achieve little with low-grade patients'

4.9 and 4.10 manifests itself in a tacit acceptance of prevailing ward conditions (Figure 4.11).

Differences in response between trained and untrained staff for two other statements are, like those presented above, statistically significant. These two statements are 'Doctors in this hospital just don't know what it is like on the ward first thing in the morning' (Figure 4.12) and 'Mental subnormality often leads to mental illness' (Figure 4.13).

Chi-square data for all statements are presented in Appendix 5, including that for the remaining nine statements. The salient points of these statements are summarised below:

i 46 per cent of staff agree that over the years the type of patient has become more difficult to care for; 44 per cent disagree; 10 per cent are uncertain (statement 1).

ii 94 per cent of staff agree that patients in their hospital can respond to care; 3 per cent disagree; 3 per cent are uncertain (statement 6).

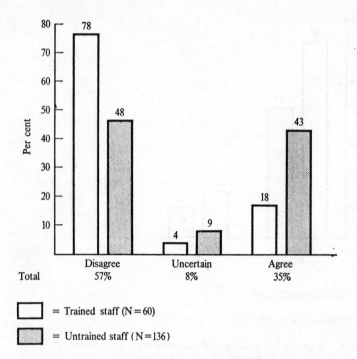

Figure 4.8 Responses of trained and untrained staff to statement 19:
'Little can be done to help low-grade patients to improve'

iii   97 per cent of staff agree that nursing experience should be appreciated by doctors; 3 per cent are uncertain (statement 7).

iv   96 per cent of staff agree that routine habit-training is essential for patients; 1 per cent disagree; 3 per cent are uncertain (statement 8).

v   58 per cent of staff agree that it is best to isolate low-grade patients from those not so bad; 28 per cent disagree; 14 per cent are uncertain (statement 12).

vi   58 per cent of staff agree that patients should not be treated like young children; 24 per cent disagree; 18 per cent are uncertain (statement 13).

vii   47 per cent of staff agree that most patients will never know right from wrong; 45 per cent disagree; 8 per cent are uncertain (statement 18).

viii   30 per cent of staff agree that it is not right to expect un-

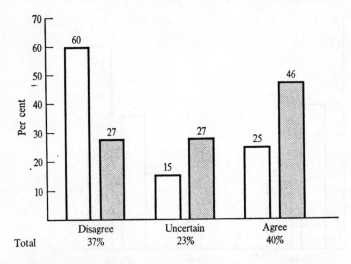

Figure 4.9 Responses of trained and untrained staff to statement 9:
'No one really knows why patients improve'

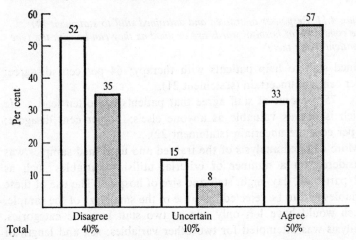

Figure 4.10 Responses of trained and untrained staff to statement 17:
'We cannot expect to understand the odd behaviour of patients'

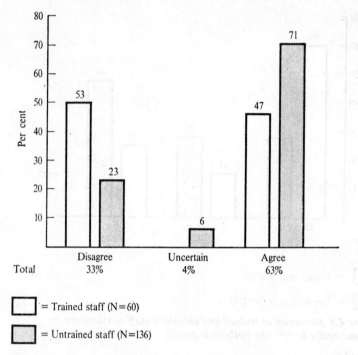

Figure 4.11 Responses of trained and untrained staff to statement 14:
'The conditions of hospital wards are as good as they can be with the type of patient living there'

trained staff to help patients with therapy; 64 per cent disagree; 6 per cent are uncertain (statement 21).

ix   75 per cent of staff agree that patients can often lead a life which is just as valuable as anyone else's; 14 per cent disagree; 11 per cent are uncertain (statement 22).

More detailed analysis of the trained and untrained samples was considered on a number of criteria, utilising variables such as full/part-time, day/night staff and size of hospital. The use of these variables had to be rejected, because of the small size of the sample, which would have left only one or two staff in some categories. Analysis was attempted for two other variables: sex and length of subnormality nursing service. This is not reported in detail, because the results again were too small in some instances to provide useful evidence. However, there were some indications that male staff were more optimistically oriented than female staff, and that untrained staff with long service, as might be expected, stressed kind-

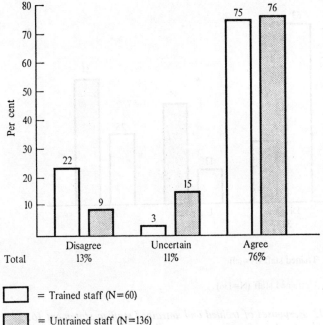

☐ = Trained staff (N=60)

▨ = Untrained staff (N=136)

Figure 4.12 Responses of trained and untrained staff to statement 2:
'*Doctors in this hospital just don't know what it is like on the ward first thing in the morning*'

ness and experience rather than training. These are issues which would be worth further research.

Summary

1 A Likert-type 5-point scale for the measurement of the attitudes of nursing staff in hospitals for the mentally handicapped was devised and applied to a one-in-four sample of staff of all grades.
2 For the purpose of analysis, staff were divided into two main categories, 'trained' and 'untrained'. Staff in training as student or pupil nurses were excluded.
3 Many staff still believed that there was a sharp dividing line between 'normal' and 'mentally subnormal'. This attitude was more common among untrained staff than trained staff (Figure 4.1).
4 Attitudes to patients' sexual behaviour were unclear. A minority

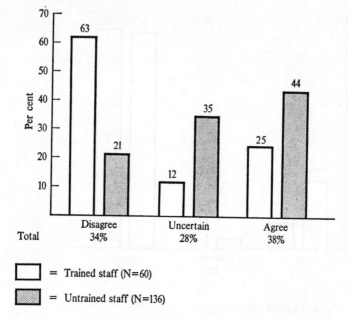

Figure 4.13 Responses of trained and untrained staff to statement 16: 'Mental subnormality often leads to mental illness'

(though a substantial one) of both trained and untrained nurses believed that patients should be sterilised. Nearly half the untrained nurses thought that 'promiscuity and mental subnormality go hand in hand', but a sizeable group of both trained and untrained nurses were uncertain on this issue. We were unable to ascertain whether the uncertainty related to the question itself or to the form of wording chosen (Figures 4.2 and 4.3).

5   A majority of nurses in both groups were emphatic that training alone was not enough to ensure the good care of patients. Both groups rated 'ability and commonsense' more highly than formal training. In the case of the untrained staff, the proportion taking this view was 93 per cent of the whole group (Figures 4.4 and 4.5).

6   There was a greater emphasis on kindness than on therapeutic programmes (again more notable among untrained staff), but there was substantial disagreement with statements which implied that low-grade patients were incapable of improvement (Figures 4.6, 4.7 and 4.8).

7   There was no very clear response to questions suggesting that

patients' behaviour was incomprehensible, though trained staff were more inclined to look for a rationale than untrained staff (Figures 4.9 and 4.10).

8 More untrained staff than trained staff were satisfied with present ward conditions (Figure 4.11).

9 Three-quarters of both groups thought that 'doctors in this hospital just don't know what it is like on the ward first thing in the morning' – a reference both to the hectic nature of the morning routine and to an assumption of medical non-involvement with difficult ward problems.

10 Untrained staff were more likely than trained staff to associate mental handicap with mental illness.

11 Overall, untrained staff were more likely than trained staff to be pessimistic in orientation.

12 A majority of ward staff, whether trained or untrained, placed more importance on what has been loosely termed 'experience' than on formal training. For many trained staff, training was a source of professional pride, but it was not always directly related to the daily task.

5   Problems of the 'back wards'

In chapter 2 we outlined our findings relating to what we called
'back wards' – wards which did not share in the improvement in
the quality of life found on other wards, and which seemed to us
to have special problems.

Such wards are not exceptional, though some hospitals have been
more successful in dealing with the problems than others. Nor are
their features as distinctive as nursing staff sometimes suggest. The
adverse features of ward management which they exhibit may be
found in greater or lesser degree in many other wards; and they
may become more common – for as the 'good', high-grade patients
are discharged to community care, so the hospitals will increasingly
have to focus on the care of those perceived as 'low-grade'. Their
numbers will increase, because the population is rising and the
mentally handicapped are living longer.

Whether nursing staff like it or not (and the majority, for obvious
reasons, do not), the future of hospital nursing for the mentally
handicapped is more closely related to the management of the kinds
of patients to be found on the 'back wards' than to the more stimulat-
ing, and more rewarding, work of the 'good wards'. The former hold
the patients they are likely to keep; the latter hold the patients they
are likely to transfer to community care.

If we concentrate in this chapter on the problems of the 'back
wards', it is not because we regard them as typical of all hospital
wards for the mentally handicapped. We know how hard many
nursing staff have fought to eliminate such patterns of behaviour.
We are deliberately concentrating on the worst in the system and
excluding from analysis much that is good and progressive, for
two reasons: this is where the long-term problems of the hospitals
lie, and the problems need to be brought into the open and studied
in depth. Purely normative control – the presentation of high standards appropriate to less severely handicapped patients, and the
denial of difficulties – simply does not work.

We begin with an extreme case. It is taken from outside the

Gateshire Region, and is based on a preliminary study undertaken by one member of the team while working as a nursing assistant in preparation for the project.[1] We did not find problems of this order of magnitude in any hospital in Gateshire; but the problems were there, and we believe that they are common to almost all hospitals for the mentally handicapped in some degree.

Ward 99

The ward consists of a large octagonal day room, two dormitories, washroom facilities, a bathroom and toilet area, a kitchen, two annexes (one for visitors and one for storage) and two airing courts, one of which is railed in. There is a medical room, and an administrative office for the sister/charge nurse.

Ward 99 has recently been redecorated and upgraded and the overall effect of the environment is very pleasing. By any criteria used to evaluate physical environment and amenities, Ward 99 would score highly.

The patient population of the ward consisted of 47 severely mentally-retarded, handicapped males aged 16 and over. In addition to their basic mental handicap, 12 of them were epileptic, 2 diabetic, 10 spastic, 3 mongol, 3 blind, 8 dumb, 1 deaf and dumb and 1 epiloiac. Nine were in wheelchairs, 28 were on medication every mealtime, 15 had to be fed and 42 were doubly incontinent. As these patients fall within the classification of 'high dependency', there should theoretically be a staff–patient ratio of 1:1. This was never achieved or even approached, except during the changeover hour from 1 p.m to 2 p.m. (the staff work on a three-shift day). There were rarely more than four or five staff, including the sister or charge nurse.

Nothing prepares the new (and often untrained) member of staff for the conditions on Ward 99. It is possible to get used to distressing sights and even to the continual deafening clamour which assails the ears. Even the regular staff did not get used to the smell, and all except one (who boasted of the fact) occasionally had to wear surgical masks when changing incontinent patients – a task which was to dominate the day's routine.

A brief outline of the schedule on Ward 99 follows, and one aspect of it, the washing and shaving ritual, will be described in some detail:

7.00 a.m. Report for morning shift, help night staff finish dressing patients (usually about 4 or 5). Prepare breakfast, i.e. toast, and the meal for the 'softs' (those who have to be fed – scrambled egg, diced bread and warm milk mixed into a tasteless compound).

7.15 a.m. Start presenting breakfast, special attention to feeding the 'softs'.

8.15 a.m. Breakfast finished and all patients taken to washroom to be shaved, washed and changed ('the shaving ritual').

8.55 a.m. Trainer calls for the 15–20 patients who make up the 'work party' (a euphemism, see below for explanation).

9.30 a.m. Finish shaving and changing the majority of patients who are then placed in the airing courts if the weather is fine. If it is raining, then they are kept in the annexe alongside the day room until the cleaners have finished. Fleeting visit by doctor.

9.45 a.m. Start the nine daily baths, shave and change.

10.45–
11.30 a.m. 'Observation' in either court, wash and change patients who require it.

11.30 a.m. 'Work party' returns and lunch is prepared and served. Once again preparation of 'softs' meal, this time mince replaces scrambled egg.

12.30 p.m. Lunch finished, wash and change those who need it.

1.00 p.m. Afternoon shift reports for duty.

2.00 p.m. Morning shift finishes.

2–4 p.m. 'Observation', wash and change patients who require it, baths (weekly rota for all patients; the only established pattern is for 9 patients who may have visits on Sundays. For the others there is no system – you bath who you see and who hasn't been done that week).

4.00 p.m. 'Work party' returns and is placed in railed airing court.

4.30 p.m. Tea – once again preparing the 'softs' meal.

5.30 p.m. Wash and change those who require it; place in appropriate court.

7.00 p.m. All but 10–12 patients put to bed (difficult to get them to settle because sun is still out). Wash those who need it – put to bed naked.

8.30 p.m. Half-an-hour before night staff come on duty, check beds. Bath and change beds of those who have been

doubly incontinent. Issue buttonless pyjama jackets or
short nightshirts.

9.00 p.m.   Afternoon shift finishes and night staff attend to
patients still up.

The washing and shaving ritual illustrates in some detail the difficulties encountered in 'nursing' the low-grade patients in Ward 99.
After breakfast the practice was for all but 5 patients (who assisted
the domestic staff) to be taken and locked in the main washroom,
along with three members of staff, for washing, shaving and changing.[2] The washroom was either locked or jammed by placing a heavy
chair in front of the door on the outside of the washroom, the door
opening out into the day room.

Justification for this was that (a) it kept all patients together and
facilitated shaving and washing as patients could not wander off,
and (b) it kept patients out of the way of domestic staff. Whatever
the justification, the result was that 42 patients were confined in an
'L'-shaped washroom, one wing of which consisted of WCs. As 9
patients were in wheelchairs, and there were also the three members
of staff, there was barely room to move – a situation which excited
many who remained calm and placid when they had adequate space
for free movement.

First priority was to get the 'work party' ready for the trainer to
collect at 8.45 a.m. ('Work party', as mentioned in the ward schedule,
was merely a euphemism for a system whereby 15–20 patients were
walked round the grounds, or taken to 'the hotel', a covered en-
closure, if raining, in order to alleviate the pressure on the nursing
staff.) The patients involved had to be got ready, and theoretically
their faces and hands were washed. In fact, faces and hands were
usually only hastily wiped over with a damp flannel. This was for
two reasons: distractions provided by other patients, and difficulties
associated with shaving.

Distractions by other patients could take many forms. For example, one of the patients might start to undress himself, while
another might start to go into an epileptic fit, while yet another
might be attempting to get into the linen cupboard which opened
into the washroom and was kept open at this time because of the
inconvenience of continually locking and unlocking the door.

The list of possible incidents could easily be extended, but the
point is that all required attention, which meant that the patient
being attended to had to be left. However, observing an incident

and getting to it so that effective action could be taken were not at all the same thing.

Immediately behind the washbasins where the nurse was washing a patient were all the wheelchair patients – this was the only area of space where they could be placed in the limited confines of the washroom. So to reach Paddy, who was, for example, going into an epileptic attack, the nurse had to negotiate the wheelchairs as well as the rest of the patients who milled aimlessly around. Having reached Paddy and loosened his trousers (loosening the collar of patients in Ward 99 was never appropriate in these circumstances because their collars were always open), the next problem would be to get him out of the washroom and out of sight.

An attack often had the effect on other epileptics of fire in dry undergrowth – it spread. But getting Paddy out, like getting to Paddy in the first place, was easier said than done. The rest of the patients and the wheelchairs had to be encountered yet again, this time with the encumbrance of a dead weight. Also the door, if blocked by the chair, had to be opened by force – no mean feat in itself. When Paddy was eventually put to bed, and the cot sides placed in position, the nurse might return to the washroom only to find the patient he was washing had wandered off and had to be brought back to the washbasin.

All this immediately after the strain of feeding 47 low-grade patients and in an atmosphere of deafening and meaningless noise. But the problem did not end there. When the wandering patient had been retrieved, he had to be shaved. Shaving poses its own peculiar difficulties when carried out in a low-grade ward.

There were two alternative methods available – either 'wet' – with a safety razor – or 'dry' – with a modern electric shaver – but in practice the electric shaver was virtually useless. Long-stay patients have been shaved in every conceivable direction, with the result that their beard growth is tough.[3] So much so, that to give an effective shave with an electric shaver it would be necessary to devote about 10–15 minutes to each patient. As time is scarce, only those with whom it is impossible to give a 'wet' shave are shaved with an electric shaver – for example, those who are old and whose skin hangs in empty folds, or those with a skin rash such as the butterfly rash associated with epiloia. Four patients (in addition to the 5 'helping' the domestic staff) had a 'dry' shave and they were left to the end. This left 38 patients to have a 'wet' shave, each of whom presented a particular difficulty: one could not keep his head still; another was without teeth and struggled violently when an attempt was made to place a finger behind the upper lip to provide a firm base for shaving it.

This situation was not helped by the fact that only two razor blades were issued each day for the 38 patients, and there were times when no supplies were available for weekends, when the hospital stores were closed. The point about growth being tough for the electric shaver also applies here. After four or five shaves the blade was blunt, although by honing on a piece of glass or the edge of the palm it was possible to get another two or three shaves.

This meant about 16 decent shaves from the two blades; for the rest it hurt; but the razor blade was still used in preference to the electric shaver not only because it was quicker to give a 'wet' shave, even with a blunt blade, but also because a blunt blade showed that the nursing staff had made an effort even if it only showed in the form of cuts.

After shaving a patient, it was necessary to change his clothes. If the laundry supply was low and his clothes were clean, then there was no bother – the clothes were not changed. If the laundry supply was low and his clothes were not clean, then a compromise was made – for example, pyjama jackets were used instead of shirts.

With luck, and the cutting of corners, the 'work party' was ready when the trainer called to collect them, and it was possible to concentrate on the remaining patients, placing them in their appropriate airing court – unrailed for those not likely to wander off, or in a wheelchair, railed for those inclined to wander off, or the potentially violent or epileptic.

The same shaving ritual was followed as for the 'work party' patients; and the same problems were encountered. Once the ambulant patients were finished the 9 wheelchair cases could be taken to the bathroom for their daily bath.

This exhausting routine was followed by 'observation' in one of the courts. This usually meant taking a breather before preparing for lunch. If, however, it was either raining or too cold, the patients could not be placed outside in the airing courts. They had to be placed in the annexe along one side of the day room until the domestic staff had completed cleaning. Only one annexe was used, rather than both, because the other was kept as a lounge for visitors. The fact that the annexe was used to store discarded wheelchairs added to the general chaos and pandemonium when the patients were placed in there – and the incidence of double incontinence increased.

In such a situation it would be expected that it would be much more difficult to 'take a breather'. This was not the case. Staff disappeared, for example, into the kitchen for a smoke, or presented an aura of conspicuous activity, such as preparing medication. The term 'observation' implies that staff are not expected to relate to the patients, and once all patients have been washed, shaved and changed after breakfast, the staff are only involved with the patients who are doubly incontinent. Those who were singly incontinent were left until lunch was concluded when, so it was argued, they would wet themselves again, so 'why take up time changing them every few minutes when it'll only have to be done later?'

This response must be placed in context. The washing, shaving and changing procedure outlined above is referred to as a 'ritual' because the staff approach it without thinking. While the details of the procedure are constantly bemoaned, for example, 'Why can't we have more than two razor blades each day?' – the procedure itself, which heightens the difficulties of shaving by its congestion of both time and space, is left unquestioned. In all but the ritualistic adherence to such procedures, the staff had opted out of the ward situation. This reaction could be observed at the three different levels of the staff hierarchy on the ward.

At the sister and charge nurse level, 'opting out' was manifested in lack of contact, both physical and emotional, with the patients. However, while the reaction was common to both sister and charge nurse, it was compensated for in different ways. Sister had a great concern that everything should be done according to the book. Although it was easier to feed a patient from a bowl rather than from a plate, the latter always had to be used. The charge nurse, on the other hand, was prepared to tolerate irregularities short of total chaos. Rules could be bent or ignored – for example, the patients' afternoon tea-break might be omitted. Both the sister and the charge nurse were seldom actively involved in the ward: both avoided situations which brought them into contact with the patients.

The situation for the student and pupil nurses was different – they were in the ward for a definite period of three months before being transferred. While they could not, like the sister and charge nurse, withdraw from physical contact, they could withdraw from emotional contact. For them, Ward 99 was a place to be endured, a ward where knowledge learned in the training school was inapprop-

riate, and from which, with luck, they would ultimately be transferred to the hospital wing as compensation.

The nursing assistants, like the student and pupil nurses, had to
make physical contact with the patients, but like the sister and charge
nurse, they were in Ward 99 for an indefinite period. In most cases,
their expectations rose no higher than a hope of getting through
their shift with as little bother and effort as possible.

To justify and rationalise this 'opting out' or patient avoidance,
an elaborate system of defence had been constructed. Staff attitudes
to patients in Ward 99 were based on three premises:

1 Patients are insensitive.
2 Patients cannot meaningfully discriminate.
3 Patients cannot be taught.

To illustrate how these beliefs were put into operation, one incident
will be cited in each category:

1 *Patients are insensitive* Mr Pelham, a severely subnormal
patient who is paralysed from the waist down, had been put to bed
at 7 p.m. and at 8.30 p.m. had been checked just before the change
of shift. He had been doubly incontinent and was bathed and the
bed changed. When put back into bed, he was taunted and teased
by Mr Nelson, a nursing assistant. Mr Newby, a pupil nurse, balanc-
ing on the end of the bed, then flung himself across Mr Pelham's legs.
Mr Pelham then wet himself. The suggestion that this was a good
example of how incontinence could have an emotional basis was
dismissed by an emphatic 'no – he's just a dirty—' from Mr Newby.

2 *Patients cannot meaningfully discriminate* Ward 99 had recently
been redecorated and upgraded, presenting a very agreeable physical
environment which had every facility to cope with a difficult and
often nauseating job; it made the nurses' job much easier in dealing
with doubly incontinent patients. While this was acknowledged by
the staff, it was still resented that difficult patients should be in a
ward with such an agreeable environment: 'They can't appreciate
it. It's wasted on them. It's much better to put some of the old-
timers in these "new" wards. They've worked hard some of them,
and they know what it means to be in a ward like this.'

3 *Patients cannot be taught* Mr Potter had been doubly incontinent. Now he was one of only 5 in the ward who were not. When
asked why, Mr Newby replied, 'It just happened. No one really
knows why.'

Ward 99 held a curious position in hospital folklore. Throughout
the hospital, there was a widely-held belief that, since the Mental

Health Act, 1959, the overall standard of patients had been going down, for example, the hospital was catering for an increasing proportion of low-grade patients. Whether this is so objectively is irrelevant, it was believed subjectively and is therefore meaningful with regard to the behaviour of the staff.

Ward 99's position in this belief was that it *could* reflect the type of patient that the hospital would increasingly have to cope with. The nature of this type of patient is well reflected in the hospital reference to Ward 99 as 'the farmyard', or a derivative. A knowing grin always followed the revelation that a nurse had been allocated to Ward 99 and an inquiry made as to whether he had brought his bucket and spade.

This view of the ward situation in Ward 99 meant that the staff expected special compensations for working there. For instance, food was pilfered on other wards, but there was a token acknowledgment that this was against the rules, and spoils were eaten surreptitiously behind the pantry door in the kitchen.

In Ward 99, no effort was made to hide the fact that staff were eating the patients' food, except during visiting on Sunday afternoon. The logic was that they were justified in taking patients' food in the first place as a 'perk' of the job and that, secondly, they could eat it openly not as an act of bravado, but as compensation for what they had to do in the ward. Though this was officially against the rules, it was expected that it would be overlooked by senior staff because of the general recognition that Ward 99 was 'the farmyard' and 'difficult'.

Were the patients as difficult to handle as the folklore implied? It is difficult to say, because low expectations create low standards of performance. From Ward 99:

   i   no one ever went to industrial or occupational therapy;
  ii   no one ever went to church or on outings;
 iii   only 5 patients ever left the ward unsupervised;
  iv   no one was ever discharged.

The 'back ward' syndrome

As shown in chapter 2, the research team encountered many of the problems of Ward 99 in the main survey, though not in such an acute form. In the remainder of this chapter, which is based on material from the survey hospitals, we attempt a sociological explanation of the social life of 'back wards', based on eight factors, all of which emphasise and are conducive to routine management – the dreary round of toileting, washing, dressing and feeding which becomes a mode of life.

1 The staff image of patients

Patients on these wards are at the bottom of the pecking order. They are usually labelled 'severely subnormal', and it is assumed by all staff, from the consultant through the senior nursing staff and the ward staff to the domestic staff, that they cannot learn. Nurse training has a strongly medical component, which lays emphasis on severe subnormality as a condition which is fixed and irreversible. This gets watered down into statements like 'These patients don't have a brain' and 'The difference between these patients and psychiatric patients is that psychiatric patients have a mind but have lost it temporarily, but these never had a mind to begin with'. Without a brain to think with and without a mind that can assimilate and interpret experiences, the patient becomes located in a situation in which development is impossible. A model of severe subnormality based on medical knowledge focuses upon physiological and neurological structures and processes which are unalterable in the light of existing theory.

But if we examine other models which lay less stress on immutable constitutional factors, such as those derived from psychology and sociology, there may be grounds for greater optimism. It is fairly well established that belief in the existence of mental handicap in a patient can result in lower scores on standard intelligence tests,[4] and that varying operational definitions of the terms 'subnormal' and 'severely subnormal' result in some patients being allocated to the latter group when they might have followed very different careers in the former.[5] Sociologists have drawn our attention to the adverse effects of labelling; the application of the term 'severely subnormal' to a patient leads to a significant devaluation of his potential by those who come into contact with him.[6]

Our observations confirm that while patients on 'back wards' are perceived as a homogeneous group, they may not in fact be so. Severely subnormal patients are defined by their extremely low level of intelligence in comparison with the norm for all persons of a particular age in a population. Where standard intelligence tests like the Terman-Merrill tests are used to assess the intelligence quotient, the cut-off point demarcating severe subnormality is usually taken to be a score of 50 or below. Thus, adult patients with an IQ of 50 or less can be said to be severely subnormal in comparison with the achievements of persons of the same age.

However, this relatively clear line of classification is more of a myth than a reality. It is by now well established that IQs are not fixed, and that individuals may advance ten points or more in a relatively short space of time; that intelligence tests are much more accurate in measuring the middle range of intelligence than in measuring either very gifted people or those of very restricted intelligence;[7] but in addition to these factors, there are those which are particular to patients in hospitals for the mentally handicapped: psychologists are in short supply, and many patients have not been tested for years – if at all; some cannot be tested at all because of physical problems, such as cerebral palsy.

Classification often takes place on the basis of less objective factors: a patient may be placed on such a ward because there is no room for him elsewhere at the time of admission; as a punishment; because he is incontinent or difficult to handle. In this way, wards may take on a special identity because of the characteristics of a small nucleus of patients, and may thus acquire transfers from other wards wishing to get rid of similar types of patients. In one hospital, the 'back ward' may house aggressive and hyperactive patients, whose identity colours staff perceptions to the extent that other less dangerous patients on the ward come to be seen in the same light. In another, it may house the most dependent patients, and thus include the old and infirm as well as the most retarded.

Whatever the original basis, the 'back ward' acquires a separate image as 'low-grade' or 'severely subnormal' or 'difficult' or simply 'bad'; and once it is so defined, the image is self-reinforcing.

2   The lack of specific techniques for treatment

The labelling of a ward and its patients involves a devaluation of the professional identity of ward staff. They have been taught what subnormality nursing is according to the norms employed in the rest of the hospital; but they can see no way of using such knowledge in relation to patients who 'have no brain' and do not show signs of improvement. 'This isn't a hospital, and we are not bloody nurses, are we?' 'We have to do everything for them – feed them, dress them, take them to the toilet ... but more than that, we have to think for them.'

It was notable that charge nurses on such wards would often point to deviations from professional practice in the performance of their work. The General Nursing Council lays down clear procedures for dispensing medication, for instance, but nurses often developed innovations which circumvented the official procedures. Similarly, they would point to techniques which they had devised for performing treatments which they considered more effective than the techniques taught in nurse training schools. We came to call this procedure *shelving*: the nurse accepted largely without criticism everything he had been taught in training school, and stoutly maintained that the received doctrine was useful, valuable and true to experience; but adding 'of course, it doesn't apply here – this ward is different'.

The only times when specifically nursing techniques are employed is when a patient injures himself, or is physically sick. At other times, the training is shelved, and the nursing image rejected.

The range of techniques for teaching patients to care for themselves is thought by nurses to be extremely limited. The most fundamental of these is *repetition*, which in practical terms refers to the imposition of a heavily structured schedule of activities upon the patients in each ward. Set events such as toilet training occur at fixed intervals throughout the patients' day. The belief is that repeated practice will firmly implant the routine in the patient's mind and thereby condition him to respond appropriately. Repetition as a technique for teaching elementary social skills thus provides one of the foundations upon which wards become organised around more or less immutable routines. This has the further implication that threats to routine are thought by nurses to undo the learning gains that patients have accrued and are by that token to be resisted.

Repetition is employed in relation to the basic needs of patients as seen by the nurses, rather than to expand the patients' capacity to look after themselves. For example, on many wards no attempt is made to teach male patients how to shave themselves. The rationale for this is threefold:

i   Most could not learn to master the technique of shaving.
ii In the process of shaving, they would mutilate themselves.
iii Razors are dangerous and hence should not be put in the hands of people who have a limited understanding of the consequences of their own actions.

The same selective pattern of application of repetition to the training of patients can be seen with regard to activities like teeth-cleaning or dressing, although the rationale for their nonutilisation would be somewhat different.

Thus, with toilet training (i.e. the practice of taking patients to the toilet at regular intervals throughout the day), bowel and bladder control are thought to be skills patients can learn through repeated practice. This belief is reinforced by the fact that patients may well remain continent during the day, an outcome that is rewarding to staff who do not have to change and wash patients who have dirtied themselves. However, the efficacy of repetition as a learning device is robbed of value when it is realised that patients who are continent during the daytime are frequently incontinent at night. That is to say, they have not so much learned to respond to their own physiological needs as to the command of the nurses.[8] What is perceived by nurses as a mode (the only mode) of learning is in reality a block to learning.

3   *The adoption of a parental role*

We have already seen that many nurses in hospitals for the mentally handicapped see themselves as parents, and their patients as children. On 'back wards', this is probably the best model for staff–patient interaction which many staff have.

Family-linked metaphors are often evoked. Terms like 'creating a homelike environment', 'a warm and happy atmosphere', 'trying to make the ward into a proper home for them', all reinforce an image of the ward as a setting in which family-like relationships flourish: 'We are like father figures to them or parents, and no more like nurses than that. No, this isn't a hospital it's a community, and this ward is their home.'

The family model is the one most readily to hand, since it is the one of which most staff have personal experience. It has considerable legitimacy, giving them a mode of helping dependent people and a set of criteria by which they can be evaluated; but there are other consequences which are less desirable.

First, like real-life parents, they may come to expect to exercise a diffuse authority over all aspects of their charges' lives. Nurses feel that they have the final responsibility for all that happens to their patients, and they may become resentful of others who would arrogate some of this authority. The patient's natural parents, occupational therapists and other visiting specialists, even members of the nursing hierarchy, may be criticised because their actions affect the lives of the patients and they do not have to take responsibility for the consequences. It may be relevant to recall Professor Garth Plowman's comment that the natural family is, after all, the most total of total institutions for dependent children.[9]

Second, nurses feel that patients should be treated like their own children, and subjected to the same rules that they apply to their own families. This means that the use of punishment is seen as reasonable and just. Charge nurses commented on a number of occasions that if their own children at home misbehaved, they would not hesitate to slap them, since this was a just and immediate punishment readily understood. Most of them do not come from those sections of society where a more permissive attitude to children is considered desirable,[10] and they employ the norms they know:

> The doctors say we should treat them as our own kids, so that's what we do. If my son does something wrong I tell him to stop it, and I warn him that if he does it again he'll be for the high jump. If he carries on with it I warn him again and if that doesn't work I give him a slap and that soon enough stops him. It's the same with the patients.

Very often, too, nurses invoke the family rule of 'no favouritism', which means that all patients should be treated the same, and none should get special attention. To single a patient out is generally frowned upon as 'spoiling'. Yet it may be precisely the quality of special and individualised treatment which is necessary if a patient is to show improvement. Therapy and the family model pull in opposite directions.

Third, the model of hospital wards as homes and nurses as fathers and mothers is strained at several points by the fact that patients on 'back wards' do not mature like children, and sometimes perform grossly deviant acts. This can cause a violent rejection of the model and the adoption of a more derogatory one: 'A lot of them can't talk the same as animals can't. I've always maintained that what they want here is a vet, not a psychiatrist.'[11]

Particularly sharp responses were found when the patient's behaviour was of a particularly 'dirty' or unpleasant kind. One male patient who masturbated rectally was classed as a 'filthy' person, and nurses felt that it was quite legitimate to beat him, even though such action was regarded as extreme. Intense feelings of disgust and anger are not easily contained within the concept of a parent–child relationship.

Fourth, staff expect patients to respond like children to their care: with affection, obedience and gratitude. Even the most severely handicapped patients are not exempted from this obligation: staff will look for some sign that they recognise and appreciate what is being done for them.

The following example is taken from a ward for spastic patients, and the nurse is commenting on a mute, bedridden patient who is doubly incontinent: 'When you have to change her you know she is grateful even though she can't say anything because she has a certain look in her eyes.' From another nurse on the same ward: 'In the morning when you come on duty they are all pleased to see us, it's just the way they look, you get to recognise little signs like that after a while.'

Patients are expected to play some part in the ward, even if this is restricted to something as insignificant as a look of recognition or gratitude; and it is understandable enough that most human beings doing a difficult and sometimes unpleasant task need some minimal sign of appreciation to find it worth while. A young male assistant nurse recounted how he had tried to establish contact with a par- ticular patient for several weeks without success. When he had given up hope, the patient walked up to him and gave him a cigarette – 'and I nearly burst into tears'.

Many staff feel that affectionate behaviour by patients is morally correct – it reinforces the childlike image and their own status as surrogate parents. It is also a basis from which to develop willing compliance. An affectionate patient will often do what is wanted of him without trouble.

'Dirty' patients both offend family rules of good behaviour and discredit the image held of the staff, since their 'dirtiness' (e.g. incontinence, eating or smearing faeces, masturbation in public, picking and eating food from the floor, etc.) is easily observable.

4 An emphasis on patient compliance

The authority that nurses, particularly charge nurses, claim over their patients is legitimised by their assumption of the parent's role rather than by any special knowledge or expertise they have acquired in training. The converse side of this equation is that patients are expected to do as they are told. Like children who do not appreciate the meaning of their own actions, patients are fostered in a compliant role which is superimposed on their already limited potential. For example, nurses may reinforce their own position by giving patients approval for engaging in actions that demonstrate their lack of understanding and self-respect:

Nurse: What are you, Pinky?
Patient: I'm a silly twit-twat.
Nurse: That's right, and why are you a silly twit-twat?
Patient: Because I haven't got a brain.

To the extent that staff control a wide array of features in the ward situation, it is reasonable to expect that patients will become more dependent and compliant because they must turn to the staff for many of the things 'normal' people can do without having recourse to others. There is very little in the ward situation that lies within the patient's immediate control. Compliance helps to stabilise relationships between staff and patients by generating evidence that confirms the nurse's initial assumption about the nature of patients.

However, patients may be both affectionate and compliant; affectionate but not compliant; compliant but not affectionate; or neither. The diagram in Figure 5.1 combines both elements of patients' attitudes and predicts the probable staff reaction.

This model locates all patients in one of five groups:

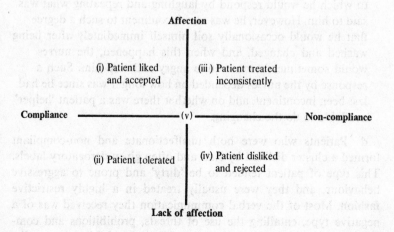

Figure 5.1 Nurse-patient interaction

E

a Patients who are both affectionate and compliant are likely to receive more attention of a positive kind, to be liked by staff, and to be the recipients of special rewards – extra cups of tea, exemption from certain routines like going out into the airing courts, being allowed to stay up and watch television. They represent the desired norm of patient behaviour. Such patients may dance to music when asked, stroke the heads and arms of nurses, or perform simple tricks on demand. One of their most salient characteristics is the ability to smile and laugh in response when staff joked or played with them. For example, one patient who was the recipient of greater attention than most on a certain ward was by far the most physically unattractive patient on the ward; but he was the object of much gentle teasing from the nurses, to which he would smile broadly and respond by saying 'I like you, mister'.

b Patients who showed no affection but were generally compliant were tolerated and might sometimes receive special rewards, but only to the extent that their unfriendliness was not translated into open aggression.

c Patients who were affectionate in their relationships with staff but who were generally unhelpful, i.e. liable to create extra work, tended to be viewed ambivalently by staff, and in consequence received inconsistent treatment. The case of Paul Perkins illustrates this category:

> Paul was the frequent focal point of staff banter and joking,
> to which he would respond by laughing and repeating what was
> said to him. However, he was also incontinent to such a degree
> that he would occasionally soil himself immediately after being
> washed and changed, and when this happened, the nurses
> would sometimes become quite angry and slap him. Such a
> response by the nurses depended on how long it was since he had
> last been incontinent, and on whether there was a patient 'helper'
> available to do the changing.

d Patients who were both unaffectionate and non-compliant formed a cluster disliked by staff and often given derogatory labels. This type of patient tended to be 'dirty' and prone to aggressive behaviour, and they were usually treated in a highly restrictive fashion. Most of the verbal communication they received was of a negative type, entailing the use of threats, prohibitions and commands designed to limit their actions. Patients of this type are disliked not only because they disrupt ward activities and offend moral sensibilities, but because they are seen as directly challenging the authority of nurses. Incontinence, for example, may be construed as a deliberate attempt to make the nurse's life more arduous and unpleasant.

Once a patient is located in this category, it is remarkably difficult for him to get out of it; it is easier to see a patient who is slow at finishing his meal than to recognise that he has finished at the same time as the other patients. Similarly, it is more readily recognised when a patient is incontinent than when he remains clean and dry for long periods of time, or when he is hyperactive rather than when he sits quietly with the other patients. Against a background of compliance, non-conformity becomes more visible than conformity.

e   The fifth group represents the real norm of ward behaviour – patients who are not noticeably affectionate or unaffectionate, not particularly compliant or resistant. They form the great majority who move hither and thither in response to routine demands, unlikely to develop any kind of personal relationship.

5   Constriction of learning opportunities

From compliance springs a very negative pattern of ward culture. Patients learn (and they do learn) that they are valued for their ability to do what they are told to do when they are told to do it; and this constricts any other opportunities for learning, because new or innovative behaviour is likely to be seen as non-compliance.

A notable feature of these wards is the almost complete absence of patient–patient interaction. For the most part, patients keep to themselves and only recognise each other's existence for brief periods. For example, a patient may sit down next to another and stroke his or her arm or face, and then after a few minutes get up and sit somewhere else. Or one may tease another by pulling his hair until the latter runs away or attracts the attention of a nurse. Joint play is extremely rare, and any form of mixing tends to occur only at the request of staff.[12]

Social behaviour is essentially egocentric, and entails little of the give and take that can be found among normal adults, or even among high-grade patients. An instance of this is hoarding behaviour. Certain patients hoard toys or pieces of food or simply odds and ends that can be found in dustbins or on the floor, such as pieces of paper, matchboxes and bits of string. Patients may hide these scraps away, or carry them around. They are usually extremely reluctant to show them to staff, and will resist having to give them up.[13]

Again, patients will often overconsume, eating all the food or smoking all the cigarettes that come into their possession within a very short time span. Such behaviour may reflect an attempt to assert personality in a depersonalised atmosphere; or it may be a reflection of material deprivation, and the fears of theft or loss which must be very real on large wards. In situations where rewards are scarce, and no informal social structure exists to cope with the scarcity, such behaviour is perhaps predictable. It serves to weaken still further the possibility of social relationships through which patients might learn; for if exchange is the basis of social bonds, then its absence will inhibit the formation of friendships.[14]

The absence of sociability and the prominence of egocentric behaviour among patients may be largely a function of their relatively low intelligence, which hinders the development of reciprocal relationships. However, it does seem likely that aspects of ward organisation compound this initial deficiency and serve to limit social development still further.

While, as we have seen, many staff hold to the 'family' model of ward organisation, they tend to see this exclusively in terms of parent–child relationships, and not in terms of sibling relationships. Patients are encouraged to relate to them, but not to each other; indeed, certain types of play and exploratory behaviour which would be expected in real families may be frowned on as interfering with the performance of routine, or leading to a state of overexcitement.

Female staff seem rather more ready to permit play and other forms of interaction than male staff, and it may be that this difference stems from the belief that men should be firm disciplinarians, while women can play a more nurturant and affectionate role.[15] It was noticeable that on male wards, female domestic staff often took on this role, stopping in their work to talk to patients and encouraging simple types of interaction between them.

Staff tend to fear that when patients become too animated, they become less controllable, and may trigger off collective disturbances in which injuries and accidents are likely to occur. Orderliness of patient behaviour is desired not as an end in itself, but as a means of preventing such upsets.

An equally important factor which inhibits the staff's motivation to engage in games with patients is simply that they do not feel that patients can learn to play. The following quotation from a charge nurse illustrates this:

> At Christmas we buy them toys and give them out but they just break them or don't even look at them. It's stupid really, because they are good toys and they are wasted on these, they don't know what they are for. I can guarantee that by the end of the day you can get a dustpan and brush and sweep them all up . . . they just break them. It's the same with football. We used to have a patient team here but it's no use now. Neil [one of the nurses] takes them out on to the field when it's fine and tries to get a kick-about going but they just stand there and watch and it ends up with him playing by himself.

Staff pessimism about the patients' capacity to learn reduces their interest in pursuing this type of endeavour as does their tendency to define only large-scale improvements in behaviour as indications of learning. Less significant learning tends to be overlooked, with the result that patient responses on which more complex skills could be built are not recognised.

Patients' learning opportunities are further constricted by the limitations of the 'normal' adults they are able to observe. Ward visitors are few, and the behaviour of the nurses is therefore their chief source of information; but on 'back wards', as noted earlier, staff behaviour to patients is often of an exaggerated and author-itarian kind. Commands are not spoken, they are shouted. Gestures are not simply made, they are acted out so that their meaning is unmistakable. Since most interactions tend to have this aggressive character, it would follow that if patients learn from staff they will learn to be submissive in interaction with them and dominating in their contacts with one another.

Thus, on wards where this kind of authority relationship is very pronounced, higher-grade patients take on the characteristics of the staff in their interactions with one another, using a similar volume and tone of voice and similar speech patterns. Phrases like 'Sit down!', 'Shut up!', 'Close the door!', 'I'll thump you one, if you don't. . . .', closely mirror those used by nurses, while gestures such as walking up to another patient and standing very close to him and at the same time leaning forward are equally frequent among those patients who lack verbal skills.

In effect the styles of interaction used by staff are 'picked up' by patients, even though they are in some sense inappropriate. Because patient–staff relationships tend to be structured around considerations of authority, patients by imitating them tend to weaken any basis on which friendships might be formed and developed. For example, if affection or feelings of fondness are important bases on which reciprocal peer relationships can be formed, then if such expressions are absent in staff–patient interactions patients will have little opportunity to acquire them. Instead they develop styles of interaction which serve to inhibit the growth of mutual affection by introducing threats and the consequent fear of punishment. Where patients have learned to obey commands and to expect discomfort to follow from threats, the presentation of such stimuli to them by other patients will tend to produce compliance and withdrawal. Relationships among patients, then, modelled as they often appear to be on staff behaviour, weaken the possible bases upon which sociability can grow and thus contribute to egocentric, self-seeking patterns of behaviour.

6　*Minimal task performance by staff*

Because patients' learning opportunities are constricted, and only predictable behaviour is required, the ward becomes a very dull place, without a spontaneous life of its own. Staff have no motivation to complete their tasks at anything more than the minimum level necessary to retain the approval of the sister or charge nurse; and the range of tasks which they are called upon to perform is neither varied nor skilled. Apart from specifically clinical treatments, the work, though often arduous, is not complex. Bathing, feeding, dressing, toileting are tasks well within the capacity of most adults, and they require little training.

Work patterns for staff tend to be highly predictable. Days when special tasks have to be performed, for example sending clothing to the sewing room for repairs or 'condemns', are usually specified by hospital policy. There is little opportunity for initiative.

Nor is there room for much interaction between the nurses. The performance of routines requires little active co-operation, since tasks can be performed in parallel.

To give an example, two nurses can each independently bath and dress patients without either one having to depend upon the speed or manner in which the other works. If one is slower at this task, this may indirectly affect the other by increasing his work load, but provided that there are two bath tubs, it will not directly interfere with his ability to do the job. The same could be said of other routine tasks carried out on the ward and to the general supervision of patients which occupies a large proportion of the staff's working day. At meal times, where several nurses distribute the food and help to feed patients, the need for co-operation is small; for once each nurse knows the type of diet each patient receives, he can carry out the task without reference to what the others are doing. If a patient struggles and resists being fed, help may be required from one of the other nurses, but this type of co-operation is of a short duration and is not necessarily reciprocal.

Nurses thus have very little motivation to improve their own standards of work. The internalised professional motivation which plays a large part in maintaining high standards in many professions, including nursing, is missing because training (the source of this motivation) has been largely rejected. The inherent nature of the job does not encourage them, because it is often boring and disagreeable. The patients do not provide a stimulus, because their own social standards are far lower; and the job neither requires nor fosters a team spirit.

7 *Low staff solidarity*

Low standards and low levels of solidarity go hand in hand. They are manifested in such reactions as the willingness of a nurse to leave a task for someone else to do, even though he has the time to do it himself. For example, a nurse, on noticing that a patient had soiled himself, commented to another member of ward staff: 'Norman can do that when he gets back from breakfast. I've already changed him once this morning.' Neither of the two nurses was doing anything except general supervision at the time. Again, on one ward the bathing of patients was postponed because there were not enough staff on duty. Rather than start by bathing a few of the patients, the two nurses on duty decided to leave the whole task for the next day's shift, when neither of them would be at work. Such examples, involving the shirking of work which would have to be carried out by other staff, were very common on 'back wards', and rare on other wards.

8 *Alienation*

Erving Goffman, in a well-known analysis, talks of social distance between staff and patients, and of the development of 'two different social and cultural worlds ... jogging alongside each other with points of official contact but little mutual penetration'.[16] But while this picture of a staff life and a patient life (or 'under-life') may be appropriate to mental hospitals and prisons, and perhaps to other wards of hospitals for the mentally handicapped, we do not think it is applicable to 'back wards'. Even this degree of social cohesion is lacking. Nurses maintained social distance from patients, between patients, and also from each other. The poverty of human relationships was general.

A more convincing explanation is that of Dr Rose Laub Coser, who, in a study of nurses' self-images on a ward for incurable patients, postulates that where staff cannot 'heal' or 'cure' their patients, they become alienated, withdrawing into an impersonality which protects them from what is seen as failure.[17]

The position of charge nurses and sisters on such wards was often one of extreme difficulty. There appeared to be only one rule: *the charge nurse cannot win.* So far from exerting leadership or promoting social cohesion, the charge nurse was isolated from the other staff by the nature of his work, his superior status and his larger pay-packet.

Most charge nurses stayed in the office for much of the time, stressing the administrative nature of their work. The following is a comment on such a situation from a female SEN:

> I don't begrudge him the money he earns, anyone who does
> this work deserves every penny they get. What makes it unfair
> is that he does less work than any of us ... he stays in his office
> and drinks tea all day and never comes out and lends us a hand,
> even when we are down to just two of us and all the feeding
> to do. He says he's got a lot of paper work to do, but I've been
> in there when he's not been around and the paper work turns
> out to be his football pools or a novel.... I'm not complaining
> about the money I take home, but I don't think it's right that
> he gets that much more and doesn't have to do anything for it.

The twin convictions – that charge nurses were overpaid, and that the claim that their days were occupied by 'paperwork' was not justified, recurred in one ward after another; and it seems unlikely in fact that the 'paperwork' was very heavy. The population of these wards was very nearly static; few of the patients went out, or spent their own pocket money; there cannot have been much to be entered on clinical records; and other charge nurses on similar wards found it possible to spend time with the ward staff and patients.

To do so might make for a grudging commendation, like the following statement from a male SEN:

SEN: He's very fair as charge nurses go.
Interviewer: Why is that?
SEN: He's willing to come out of the office and give you a hand ... he's not like some who stay in the office all day and leave the running of the ward to a SEN who thinks he can boss everybody around.

However, if the charge nurse did come out on to the ward and 'lend a hand', he risked devaluing his status; for, as we have seen, he has no specific techniques to offer, and his performance of the basic tasks of toileting, washing, dressing and feeding is unlikely to be superior to that of an untrained nurse with a few weeks' experience. There may occasionally be satisfying professional tasks to perform, like taking a patient's blood pressure, suturing a wound or treating a laceration, but such opportunities of demonstrating expertise are comparatively rare; and the general tendency among nursing staff to derogate the importance of training in favour of ward experience means that there will be no great respect for his formal qualifications.

To escape from this double bind requires remarkable qualities of personality and administrative understanding; but people with these qualities are more likely to be promoted to the nursing hierarchy than left in charge of 'back wards'.

In Figure 5.2, we show the eight factors which have been listed in the form of a vicious circle; the circle is completed by the fact that it is alienation (the maintenance of social distance) which makes possible the creation of antagonistic stereotypes, and it is the stereotyping of patients which sets off the whole movement again. But it is more than a vicious circle; for each of the eight factors affects and reinforces the other seven, and all point to and are reinforced by the central fact of routine management.

The centrality of routine

Routine is necessary because patients are held to be incapable of anything else – what else can you do for people who 'haven't a brain'? The fact that the patient is on the 'back ward' may be held

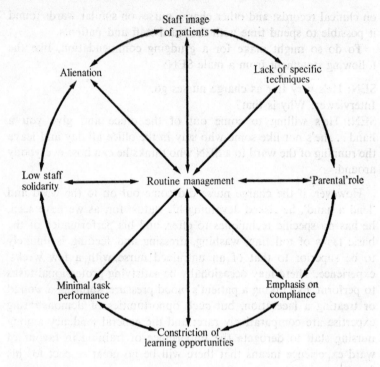

Figure 5.2 The 'back ward' syndrome

as prima facie evidence that nothing else could be done for him: if it could, he would be on a 'better' ward. He can only learn, if at all, through ceaseless repetition.

Routine is necessary because the patients need 'everything done for them'. They have to be toileted, washed, dressed and fed, and with staff shortages, this takes up the whole day.

Routine is necessary because they are 'like children' and parents must not have favourites.

Routine is necessary because patients have to 'do as they are told', and behave like good children.

Routine is necessary because there would be 'no end of trouble if they did as they liked'. They might injure themselves, and the nursing staff would get the blame.

Routine is necessary because 'it's a lousy job, anyway', and it doesn't really matter how it's done.

Routine is necessary because 'the other staff will duck out of their share if they get the chance'.

Routine is necessary because 'we don't work as a team – why should we?'.

Routine makes for a smooth-running ward, minimises disturbed behaviour, provides automatic checks that necessary procedures have been carried out for all patients, and prevents or lessens the effect of incidents; and above all, routine makes it possible to satisfy one's superiors.

Satisfying consultants and nursing officers that the ward is run competently is of great importance. On them depends the staff member's chance of promotion and perhaps of transfer to a 'better' ward. Consultants may not spend much time with these patients – their main attention is necessarily directed to diagnosis, assessment and active treatment – but nursing officers will visit the ward frequently, and their standards and expectations will count heavily.

The following quotation is from a nursing officer with responsibility for a group of wards for the severely subnormal:

You can tell if a ward is well run by the patients ... on these wards they are all doubly incontinent and you can tell if there is slacking by whether they are all sitting wet through in their trousers ... if you see that, you know there's a lot of slacking ... you can tell by whether they are clean and dry whether the staff are doing their job. There isn't much more that you can do for these lads than that. ... On a fine day, you can take them out and kick a football with them, but they lose interest after a little while. Or you can give them toys, but they break them and throw them away after a few moments ... you see, you can't hold their attention long enough. You can give them TV to watch, but most of them don't bother to watch. As I say, there isn't much you can do apart from feed them and keep them clean and dry.

The cleanliness of patients, the absence of stubble on male chins, and the general appearance of both patients and the wards serve as key indicators that a ward is well run; and, as the quotation indicates, non-routine events such as football or play with toys or television are seen as peripheral and not susceptible of evaluation.

The overruling importance of 'orderliness' and 'neatness' has been fully documented elsewhere.[18] One of the team had experience of a children's ward in which the children were not allowed to play with balloons given by a visitor because they popped (which 'caused excitement') and being hydrogen-filled, stuck to the ceiling (which 'made the ward look untidy').

Making patients presentable in terms acceptable to the outside world becomes the dominant part of the staff's work because it is an easily observable indication that the ward is being run efficiently and that patients are cared for. On both a formal and an informal basis, nurses are made aware that any efforts they may make to engage the patients' attention and involve them in activities outside this unvarying cycle of events may be held to detract from its faithful performance.

As far as ward staff are concerned, routines thus have a certain sanctity that is buttressed both by their own perception of the patients and the ward situation, and by the social and professional pressures exerted on them. Given this sanctity, events that tend to upset routines or threaten to change them significantly come to be opposed. For example, the presence of voluntary workers can be resisted by nurses:

> I think they do have a place in the hospital, but only if they do certain things. As long as they are prepared to work along with the staff I welcome them with open arms, but most of the time they come here and just play with the patients till they get so worked up they won't do as they are told. I know it's good for the patients to have this kind of contact, but when they get so excited that they won't sit still to eat their tea, knock things over and stop us from getting the work done, then I am going to draw the line at that.
>
> (Ward charge nurse.)

Similarly physiotherapists, speech therapists, occupational therapists, social workers, chaplains and patients' relatives may be seen as ward intruders, bringing alien and threatening values into a closed world of precarious stability.[19]

The situation we have described is one of great complexity and tension. Unfortunately, it has produced polarised reactions. Sociologists, journalists and senior members of the health services, doctors, nurses and administrators alike, are inclined to take the view, when an Ely or a Farleigh hits the headlines, that such conditions are scandalous, and must be stopped. But their prescriptions for change – 'better furnishings', 'more training', 'more staff', 'more volunteers', 'more publicity', stop far short of tackling the causes. Most of these wards are now quite well furnished (some such wards, where there are incontinent patients, are carpeted, and a great deal of energy goes into preserving the pristine state of the carpet). More training might help – but what sort of training, since it appears that trained nurses are as helpless in such a situation as untrained ones, and training is 'shelved' as inappropriate? More staff might help – but what sort of staff, and how are they to be motivated? Volunteers, as we have seen, are likely to be resisted, or confined to tasks of a routine nature. Publicity produces some remarkable displays of public self-righteousness which serve only to exacerbate the strains and to tighten the defensiveness of ward staff.

For there is a good deal in what they say. Patients do have to be kept clean and tidy – no one is suggesting that they should be physically neglected. They do have very limited capabilities. Superiors do have to be satisfied – that is a fact of any kind of working situation. These wards are short-staffed, and they do not always get the best staff because they are at the bottom of the pecking order; and the job is not only stigmatised – it is hard and often unpleasant. Most of the critics would be hard put to it to sustain it even for a day. People who do it year in and year out, with neither professional nor public support, and with only a very limited job satisfaction, are performing a very underrated public service.

So the situation goes on – officially denied or disapproved of, but a living daily reality for many patients and staff up and down the country. Considerable efforts are made to change it from time to time by senior staff and specialists, but the sub-culture of the 'back wards' remains resistant to change, even in small ways.

For instance, a consultant, commenting on a ward for spastic and severely subnormal patients, found that nursing staff blocked his recommendations about feeding patients:

We have given them instructions on how to feed patients, but they never follow them. What they do is stand behind them and then bring the spoon up to their mouths from the side, so that they can't see the food coming to their mouths, and then they just shovel it in so they don't have a chance to chew it. We wanted them to stand in front of the patients, so that the patients could follow the movement of the spoon with food on it, and then place it on the tongue so that they could exercise it and help develop the muscles. They don't do this, though, they always have some reason – it's too long to do and they are rushed, or they think it's a waste of time. They want to see an instant improvement before they are convinced that it's of any use.

The same consultant commented that much of his work had little lasting benefit because remedial treatment given to individual patients was not followed up on the wards by the patients:

> If we spend ten minutes three days a week with one patient, this isn't enough, because these exercises need to be followed up on the ward ... they have to be kept up consistently, or all the benefit is lost. We give demonstrations to the nurses and they seem quite interested but somehow when they get on the ward, they lose that interest and don't bother to keep it up.

Occupational therapists and psychologists have reported that resistance to the introduction of new forms of treatment and learning was so great that they had to withdraw from such wards. One charge nurse speaks for many:

> All these so-called new ideas have been tried before. People come up with some bloody daft ideas and then expect us to make them work. They are only out to make a name for themselves by coming up with a theory that no one has thought of before.

Conclusion

Individual and local action on particular wards seems unlikely to have lasting effect. We think there are three main ways out of the impasse:

1 *Breaking up the sub-culture* Some members of the research team were of the opinion that the only practical and effective action would be to move either the patients or the ward nurses or both. It would be possible to scatter the patients among other wards of the hospital, and some at least might show a surprising improvement as a result. The staff might be left on the ward, but be given high-grade patients to care for so that they could see some results for their efforts. Again, it would be possible to transfer the nursing staff to other, more innovative wards, and to bring in other, more innovative nurses; or it would be possible to scatter both, leaving only the physical structure of the ward which, with a new name, might acquire a new identity.

On reflection, we do not recommend any of these modes of action.

We have seen that Ward 99, or its equivalent, is often a necessity for the hospital. Other wards are enabled to be 'good' and progressive because the 'back ward' exists as a last resort. To abolish it might upset the equilibrium of the whole hospital; and certainly the presence on other wards of its patients and/or staff would serve to depress standards. While individual patients or nurses might greatly benefit from transfer (and most nursing officers are already alive to this possibility), we think that the sub-culture has to be treated as a whole. It cannot simply be wiped out of existence.

2 *Minimising routine* We think that routine procedures have to be carried out, but that they need not bulk as large in the life of the ward as they do, and that they can be dysfunctional. Some patients could be taught to acquire bowel and bladder control for themselves, to wash, dress and feed themselves; and they might benefit from being attached to other wards, where they could imitate other patients who have these capacities, provided that this was done in small groups, for short periods, with a special nurse attached to them. For those who remain incontinent, the use of incontinence pads and other special equipment could prevent many of the unpleasant effects which mar the ward day. There is no reason why 'cleaning up patients' should become the central activity as it often is. The account of shaving rituals in Ward 99 provides another case in point. Some at least of the problems could have been obviated by the issue of a few more razor blades.

A nursing officer in one hospital embarked on a study of 'administrative nonsenses' – small time-wasting rituals which persisted in her own hospital without justification in either economy or reason. In a few weeks, she discovered thirty-six such rituals.

There may be ways of smoothing and minimising routine procedures on a given ward, and the staff themselves could pinpoint some of the difficulties if they were asked. Small things like rehanging a door to open in the opposite direction, providing extra storage space, handling patients in small groups rather than in the mass (was it really necessary for 42 patients in Ward 99 all to be washed at once?), could make a great difference. It should not be below the professional dignity of senior members of the medical and nursing staff to suggest and initiate such changes – good administration consists of attention to small issues as well as large ones, particularly when the small issues may be key factors in major changes.

3 *A new technology* Somehow, the vicious circle has to be broken, and it may be that this could be achieved if some new

element in treatment were introduced.[20] It is not that there are no new ideas available. Ideas do exist, but they have either remained at the research stage, or have been developed in other fields and not applied to the care of the severely mentally handicapped.

A Lancashire hospital recently operated a 'Seek and Find' policy. Members of the nursing staff were sent out to other hospitals to seek out new ideas and bring them back for trial and experiment. This kind of receptiveness to innovation could be fostered more widely.

We think that there are three main areas in which a search for a new technology might be successful: each would require careful and controlled experimentation.

a   Modelling theory

We use the term 'modelling theory' to denote systems of patient care and management which seek to capitalise on the parent–child concept by using the nurses as models whom the patients can imitate. Experimental projects such as Professor Tizard's Brooklands study[21] or the research of King, Raynes and Tizard[22] are based on the assumption that subnormal people are in need of closer and more affective relationships than are provided in the typical hospital setting. They suggest that attention-seeking and a desire for affection on the part of patients are not abnormal personality traits, but a natural response to institutional deprivation.

In the Brooklands project, staff were assigned to small groups of children for whom they had full responsibility, thus facilitating close and personal interaction. There was a particular emphasis on developing skills of speech and play, since these were basic to the fostering of patterns of sociability.

Albert Bandura, an American social psychologist, conducted numerous experiments on modelling in an attempt to discover the conditions that encourage learning through imitation. He concludes that a nurturant relationship is not a necessary condition if learning is to take place, but it does encourage the acquisition of new speech patterns and verbal skills. This proposition is consistent with Tizard's finding that children in the Brooklands unit made relatively large gains in verbal mental age in comparison with a control group of children in a hospital setting, but did not make comparable gains in non-verbal mental age.[23]

One difficulty in applying these findings to wards for adult patients labelled as severely subnormal is that they have been developed primarily in relation to children; and, as we have noted earlier, adult mentally handicapped people are not children, though they are often conceptualised as such. They may have a fully developed sexuality. Their emotional and intellectual development is not so much retarded at the 2-year-old or 3-year-old level (though this is a popular belief) as unevenly developed and fragmented. We have commented on the dangers of using the parent–child model for adults at some length; and while some of these relate to the particular *kind* of parent–child model which is employed – a restrictive and authoritarian one for the most part – we are not convinced that treating mentally handicapped adults as children, even in a warm and permissive relationship, would be constructive.

However, the principles of modelling theory seem distinguishable from the particular model which has been applied so far. Adults do learn from other adults, and the family is not the only model for social group-formation. The application of small-group theory might produce ways of developing personal interaction which have so far been overlooked,[24] but this would have to be done in a research situation, and the skills transferred to nursing staff.

b *Learning theory*

A different approach, focused on the individual rather than the group, is that derived from theories of behaviour modification. In the attempt to develop a general theory of learning processes, psychologists have been led to examine subnormal people both in terms of their capacity to learn and the methods of learning they employ. For example, Sidney Bijou defines mental retardation as 'a limited repertoire of behaviour shaped by events that constitute a person's history',[25] thereby shifting the focus away from biological factors towards external stimuli which impinge upon the individual. In doing this, the salience of a wide array of situational and psychological variables to problems of slow learning can be seen more clearly. The focus shifts from what a person is (for example, a mongol or a Klinefelter) to what he does, and hence to a more complex appraisal of his condition. A behavioural science perspective on mental handicap carries with it a basic assumption that this is a condition that can be modified through a conscious manipulation of an individual's social environment.

While behaviour modification also has its dangers when employing aversive techniques (and we emphatically do not recommend the use of such techniques, which can be very cruel in the hands of insensitive practitioners), it is possible to confine it to the use of positive reinforcers which offer the patient small rewards for appropriate actions. This approach can offer an alternative to ceaseless repetition and a short cut to learning with very positive results and no risk to the patient.

A number of studies have concentrated upon such issues as teaching patients to acquire bowel and bladder control, to develop a basic vocabulary, to control aggressive and violent tendencies. The techniques depend for their effectiveness on the kinds of reinforcers used and upon the frequency and timing of their distribution. Sweets, cigarettes, the opportunity to play, and verbal and physical expression of affection have all been used by research workers, but the most effective reinforcer may be different for each person. The frequency of reinforcement has been examined in relation to subnormal people's ability to learn and, although some discrepant findings have emerged, there is a fundamental consensus concerning the effectiveness of intermittent reinforcement.[26] Where a desired form of behaviour is rewarded at either fixed or variable intervals, rather than after each occurrence, learning tends to take place more rapidly and to persist for longer periods. The timing of reinforcement is also vital, and (like the 'clip on the ear' – an aversive technique which has conditioned many a patient into passivity) the sooner it is dispensed after the occurrence, the more effective it will be.

By the use of these methods, psychologists have been able to develop quite complex and valuable skills in subnormal people where other methods have failed. Simple skills can be built into quite complex 'chains' – for example, in teaching patients to dress themselves, each separate phase of the process can be taught independently until the patient knows how to perform all of them. Once these have been learned, the emphasis can shift to relating the component actions to form a complete pattern.

In much of the same manner, behaviour that is disruptive or obnoxious can be 'extinguished'. One of the premises of behaviour modification is that no behaviour persists unless it is or has in the past been reinforced, so that behaviour that is obviously maladaptive, such as self-mutilation, will only be repeated to the extent that the individual finds it rewarding. We have already seen that hostile and non-compliant patients are likely to get more staff attention than the quiet mass who do not show strong reactions of any kind.

In such situations, attention from staff is a reinforcer, and it is being applied to perpetuate the antisocial behaviour. By controlling such sources of reinforcement and encouraging alternative responses that are incompatible with the original activity, it is possible to 'extinguish' the undesirable behaviour.

In general, the application of theories of behaviour modification have produced two conclusions pertinent to the problems of 'back wards'. The first is the belief that severely subnormal people can learn, provided that the right kinds of reinforcer are used. If an individual fails to learn, the theory calls upon its user to seek for failures in the application of the technique rather than to reject the patient as someone incapable of learning. In this way, it develops patience and tolerance on the part of the user, and provides an impetus to innovation. The second is that such techniques can be readily taught to 'non-experts', that is, to people not trained in the behavioural sciences. Ayllon and Azrin, for example, taught nurses to manage a ward for adult schizophrenic patients by using these techniques.[27] Tharp and Wetzel taught parents to use techniques systematically at home with behaviourally disturbed children[28] and Birnbrauer and Lawler passed the techniques to teachers in a school for mentally handicapped.[29] Gray and Kasteller blended behaviour modification and modelling procedures in an experiment where retired people from outside the hospitals were paired with mentally handicapped children and briefed in reinforcement techniques.[30]

If it is possible to use such techniques in settings where close supervision is not feasible, it should certainly be possible to organise them in a ward setting where staff are in close contact with nursing officers and psychiatrists, who can offer expertise and advice. Some supervision would also be necessary to ensure that reinforcement techniques were not used to promote undesirable behaviour – for example, the 'rituals' earlier described as exaggerating a patient's child-like status. Staff activities would need to be related to clear-cut programmes and goals with a positive value.

c   *Special skills*

A third source of a new technology might be found in the application by nurses of simple skills derived from those 'ward intruders' whose presence and values are often rejected. Physiotherapists, occupational therapists, speech therapists and other specialists have skills to offer which are not fully used for three reasons: the specialists themselves are in very short supply and their work concentrated on patients who are possible candidates for discharge; when they do go to the closed world of the severely subnormal ward, they often find the nurses unco-operative; and they themselves are frequently resistant to teaching techniques to nurses for professional reasons, emphasising the exclusive nature of their own skills and qualifications.

We would like to see a situation where nurses welcomed such staff as offering new and valuable skills, and the staff for their part were prepared to act as consultants and teachers to nurses, passing on the simpler of their skills to members of the nursing profession. They have nothing to lose but professional restrictivism, and everything to gain in the way of status and efficiency.

We believe that the search for an effective new technology offers the best hope of breaking through the 'back ward' syndrome, and that this should be a priority in research. The methods suggested here require imagination, an initial input of scarce skills, and careful supervision; but they point to ways of salvaging human potential and improving the quality of life on the wards where the orthodox methods have manifestly failed.

Hospital and community

One of the major points of criticism of hospitals for the mentally handicapped has been their physical and social isolation from the surrounding community; and since the introduction of the first community care plans in the early 1960s there has been much government encouragement of the development of community links. This has taken several different forms – the general encouragement of volunteers and voluntary organisations as part of the health and social services which was reflected in the Aves Report;[1] the recognition by the DES and DHSS of courses in community work in universities and Colleges of Further Education, and the employment of community workers on the Home Office-sponsored Community Development Projects set up in 1969;[2] the specific encouragement of voluntary work in hospitals contained in three DHSS circulars,[3] which has led to the appointment of voluntary service organisers (VSOs) in the London teaching hospitals and elsewhere, and the creation of a Standing Conference of VSOs; and the application of all these new ideas to hospitals for the mentally handicapped.

The circular *On Improving the Effectiveness of the Subnormality Hospital* (1965) recommended that 'contacts with the community life of the area should be promoted in all possible ways . . . to bring the geographically isolated subnormality hospital into closer contact with the community it serves'.[4]

Better Services for the Mentally Handicapped stresses again that 'contact should be maintained with life outside the hospital through contacts with the local community around the hospital as well as with patients' families,'[5] and devotes a whole chapter to voluntary service – 'the contribution of the private citizen' – which lists a number of ways of developing links. These include friendship for individual patients, the running of group activities such as drama, music, painting and horse-riding, raising funds for amenities and the development by voluntary service organisers of new types of helping groups – school-children, university students, the 'regulars' at a pub or club.

This development of official encouragement has taken place against a background of continuing criticism. The report on Ely Hospital noted the lack of community support for the hospital, and concluded: 'A determined effort needs to be made to associate the work of Ely with the surrounding community so as to secure a more effective pattern of community care and greater participation by voluntary associations in the work of the hospital.'[6]

Dr Pauline Morris makes a similar point,[7] and a more disconcerting one. In her national sample of hospitals, there was a good deal of apparent activity by voluntary organisations and volunteers, but the dividend in enriched human relationships was remarkably small.[8] Volunteers raised money, provided entertainments, decorated the chapel, made tea for visitors, but they rarely entered into personal relationships with patients. One is left with the impression that staff satisfaction with the arrangements was considerably higher than patient satisfaction.

Research design

In the Gateshire survey, we decided to concentrate on this issue of personal relationships: to collect data not in terms of the links between hospitals and organisations, but in terms of what these meant for individual patients. We hoped in this way to get beyond the public-relations picture ('Community links are very good – the WRVS and the League of Friends come in every week') to a more realistic assessment of the situation.

We started by taking three kinds of contact which patients might have with the outside world:

i *family and personal contacts,* i.e. those naturally arising from the patient's home situation and life-pattern;

ii *neighbourhood contacts,* i.e. those arising from the location of the hospital. This category included both informal contacts (e.g. visiting shops or the local pub, visits to the hospital by individuals in the area and organised contacts by voluntary societies and groups;

iii *official contacts,* i.e. those planned and organised by the hospital.

These were studied in six selected hospitals chosen to reflect the variables of size and geographical location: one large, one medium-sized and one small in an urban and in a rural setting. These are shown in Table 6.1.

Table 6.1 Situation and size of hospitals in community survey

Size	'Rural'	'Urban'
Large (over 300 beds)	Laker Institution	Lamprey Institution
Medium (100–300 beds)	Milan Grange	Marathon Grange
Small (less than 100 beds)	Sycamore House	South House

Family and personal contacts

This form of patient–'outsider' contact, mainly with relatives, has been for many patients traditionally their only link with the outside world; and it remains the main method by which the outside world reaches into the hospitals. It is important not merely as a lifeline for community relations, but on a more practical level in providing a home base for the patient, a physical reference to another living place.

One has only to imagine the consequences of the severance of all present family links to perceive their importance; it would mean the loss of nearly all meaningful contacts for most patients.

The potential of this form of contact is enormous. The simple fact that it concerns large numbers of 'outsiders' as well as patients points to this. It is important to assess this potential, to discover how it might be best exploited, and to indicate the constraints at present at work. In all, the six hospitals contained 1,508 patients. Table 6.2 indicates how often they were visited by relatives and friends and how often they were able to return to a family home.

Although this is the most extensive channel of 'outside' contacts, as Table 6.2 indicates, only 26 per cent of patients are visited more than once per month and only 6 per cent go home more than once per month. Conversely 38 per cent are never visited and 78 per cent never go home.

About two-thirds of those patients visited regularly have weekly visits and a small proportion are visited two or three times a week. Many of those patients who go home regularly are 'parole' patients, who visit relatives at weekends unaccompanied.[9] There is a large

*Table 6.2   Patients' contacts with families and friends
(six hospitals) (N = 1,508)*

| | Frequency (%) | | | |
	Regularly	Occasionally	Rarely	Never
Visited	26	24	12	38
Returned to family home	6	7	9	78

Notes
1. 'Regularly' = more than once a month.
   'Occasionally' = once a month to three times a year.
   'Rarely' = less than three times a year.
2. Numbers 'going home' do not relate to length of stay at home, which can
vary from an afternoon to several weeks, but solely to the number of times
the journey is made. The act of leaving hospital is considered here as the
relevant factor.

divergence between the numbers of patients visited and those going
home. This no doubt reflects to some extent the real difficulties of
taking some of the more severely handicapped patients out of the
ward situation, but it may also reflect the feelings of both relatives
and staff that there is nothing to be gained from removing patients,
even for a short time.

In spite of recent attempts in some hospitals to make staff more
aware of the value of personal and private contacts, most hospital
staff seem ambivalent about all but the most dramatic or obvious
cases. They will respond with passion to the neglect of a 4-year-old
child, but not to that of a 50-year-old man with no contact in over
twenty years. Linked with this ambivalence is a general lack of
provision for visitors in terms of where to take patients and what to
do with them. Most visitors are confined to meeting their patient
in the ward day room, especially when the patient is seriously mentally or physically handicapped or the weather is not fine enough
to use the grounds. In such circumstances it is difficult to have a
private and meaningful conversation.

In the great majority of cases the concern and involvement of
families is directed solely towards their particular patient to the
exclusion of all others. However, there are cases where other patients
are involved. For instance, where two patients are firmly attached,
a visit to one means a visit to the other. In very rare cases, family
involvement is more generally philanthropic and concern and in-

volvement for other patients will result. At Lamprey the relatives of one patient tend to care more for the welfare of the whole ward, giving parties, taking patients home and providing money for material comforts. A patient's relative at Milan Grange takes most of the patients from her son's ward on outings three or four times per year. Other isolated examples could be cited from Marathon and Laker. The fact that patients' families usually form the nucleus of organisations like the NSMHC and the Leagues of Friends points both to the strength and to the potential of family involvement.

Patients' contact with families tends to depend on their age and the length of hospitalisation. Tables 6.3 and 6.4 indicate that both visiting and home-going rates tend to fall with increasing age and length of hospitalisation of the patient.

Contact is largely with parents, and both tables reflect the loss of parental support in the middle years through parents' age, infirmity and death. Though the youngest patients have contacts with the

Table 6.3   *Visiting, by age groups (N = 1,508)*

Age	No. in age group	Age group visited (%)	Age group home-going (%)
0–19	264	72	30
20–39	522	69	25
40–59	492	53	23
60+	230	48	18
Total	1,508		

Table 6.4   *Visiting, by length of stay*

Length of stay (years)	No. in length of stay group	Length of stay group visited (%)	Length of stay group home-going (%)
0–5	269	73	34
5–10	246	76	29
10–20	460	61	19
20+	533	52	17
Total	1,508		

wider family – brothers and sisters, uncles and aunts – the involvement for most patients is with parents only, and the loss of parents
means their total separation from family life.

In general, the size of the hospital appears to play little part in
determining the extent of family relationships. The critical factors
appear to be age and length of stay, mentioned above, and geographical setting (Table 6.5).

Table 6.5 indicates the difference between the urban and the rural
hospitals with regard to the distance of patients' homes. As Table
6.6 indicates, this varies from the 74 per cent and 8 per cent respectively of short and long distance at urban Lamprey to the 0 per cent
and 69 per cent respectively at rural Sycamore.

Differences are more consistent within each size pairing; Lamprey

*Table 6.5   Patients with homes: distance from home to hospital
(N = Urban: 848, Rural: 546)*

Distance home (miles)	Patients in urban hospitals (%)	Patients in rural hospitals (%)
0–10	63	9
19–30	28	56
30+	9	35
Total	100	100

Note 'Patients with homes' = those patients with addresses of next of kin
in their case-notes.

Table 6.6   Distance from home, by hospital

| Hospital | Distance home | | No. |
	0–10 miles	31 + miles	
UL[10] Lamprey	74	8	623
RL Laker	16	29	308
UM Marathon	36	9	201
RM Milan	7	39	212
US South	4	42	24
RS Sycamore	0	69	26

(UL) has 74 per cent of its patients' homes 10 miles or less distant and only 8 per cent over 30 miles distant; whereas Laker (RL) has only 16 per cent of its patients' homes 10 miles or less distant and 29 per cent over 30 miles distant. In both the medium-sized and the small hospitals the same trend is apparent, although the differences between the small hospitals are not so accentuated.

From these findings it would be expected that the urban hospitals would have more family involvement than the rural hospitals, especially in view of the greater availability of public transport in urban areas. Table 6.7 gives evidence on this point.

Table 6.7   Percentage of patients receiving visits and going home, by hospital

| | Percentage of all patients in hospital | | | | |
| | Visiting | | Going home | | |
	regularly or occasionally	rare or never	regularly or occasionally	rare or never	N
UL Lamprey	60	40	16	84	656
RL Laker	50	50	11	89	350
UM Marathon	46	54	7	93	211
RM Milan	37	63	11	89	228
US South	8	92	80	20	25
RS Sycamore	8	92	21	79	38

Where visiting is concerned, the hypothesis is confirmed at the large and medium-sized hospitals, but not at the small ones. The percentage going home is small at all hospitals, except South House which seems to have a distinctive policy. A factor to note is that being visited and going home may be viewed as alternatives – a high rate in one respect leading to a low rate in the other. Overall, the differences between the urban and rural hospitals are not as marked as one would expect from the differences in geographical location.

Closer examination of visiting and home-going patterns suggests that these are influenced by a variety of organisational factors. For instance, the large and medium-sized rural hospitals tend to reinforce the concept of the monthly 'big visiting day' by providing teas and holding events exclusively on those days. Special coaches are chartered to Laker Institution (RL) from the two nearest cities on those days specifically to ferry visitors. The subsequent increased monthly visits are reflected in the 'occasional' category figures. 32 per cent of patients at the two rural hospitals are visited 'occasionally', whereas the corresponding figure at the two urban hospitals is only 20 per cent. In the same way home-going is influenced to a large extent by the numbers of 'parole' patients. For instance, at both Lamprey and Marathon the wards with the highest numbers of patients going home are those with the highest numbers of 'parole' patients. This is not merely an indication that relatives are most prepared to have at home the least handicapped patients; it also reflects the fact that these patients do not have to be collected from the hospital.

As 'parole' is officially permitted for any outing, it is not biased towards favouring any one type of contact between patients and outsiders. However, its degree of use is affected materially by other factors. For example, Laker (RL), although no farther from centres of population than Milan (RM), is more isolated from the point of view of public transport services. This, linked with the fact that Milan has always had an older and more self-sufficient patient population,[11] has meant the far greater use of parole, and this means a higher rate of home visiting although patients' homes are more scattered.[12]

All the hospitals now officially stress that visiting the hospital is permitted at any time; but the routines for accepting visitors into the wards are firmly geared in most cases to certain times on certain days, and most visitors accept the unwritten rule. For example, even at Lamprey Institution, where visiting hours are the most flexible, a visit at any time apart from Wednesday afternoons or at weekends is rare. The evenings, which would seem to be appropriate times from the visitors' point of view, are ruled out for most patients because of ward routines – meals, bathing and early 'lights out'. The serving of tea on certain days suggests that these are the 'correct' days for visiting. At Lamprey, a tea-room has been built and is voluntarily staffed on 'main visiting days' (Wednesdays, Saturdays, Sundays).

All hospital staff seem to perceive visiting by relatives of patients as being meritable – something that has naturally always happened and naturally always will. Thus, few see need for change except where visiting impedes their work or comfort. Personal visitors are generally treated with a kind of distant respect. This, of course, is partly in consideration for privacy; but it also reflects an ingrained attitude that relatives are not directly concerned in caring for patients, and that their visits constitute an interruption to the care process. The nurse is a professional, the relatives are seen as amateurs. Many ward staff think it good for 'their' patients to have visits, but keep their professional and social distance.

In all hospitals it tends to be the same group of patients in terms of age and length of institutionalisation who are visited and who go home. As Table 6.8 shows, it is the younger patients who have been in hospital a shorter time who are generally favoured. The same tendency applies to both urban and rural hospitals, although as expected the percentages are consistently lower in the latter. An interesting feature of Table 6.8 is that home-going decreases with age in the rural hospitals but not in the urban hospitals. This again reflects the greater use of parole in urban hospitals for older patients.

The large and medium-sized urban hospitals both have a social worker. It might be expected that this would result in increased visiting, since the social worker's primary concern is with families; but in fact, though social workers no doubt do excellent work with individual patients and their families, their work does not significantly affect the visiting figures. The rather erratic relationship with local authority Social Services Departments and a necessary preoccupation with work related to admissions and discharges restricts their work to a very small percentage of patients. A much larger social work force would be necessary to achieve quantifiable differences.

Patients' relatives do exert some influence through the hospital Leagues of Friends. Leagues of Friends in the large and medium-sized hospitals have been formed and maintained largely through the support and energy of relatives. 18 out of 60 committee mem-

Table 6.8 *Percentage of patients receiving visits and going home, by age*

Age	Urban		Rural	
	Visit	Home	Visit	Home
0–19	69	19	64	16
20–39	61	13	62	16
40–59	51	11	34	7
60+	42	14	26	4

bers of the Leagues of Friends were patients' relatives.[13] This percentage would be greater were it not for the policy at Laker Institution of attempting to gain a broader range of interest by the co-option of representatives from voluntary organisations.

The formation of Leagues of Friends has brought senior staff into contact with the most enthusiastic and energetic families, but apart from this, few of the senior nursing, medical or administrative staff are personally involved with families. It is those working at patient level – the ward staff, teachers, social workers and therapists – who encounter them personally.

Neighbourhood contacts

Contacts with local individuals and organisations showed much greater differences between hospitals than contacts with patients' families, and the pattern was much more erratic. We investigated the effect of four variables: hospital location, hospital size, the types of patients in particular hospitals and staff policy. Of these, the factors of hospital size and types of patients did not produce significant results,[14] but hospital location and staff policy seemed highly significant. Findings on these two factors are given below.

Hospital location

Urban hospitals have a much greater potential for community contacts than rural hospitals. For example, Lamprey (UL) has an urban population of over half a million within a five-mile radius. Laker (RL) has no more than 3,000 people scattered within the same radius. It is to be expected that Lamprey would find far more voluntary organisations and helpers within easy reach and this is in fact the case. For instance, at Lamprey at least 10 secondary schools have been contacted within a five-mile radius. Laker has one school within the same radius and no contact.

The accessibility of the hospital is also important. The three urban hospitals all have easy access to regular public transport, both road and rail. Of the three rural hospitals, however, only Milan Grange has opportunity to use road and rail (and even in this case the railway is nearly a mile away), while Laker and Sycamore have to rely on irregular bus services alone for travel to and from the nearest large centres of population.

A third factor which creates differences between the town and the country hospitals is the attitude of the nearest community. For the rural hospitals, the nearest centre of population is the local village. Villages have a close-knit and organic life of their own. The presence of an institution, with its distinctive way of life and its alien values, tends to be seen as a threat. A town with its more loose-knit and 'cosmopolitan' structure, can set up relationships with an institution with far less strain, and the very impersonality of urban environments may be a favourable factor.

For example, at Milan Grange (RM) there is no contact between patients and people from the nearest village, apart from the occasional shopping errands of 2 of the 230 patients. Patients have been either made unwelcome or rejected in local pubs and clubs, and they take no part in local events and entertainments. The social distance between village and hospital has extended to staff, few of whom come from the local village, though some come from villages farther afield.[15]

At Laker Institution (RL), although many staff live in the local village, the same tendencies can be seen. Apart from the weekly attendance at the local Methodist church by 30–40 patients, there is no organised contact between locals and patients. Two or three patients do 'abscond' to the village shop, but as one nurse ironically remarked, 'you can't keep your eye on them all the time!' None of the voluntary workers who regularly visit the hospital comes from the village. At Sycamore House (RS) there is no evidence of past local involvement in the hospital and patients do not use the village shop (a daily mobile shop calls at the hospital). No patients belong to local clubs, visit the pubs or work locally, and only three or four patients attend the local church. The 'parole' patients of Milan Grange (RM) and Sycamore House (RS) all make for the nearest large centres of population; at Milan they usually take a train to a city twelve miles away, and at Sycamore they travel by bus to the nearest town.

At one time, many of the less handicapped patients in all three hospitals worked for local farmers during the harvest – usually for very small rewards; but this form of labour has now been withdrawn by the hospitals, and it does not seem to have led to any enduring contacts.

Conversely, the urban environment seems to favour easy movement of patients and local people between hospital and community. This is suggested by the greater number of 'parole' patients[16] in urban hospitals shown in Table 6.9.

Table 6.9   *'Parole' patients at each hospital and between urban and rural hospitals (percentage)*

Hospitals		'Parolees'	Percentage of all patients	Total percentage
Urban	Lamprey	87	12	
	Marathon	35	17	16
	South	25	100	
Rural	Laker	0	0	
	Milan	27	12	8
	Sycamore	25	70	

This may reflect the type of patient in particular hospitals and matters of hospital policy, but it also reflects the accessibility and the extra variety of an urban community.

Table 6.10 shows that more patients from the urban hospitals go into the local community for both work and pleasure.

This movement is not merely restricted to parole patients. At Lamprey (UL) groups of more handicapped patients are escorted by staff into the local shopping centre, an event rarely mirrored at Laker. All three urban hospitals have patients who visit the pubs and clubs of the local community; there is no evidence of such involvement at the two larger rural hospitals, and only marginal involvement at Sycamore House.

Staff policy

All the hospitals recognise some need to forge links with the outside world and the surrounding community. However, there are consider-

Table 6.10   *Patients going into the community: urban and rural hospitals (percentage)*

	Outside employment	Regular use of church, clubs, etc.*	Local outings*
Urban	3	5	18
Rural	0	6	10

* These two categories overlap.

able differences in the ways in which this is translated into administrative responsibility. At all six hospitals, persons other than patients' families coming into the hospital pass through the hands of one or two senior staff. At Sycamore (RS) and South House (US) the wardens occupy this boundary position between hospital and 'outside'; at Milan (RM) and Laker (RL) the hospital secretary and the senior nursing officer share this function; at Marathon (UM) it is a nursing officer allocated part-time to the charge of voluntary services; at Lamprey (UL) it is a full-time organiser of voluntary services. These hospital personnel control hospital community relations.

The VSO at Lamprey has concentrated his efforts to recruit voluntary workers largely on educational establishments, and as a result most of the neighbourhood contacts within the hospital involve schoolchildren or students. Of 80 individuals with patient contacts in the six months prior to the survey, 50 were recruited through school, college or university, resulting in the direct involvement of 3 schools with children's visits as part of the school curriculum, 7 other schools, 3 local colleges and the local university. The support of the VSO has not merely maintained and encouraged this interest, it has provided the base for other developments. School contacts have encouraged the involvement of the International Voluntary Service, who are now setting up a summer play project during the school holidays. The hospital plays a part in a 'City Challenge' course,[17] and a junior League of Friends runs twice-weekly clubs for the patients.

At Laker Institution (RL) contacts of this kind failed to develop after initial links between the hospital and the local secondary school. Neither the hospital secretary nor the teachers had clear ideas on how to allocate the school-children, and the initial interest soon died. At Marathon (UM) the nursing officer in charge of voluntary services has recognised the potential of schools contacts, but has not yet developed them. Several schools are 'in touch', but only one has encouraged children to go into the hospital. Links have been made with youth clubs, but with little practical effect so far.

Table 6.11 indicates the nature of the groups and organisations coming into the hospitals. The strong school and student basis of Lamprey Institution patient contacts is immediately evident. At the other extreme, the total isolation of South House is notable. This is due largely to a combination of the type of patients allocated to South House and the staff policy. Stress is placed on patients'

F

Table 6.11   Voluntary groups entering hospitals and engaged in direct contact with patients (number of groups)

	UL Lamprey	RL Laker	UM Marathon	RM Milan	US South	RS Sycamore
League of Friends	1	1	1	1	—	—
Nat. Soc. for Ment. Hand. Children, Spastics Soc. etc.	1	2	—	1	—	—
Social Service Groups—WIs, Rotary, Lions, Church, etc.	1	3	2	2	—	1
School/college/ university	13	1	1	—	—	—
Youth clubs/ organisations	2	1	2	—	—	—
Independent individuals or groups	3	2	2	—	1	1
Total	21	10	8	4	1	2

ability to work in normal 'outside' employment, to come and go when they please (within certain times) and to visit relatives and friends. This means that efforts to forge 'outside' links are being channelled through individual patients rather than through the hospital as a unit, and group contacts are very rare.

Most contacts with organisations occur inside the hospitals. However, even apart from the numbers and activities of the 'parolees', there are differences in the nature and numbers of contacts outside the hospitals that are actively encouraged and supported by the hospital. Some are corollaries of internal contacts (a voluntary worker usually active within the hospital may take patients out for the day), but others remain exclusively community based.

But despite the differences which have been described, there are features common to all hospitals:

1   *A lack of spontaneous involvement*   Involvement tends almost always to be at the invitation of the hospital or through the activities of an outside organisation. There are few examples of volunteers actually approaching the hospitals independently. Those that have occurred are conspicuous by their untypicality: a girl with no previous connection with mental handicap, having read an article in a Sunday newspaper about family neglect of the mentally handicapped in hospitals, approached Lamprey Institution, was put in

touch with the VSO and is now a regular visitor to one of the wards; similarly a girl from the locality of Laker Institution interested in making a future career in nursing approached the hospital independently and now helps weekly on one of the wards. This kind of approach is very rare. Involvement is largely through organisations – either special organisations for the mentally handicapped, like the National Society for Mentally Handicapped Children; or hospital organisations, like the League of Friends; or general organisations, like Women's Institutes, Rotary Clubs or the Red Cross.

2 *Membership within voluntary organisations tends to overlap* The organisations tend to have members in common, which means that interested individuals are not as numerous as might be expected from the numbers of interested organisations. This means that actual involvement and numbers are not great, though the potential certainly is. For example, at Laker Institution there is a nucleus of common membership spanning the League of Friends, the local NSMHC and a local Lions Club; at Marathon there is common membership between the school that is involved and a youth club that has had contacts; and similarly at Lamprey between the League of Friends, a church group and a social service group.

3 *Volunteers come into the hospital more than patients go out* Opportunities for patients to establish informal contacts outside the hospital are minimal. Only 13 per cent of the total patients ever go out unaccompanied, and although in all the hospitals there have been some attempts to escort out small groups of patients, this has only marginally affected the patient population. Few patients attend local clubs or events in the local communities of any of the hospitals.

4 *The involvement is generally small and erratic* Excluding the wards at Lamprey Institution, which has a full-time VSO, only 6 out of the total of 28 wards are regularly visited by volunteers who are actively involved in ward or patient activities. Where volunteers come into the hospitals for non-ward activities or functions, such as social evenings, dances or various entertainments, informal relationships are only possible with a small number of patients, and are difficult to maintain. Most of the hospitals have had the experience of voluntary workers who are seen once and then never again, and most know of individuals or organisations that have pledged support but never given it.

5 *Contacts are task-centred rather than person-centred* Staff can often identify an activity or service without knowing the volunteers involved; in other words, the activity performed by the outsider is

seen as more important than the volunteers themselves. The question of the deployment of voluntary workers in the hospitals is certainly a difficult one. Staff involved with volunteers often have no clear or consistent ideas about the nature of what the volunteers can or should do. Ward staff views regarding the activities of volunteers vary from employment in routine ward work to escorting individual patients out. All views, however, appear to assume some social distance between volunteers and patients – none assume likelihood of anything approaching equality in contacts. The volunteer is at the outset initiated with views of the necessity of activity or service and the ethos of social distance. This serves generally to label volunteers as extra staff instead of enabling them to fulfil roles that complement the work of staff.

6   *The method of recruiting and maintaining volunteers has tended to be through friends and acquaintances and by word of mouth*
This reflects the common membership of the organisations involved, referred to above; it also reflects the lack of spontaneous involvement and points to the importance of the personal face-to-face relationships in encouraging and supporting contacts with the hospital and its patients.

Leagues of Friends

Leagues of Friends exist in various stages of growth and development in all the four larger hospitals and have tended to draw on patients' relatives and previously committed groups for their active membership. Although none of them has been very successful in the recruitment of new active volunteers, they are important because they illustrate all of the above features: many of their members belong also to other organisations with interests in the hospitals and patients. Membership is not spontaneous, being usually by invitation or personal encouragement. Virtually all involvement of members with patients takes place within the hospital, and although nominal membership is sometimes large the nucleus of active members is sometimes extremely small. Most Leagues of Friends have restricted involvement with patients to the provision of services and the helping of staff, and much of the work takes the form of fund raising with no patient involvement. Finally, active membership and its recruitment has been largely the result of personal friendships and allegiances. Thus, in spite of the undeniable dedication and unselfish involvement of individuals, the general picture of the processes and structures of volunteer contacts is of piecemeal development and instability.

Official contacts

Official contacts, i.e. those directly sponsored by the hospital authorities, are traditional in character and much the same in all six hospitals. All the hospitals take out at least some of their patients, either on coach outings or on one-week or two-week-long holidays. All hospitals receive at least some visitors or parties of visitors intent on seeing the hospital or its staff rather than the actual patients, or providing hospital entertainments. Visits are more numerous and more varied in the larger hospitals, the more urban hospitals and (largely a combination of the former) those with senior staff attached to them.[18]

Lamprey (UL), Laker (RL) and Marathon (UM) receive the most visits and Milan (RM), South (US) and Sycamore (RS) are largely neglected, thus indicating the advantages of both size and urban location.

Differences in official contacts resulting from size can be seen in comparing Laker Institution (RL) with Milan Grange (RM). Apart from the normal visits to Laker of two HMC members quarterly, large groups of up to 40 persons from the school of nursing, a college and the university, all from the nearest city, visit at least annually, the college presenting an annual concert. The local College of Education also visits in smaller groups and every few months groups from other hospitals are shown around. The occupational therapy department holds sales of work three times a year, and there is an annual Open Day, to which other groups and organisations are invited.

In contrast, apart from its quarterly visits from HMC members, Milan Grange receives few visitors. Most occupational groups interested in the hospital care of the mentally handicapped visit the largest and most important hospital for the mentally handicapped in the area (Linsted Institution). The smaller Milan Grange receives few visits. There are no formal contacts with schools or other local organisations and no formal entertainments. The only events that attract outsiders are the annual Open Day, attended mainly by relatives of patients, and the annual Staff Dance which takes place in the absence of the patients. Milan is further handicapped by its lack of a school. As many groups who visit the hospitals are interested mainly from an 'occupational' viewpoint, this excludes from Milan the interest of teachers or trainee-teachers found at other hospitals. As with Laker, sales of handicraft work attracts a steady flow of visitors, although many 'outsiders' seem to be more interested in bargain-hunting than in the hospital or its patients. As might be expected, Lamprey Institution (UL) receives most visits of this nature, drawing on the greater numbers of interested organisations and an increasingly interested public (as witnessed on Open Day) found in a large city.

The arrangement and conducting of formal contacts can feature quite heavily on the timetables of senior staff, especially in the busier hospitals. One interesting feature is the reaction of ward staff to conducted visits. This reveals something of the nature of hospital–community relationships. While the ward staff need to inform 'outsiders' of the conditions under which they work, they often disguise those very conditions by giving wards or departments quick (and often temporary) facelifts before conducted visits.

As Table 6.12 shows, nearly half the patients in all the hospitals are taken on hospital holidays. However, there are significant differences in the proportions of patients taken on outings.

Patients on hospital holidays are always accompanied by staff. Only the more able and self-sufficient patients are usually taken on hospital holidays. For example, Marathon Grange sends most of its 'holiday patients' to two seaside holiday camps belonging to a miners' association but one 'higher-grade' group stays in a seaside private hotel. A similar situation occurs at Laker (RL). Milan Grange patients are taken to one of the camps used by Marathon, a camp also used by Lamprey (UL) patients. Lamprey has more variety of holiday accommodation, because of its greater numbers.

Table 6.12   Patients taken on hospital outings and holidays[19]

Hospital	Patients taken on holiday in last 2 years (percentage of all patients)	Patients taken on outings in last year (percentage of all patients)
UL Lamprey	46	77
RL Laker	43	39
UM Marathon	50	71
RM Milan	37	35

Hospital holiday figures are, of course, supplemented by those patients who go home for holidays, and all hospitals tend to favour for holiday allocation those who do not have a holiday at home. However, in contrast to these patients who never leave the hospital, there are those who have more than one holiday per year as well as being well cared for by their families and taking numerous outings.

The 'hospital holiday' has become an institution in itself, but the situation with regard to outings is less fixed. Here the numbers, purposes and types of outings, and the numbers of patients taking part, are affected to a greater extent than the holidays by finance and the provision of transport. This is not to say that they are more expensive than the holidays, it merely reflects the fact that they have not been so universally recognised as justified or desirable by either nursing staff (who direct the outings) or administrative staff (who control the finance and transport). Traditionally the trend has been to take the 'higher-grade' patients to the seaside for the day two or three times per year, explicitly satisfying to both staff and patients.

As the more socially competent patients have been discharged, there has been a decrease in outings and the allocation of finance. However, recently there have been signs of a broadening in the rationale for outings among the nursing staff and more experimentation. Trips for 'high-grade' patients to events have been supplemented in the two urban hospitals by an occasional outing of 'low-grade' patients to the seaside or country. Table 6.12 indicates that there are many patients who never leave the hospitals, and it is evident that there are large sections of the hospital community cut off from even the most marginal contact with the outside world. Both coach outings and holidays are usually organised by wards or groups of wards, which tends to change the external surroundings without disturbing the internal structures and processes of ward social life. (The interesting point here is that almost without exception staff saw this as the main form of contact with the 'outside', indicating both the past reliance on it and staff perceptions of its relative importance within a limited range of outside contacts.)

As with family and neighbourhood contacts, official contacts vary with the location of the hospital. A simple example, in addition to those given above, illustrates this: Lamprey (UL) Open Days can expect to attract large numbers of the general public; Laker (RL) has to drum up support by personal invitation and pleas to staff for the attendance of their relatives and friends.

Official contacts also vary with size of hospital. As previous observations have indicated, the patterns of social interaction at the two small units, South House and Sycamore House, are in many ways different from those in the larger units. Large and medium-sized hospitals share a distinctive 'hospital' ethos and a common pattern of administration. The small units are mainly for young high-grade and physically fit patients, some of whom work out and develop natural relationships within the area. All the patients in both units are male. They are run by wardens who, though trained nurses, fill an administrative role not unlike that of a warden in a local authority hostel.

The emphasis in the two small units is on the provision of a 'homely atmosphere' from which patients can go out into the surrounding community. The wardens make no attempt to promote outside contacts, and one felt that to do so would be wrong because it would make the unit 'less homely'. The dangers of overorganisation would be more convincing if patients were able to make their own community contacts, but this is not the case. At South House, 10 out of 25 patients do not work out and 5 do not have family homes to go to. At Sycamore House, 36 out of 38 patients do not work out, 13 do not have parole (all patients have parole at South House), 30 do not go home and 13 have no known relatives. The frequenting of clubs and pubs is discouraged by the staff in both units. There are no regular visitors to the units and no volunteers or voluntary organisations take an interest in them. As a result, some of the patients are more isolated than they would be in a large or medium-sized hospital.

Conclusions

This small and preliminary study of the relationships between hospitals and the community is not definitive; but it suggests several major points which have been largely overlooked in the current enthusiasm for voluntary work and volunteers:

1   The potential contacts between hospital and community are both varied and complex. The actual contacts are often rather simple and stereotyped.
2   Community contacts of all types – family, neighbourhood and official – are easier to create and maintain for hospitals located in urban areas. Rural hospitals may need to make a special effort: and

they may find relationships with the nearest town more productive than those with the local village.

3 Of the three kinds of contact, family contacts are the most numerous, the richest in content, and the most enduring. Much more could be done to make families feel welcome in hospital and to treat them as partners in the therapeutic process, rather than as intruders who are merely tolerated.

4 The use made of voluntary workers is often task-centred rather than person-centred. It is much easier to arrange for volunteers to go round with trolleys than to facilitate the growth of genuine personal relationships. Perhaps this cannot often be done directly – one needs some sort of task network as the basis for human contacts; but it is important that the task should be seen as the means and not the end. Volunteers are not substitutes for paid staff, and their special contribution needs to be preserved.[20]

5 Some patients have many outside contacts, many patients have none. Often it is the same group of patients which has visits, goes home, profits from the work of voluntary societies, goes on officially planned outings and holidays and takes the spotlight on Open Days. It is very easy for community contacts to be concentrated on the 'better' patients, and there is some justification for this in that these are the patients who are most likely to be discharged; but it is the group who are not likely to be discharged who have least family contacts and who most need help.

Our findings very largely corroborate those of Dr Pauline Morris:[21] there is a good deal of activity of a sort, and any senior officer in a hospital could reel off a list of ways in which community contacts are actively encouraged and pursued; but the activity tends to be organisational rather than personal, it is very easily diverted into routine channels, and it leaves very many patients untouched. We come up against the recurring question in the field of mental handicap: why does so much official encouragement and so much administrative activity yield such small results in practice?

Dr Morris attributes this to the operation of two factors: passivity on the part of the outside community, and unconscious resistance on the part of the staff:[22]

> Hostility is rare, but neutrality commonplace. . . . Undoubtedly many people are glad to have the excuse not to involve themselves, to avert their heads as they pass the hospital gates. . . . But we believe that the reluctance of the community to become involved

with the life of the hospital is part of a two-way process. There is unconscious resistance by staff at all levels to allowing the outside world to impinge on the world of the institution, and to allowing patients to leave the hospital and see the world outside for themselves. Either happening may disturb the social equilibrium of the regime in which a vital component is 'order'. 'Order' is a very fragile thing, achieved only by long and patient efforts on the part of the staff, and although easily disturbed, it can only with difficulty be re-established.

We think that Dr Morris's points are valid (though an increasing number of senior hospital staff are now very well aware of the dangers of valuing the system more highly than the patient: they have read Goffman's *Asylums,* too); but we think that the problems go rather deeper.

From the point of view of conventional wisdom, the promotion of community contacts of one sort or another seems a relatively easy task – a mere matter of commonsense and a welcoming attitude; and the surprising thing is that so much encouragement has in many cases produced such meagre results. From the point of view of a social scientist, the task is one of appalling difficulty, and the only surprise is that there have been any results at all.

The difficulty arises from two factors: first, a hospital for the mentally handicapped is 'a society within a society'.[23] Many were set up in the face of local opposition in the days when the mentally handicapped were openly stigmatised. Their successful operation depended on the creation of a team spirit among staff and patients which focused their loyalty on the hospital as a unit. The organisation operated almost without reference to, and sometimes in spite of, its immediate environment. Tradition and expediency have therefore combined to create centripetal or inward-looking systems. Recommendations for the development of community contacts require them to be centrifugal or outward-looking: and it is remarkably difficult for any system, mechanical or social, to operate centripetally and centrifugally at one and the same time.

The second problem is that official documents are often very vague as to what they mean by 'the community'. References may be to patients' families and friends; to voluntary workers, who offer their usually unpaid and unqualified services to the hospital; to voluntary organisations, which may vary from local groups of voluntary workers to the quite sophisticated services of large voluntary organisations with paid and qualified workers; to statutory bodies, such as the Social Security network or the local authority Social Services Department; to the nearest village or housing estate; or to near-mystical concepts such as 'the City of London' or 'the people of Clydeside', which include all these in unspecified combination.

The existence of the first problem means that community relations cannot be left in the hands of a senior hospital officer who, by the nature of his job, is identified with the operation of the hospital as such. Doctors, senior nursing officers and administrators have their own part to play in the hospitals' public relations, and many of them play it very well, giving public lectures, handling relations with Press and television, welcoming itinerant research workers and arranging for visits by civic and other dignitaries. This is part of their work. The creation of face-to-face relationships for individual patients is not. This is a task for a free-floating officer not too closely identified with the hospital, looking outwards rather than inwards.

The existence of the second problem means that this officer must be a specialist. The stitching of a particular group of isolated people into the fabric of the community is an intricate, technical task, involving the disentangling and combination of many strands of potential assistance. We are not convinced that this can be done by the appointment of a Voluntary Service Organiser, for two reasons: most VSOs are very sketchily trained, and do not have the necessary expertise in community work; and the job description usually involves concentration on a limited range of contacts – those with voluntary organisations and volunteers – to the exclusion of work with families, with statutory organisations, and with ward staff.

We should prefer the appointment of Community Service Organisers or Community Liaison Officers, who would be free to consider the whole range of potential contacts and, in consultation with the medical and nursing staff, to build up appropriate networks to meet the needs of individual patients. This is not social work as commonly understood, and it cannot be done from a base in the local authority Social Services Department.[24] It is an administrative task, and it must be hospital-based if the co-operation of the staff is to be enlisted. The post should be one carrying status and prestige – not a minor frill tacked on to the working of a basically inward-looking institution. We think that the creation of posts on these lines offers the best hope of translating good intentions into reality. A specimen job description for a Community Services Organiser is given in Appendix 4.

7   Community care

When local authority Social Services Departments were set up in 1971, they took over *inter alia* the social care of the mentally handicapped, both residential and domiciliary, from the Health Departments. Members of the research team visited all the local authorities in the area of the Gateshire Region in 1972, discussing policy with the senior staff of the Social Services Departments, and collecting data according to agreed schedules in all training centres and hostels for the mentally handicapped. Subsequent visits were made in 1973–4 to update the data. The eleven local authorities have been reorganised from 1 April 1974 as a metropolitan county and two non-metropolitan counties.

We were conscious that this work came at a difficult time for Social Services Departments. Directors were still fairly new in post, and were feeling their way into an unfamiliar situation with many constraints. They were short of staff, and particularly short of qualified staff. They began their work in a situation where public expectations about the quality of service had been raised, and they often did not have the resources to meet them. The amalgamation of the former Children's Departments, Welfare Departments and the social aspects of the work of Health Departments was expected to achieve a whole which was more than the sum of the parts – replacing defined and specific responsibilities for certain categories of persons in need with a responsibility for the social wellbeing of whole areas. In addition to the general duties imposed on Social Service Departments by the Social Services Act, 1970, there were new specific responsibilities – notably for 'promoting the welfare' of old people under section 45 of the Health Services and Public Health Act, 1968, and for seeking out the disabled under section 1 of the Chronically Sick and Disabled Persons Act, 1970. Mental health work had no claim to priority.

In some respects, it involved particular areas of difficulty. Medical Officers of Health and their staffs, many of whom had worked hard to build up the community mental health services ever since the National Health Service Act, 1946 (section 28) gave them respon-

154

sibility for 'the development of care and after-care ... for illness and mental defectiveness', were very concerned at the transfer of hostels, training centres and domiciliary care to a new service with no health expertise. The disappearance of the psychiatric social worker and of mental health work as a specialism in its own right added to their concern.[1]

Hostel and training centre staff, for their part, found their former links with the Health Departments disrupted, and had to work out new patterns of contact with a fresh group of administrators who, in the early days at least, had many more pressing responsibilities.

In these circumstances, the publication of the White Paper *Better Services for the Mentally Handicapped* in June 1971 made comparatively little impact. A White Paper is only an expression of general intent. There were enough urgent problems for this to be left to a somewhat problematical future.

Even in 1972 the major reorganisation planned for both the local authorities and the Health Services in 1974 was beginning to cloud the horizon. No senior member of staff in either set of authorities had more than a few months' security of tenure. It was not a propitious time for developing new schemes which might in any case be lost in the reorganisation process.

So there was a general sense of waiting; of 'keeping the services going' until 1 April 1974, when the new local authorities and the Area Health Authorities, with their newly-appointed staffs, could begin to develop long-term plans. In 1972–4 we were visiting services in limbo.

To ask questions about the priorities and forward planning of Social Services Departments was, as one member of the team noted, 'to impose rationality on organisations which could not yet behave in a rational manner'. Nearly all the eleven authorities visited saw the need to increase services for mentally handicapped people already living in the community, but none had yet given serious attention to the sweeping proposals for further discharge contained in *Better Services for the Mentally Handicapped*. Some directors thought that it would take ten or twenty years to meet the requirements of the White Paper, and were doubtful whether discharge on the scale proposed was practicable. The general feeling was that it might never happen; and that if it did, a few years of delay would make little difference. What had become a priority at national level was not yet perceived as a local one.

The ten-year plans

In 1962 local authorities prepared ten-year plans for development in community care which included estimates of actual provision planned for 1972.[2] Commencement of research in 1972, therefore, gave us a rare opportunity of studying in retrospect the relation between planning and implementation. Table 7.1 shows the findings relating to places in training centres.

Table 7.1   Planned increase and actual increase in training centre places, 1962 and 1972

Local authority	No. of places, 1962	Estimate for 1972	Actual no., 1972	Planned increase (%)	Actual increase (%)
1	25	50	60	100	140
2	—	150	60	—	—
3	—	100	75	—	—
4	56	60	80	7	43
5	35	35	50	—	42
6	260	260	350	—	34
7	30	30	30	—	—
8	200	250	330	25	65
9	126	159	170	26	35
10	125	205	220	64	76
11	717	1141	902	50	26
Total	1,574	2,440	2,327		

At first sight, most of the local authorities may be said to have fulfilled their plans. The total of places available by 1972 was very close to the 1962 projections, and six authorities had in fact exceeded their estimates. However, there were marked fluctuations, and some authorities' targets had been set very low. Authorities 2 and 3 started with no places, so that one could not calculate a percentage increase. Both fell short of their targets. Authority 7 had 30 places, planned no increase and achieved none. Authority 6, conversely, planned no increase and exceeded its non-expectations.

These comparisons give us only very limited information, since authorities started with different levels of provision, and there were no firm guidelines in 1962 as to what they ought to be able to achieve in the next ten years. Table 7.2, which relates the information from Table 7.1 to population changes for each local authority, suggests that plans bore little relation to subsequent reality.

Table 7.2 Planned increase and actual increase in training centre places per thousand population, 1962 and 1972

Local authority	Places per thousand population, 1962	Estimate for 1972	Places per thousand population, 1972
1	0·26	0·52	0·63
2	—	1·11	0·51
3	—	0·41	0·32
4	0·53	0·56	0·75
5	0·58	0·55	0·82
6	0·51	0·49	0·67
7	0·56	0·55	0·65
8	0·66	0·83	1·05
9	0·31	0·36	0·38
10	0·42	0·67	0·71
11	0·43	0·64	0·59

Health and Welfare: The Development of Community Care had suggested a target of 0·65 places per thousand population. Six authorities reached or passed this target, though only two had planned to do so. Some authorities, with a rising population had even planned a lower proportion of places for 1972 than they already possessed in 1962; but all in fact increased provision.

All the authorities had some forward plans (usually carried over from the Health Departments) for development of training centre places up to 1981. Table 7.3 compares these with the 1972 figures and also with the number which would be required under the proposals of *Better Services for the Mentally Handicapped*, which lays down a uniform standard of 1·5 places per thousand population.

Four authorities (4, 5, 7 and 8) had plans which exceeded the White Paper requirements, and six authorities (2, 3, 6, 9, 10 and 11) had plans which were very much more limited.

Better Services for the Mentally Handicapped also recommended the expansion of day places in training centres for adults coming by day from hospital. In 1972 there were only 43 such places in the Region, but plans for development by 1981 were considerable in scope, and fell not far short of the White Paper figures (Table 7.4).

A comparison between Tables 7.3 and 7.4 shows some interesting relationships between the two sets of data. In relation to places for hospital-based patients, four authorities proposed to exceed the

Table 7.3 Actual places in training centres, 1972, plans for 1981 and White Paper requirements

Local authority	No. of places, 1972	Estimate for 1981	No. required by White Paper proposals (Cmnd 4683)
1	60	140	139
2	60	120	203
3	75	195	440
4	80	200	160
5	50	130	90
6	350	570	757
7	30	105	73
8	330	485	470
9	70	260	402
10	220	320	450
11	902	2,264	2,803
Total	2,227	4,789	5,987

Table 7.4 Additional places in training centres for hospital-based patients, 1972, plans for 1981 and White Paper requirements

Local authority	No. of places, 1972	Estimates for 1981	No. required by White Paper proposals
1	2	10	19
2	—	44	27
3	—	56	59
4	4	20	22
5	—	10	12
6	14	101	100
7	—	22	10
8	10	70	69
9	—	72	55
10	—	75	60
11	13	235	373
Total	43	715	806

White Paper estimates, and three of these (authorities 2, 9 and 10) were underproviding for community-based patients. Five made proposals very close to the White Paper proposals, and only two proposed less. It looks as though the proposal for providing training places for patients *from hospital* (i.e. patients for whom this would be the local authority's sole responsibility, their board and medical treatment being provided from Health Service funds) may have commended itself more to local authorities than the proposal for expanding services for mentally handicapped people based in the community (for whom they would bear all the financial responsibility apart from Social Security payments). A similar analysis was made for hostel places,[3] and Table 7.5 shows the 1962 plans matched against achievement by 1972.

Table 7.5 *Planned increase and actual increase in hostel places, 1962 and 1972 (*=%)*

Local authority	No. of places, 1962	Estimate for 1972	Actual no., 1972	Planned increase*	Actual increase*
1	—	13	10	—	—
2	—	—	47	—	—
3	—	36	56	—	—
4	—	48	8	—	—
5	—	30	11	—	—
6	32	149	84	366	162
7	—	16	16	—	—
8	27	72	51	167	89
9	20	32	25	—	—
10	—	65	70	—	—
11	—	92	56	—	—
Total	79	553	434		

Nine of the eleven authorities had no hostel places at all in 1962, and percentage increases cannot therefore be calculated. All the authorities except authority 2 had made some plans, but achievement often bore little relation to these. Authority 2 planned no beds and, in fact, provided 47.

The total number of places available in the eleven authorities in 1972 represented approximately 0·1 per thousand population. The highest proportion in 1972 was 0·23 per thousand population in authority 10. Authority 4, the lowest, had only 0·08 per thousand population. The actual number of hostels planned and built gives a similar picture of very limited provision (Table 7.6).

Table 7.6 refers to hostels specifically built and staffed for the mentally handicapped. This does not directly relate to the number of patients, since mentally handicapped patients are sometimes sent to hostels for the mentally ill, and vice versa, and some hostels are regarded as 'mixed'. Plans for hostel beds (whether in special hostels or 'mixed' hostels) are shown in Table 7.7. All the authorities

Table 7.6   Planned increase and actual increase in number of hostels, 1962 and 1972

Local authority	No. of hostels, 1962	Estimate for 1972	Actual no., 1972
1	—	1	2
2	—	—	1
3	—	2	2
4	—	4	1
5	—	2	1
6	2	5	4
7	—	1	1
8	1	3	2
9	1	2	1
10	—	4	3
11	—	6	3
Total	4	30	21

Table 7.7   Hostel beds, 1972, plans for 1981 and White Paper requirements

Local authority	No. of beds, 1972	Estimate for 1981	No. required by White Paper proposals
1	10	10	66
2	47	80	94
3	56	96	208
4	8	98	77
5	11	25	43
6	84	194	358
7	16	29	35
8	51	74	242
9	25	98	188
10	70	136	210
11	56	146	1,300
Total	434	986	2,821

had planned for some increase in hostel accommodation, but in very few cases was this of anything like the dimensions required by the White Paper proposals.

The White Paper also envisages a considerable expansion of non-institutional community care, through boarding out or the use of lodgings.[4] Facilities of this kind were very limited indeed. In 1972 there were less than 100 places in the eleven local authority areas; but plans, as shown in Table 7.8, were extensive.

Table 7.8 Boarding out/lodging places, 1972, plans for 1981 and White Paper requirements

Local authority	No. of places, 1972	Estimate for 1981	No. required by White Paper proposals
1	13	—	16
2	10	37	23
3	—	49	49
4	—	16	19
5	—	8	10
6	30	86	87
7	—	18	9
8	10	59	59
9	1	75	46
10	22	65	51
11	6	219	315
Total	92	632	684

Four authorities actually had plans for places which exceeded the White Paper proposals. However, lodging places (which require no forward planning and no capital expenditure) may be seen as a cheap alternative to hostel building, and it is necessary to read Table 7.8 in conjunction with Table 7.7.

Plans for local authority social workers are not susceptible to the same kind of analysis. In 1962 figures for that year and plans for 1972 were given in terms of *mental health* social workers, i.e. psychiatric social workers and mental welfare officers employed in the Mental Health section of a Health Department. By 1972 these workers had been transferred to the Social Services Departments and most of them were expected to take a mixed case-load. It was no longer possible to separate mental health work from other kinds of social work. *Better Services for the Mentally Handicapped* makes this point in regard to future planning:[5]

> It is not possible to set similar targets for increasing the numbers of social workers . . . and similar staff. The need for more such staff is great, but the mentally handicapped and their families are only one group among many for whom their services are required; any estimate of numbers related to the mentally handicapped alone would not be meaningful.

The community care plans of 1963 were followed by ten years of patchy development. Most local authorities at least approached their original estimates, and some exceeded them; but the original estimates were in many cases pitched very low by the standards now nationally proposed. It is hoped that local government reorganisation and the Secretary of State's fresh initiative in asking for new ten-year plans will provide opportunities for reappraisal.

The training centres

Before 1 April 1971 both junior and adult training centres were the responsibility of the local authority Health Departments. On that date, junior centres were transferred to the Education Departments and adult centres to the Social Services Departments. The present section refers to the adult centres only.

As indicated in Tables 7.1–7.4 there was a considerable development of training centre places. Most of it had taken place within the period since 1967, and there was a sharp distinction to be drawn between the new purpose-built centres, often modern and attractive in appearance, and the older ones. Of the 25 training centres studied, 16 were new and 9 of the older type. Of the latter, five were of very poor appearance. One, already condemned by the Public Health Authority, looked more like an old prison than a training centre. Some were ex-Board schools from the beginning of the century – no longer deemed suitable for 'normal' children.

Thirteen training centres for adults were joined to junior training centres – a fact which caused some administrative confusion with the new division of responsibility. Our impression was that the adult trainees often got the worst of two worlds, since they were denied the facilities now thought appropriate for children, and yet the social organisation, perhaps deriving from the Board school image, gave them nothing like the freedom of independent workers.

Working population

All the adult centres had more male trainees than female, though the disparity between the sexes was not very great. There were 1,877 trainees in all, 1,068 male and 809 female. Most of them were young, nearly 60 per cent being under the age of 30 and over 20 per cent under the age of 20. This is what one would expect in view of the fact that the hospitals have an admission peak around the age of 40 at the time when parental care is likely to fail through parents' death or infirmity.

Most of them had been attending a training centre for a long time – over 70 per cent for over five years and more than 90 per cent for over a year. They seemed to have little hope of ever gaining outside employment – going to the training centre was a way of life in itself. Some were thought 'capable of employment'; but jobs were scarce in most areas, and employers were not always sympathetic to the special problems of mentally handicapped workers. Of 157 considered 'capable of employment', only 65 had actually been employed outside the centres for any period in the twelve months preceding our inquiry.

Only a few trainees had a severe physical incapacity. Of the total group of 1,877, only 19 were liable to incontinence, 8 were deaf, 7 were blind or partially sighted, and 33 had problems of physical mobility. This last group of problems was relatively unimportant, since the patients were seated when working. The incontinent, the deaf and the blind represented less than 2 per cent of all trainees, and the profile of the trainee population contrasts sharply with that of the hospital population, many of whom were severely and multiply disabled. But as Table 7.9 shows, the level of social skills among trainees was scarcely higher than that of in-patients.[6]

'Ability to read', in Table 7.9, means the capacity to recognise signs and simple sentences. 'Ability to write' usually means no more than copying their own names or simple written material. Probably not more than 5 per cent of the trainees were capable of writing their own letters. While 37 per cent could count up to ten and handle the basic coins, it is difficult to determine whether they could actually count in any meaningful sense, or whether they had learned the first ten figures off parrot-fashion. The trainees scored heavily in ability to wash and dress themselves, but the other figures are generally close to those for the hospital population.

Both sets of figures are based on estimates by staff, not on direct

*Table 7.9   Comparison of social skills: trainees and hospital
             patients*

	Trainees (%)	Hospital patients (%)
Ability to read	35·3	28·7
Ability to write	18·6	25·0
Ability to count	37·0	37·5
Ability to go shopping	20·0	17·8
Ability to wash and dress self without assistance	90·7	56·6

Trainees: N = 1,877.
Hospital patients: N = 1,541. Figures from Tables 3.11 and 3.13.

investigation. There may be some minor differences in definition, and it is possible that some patients had a potential of which staff are unaware; but we can generalise to the extent of saying that some two-thirds of trainees did not have the basic social skills which would make them immediately employable in modern industrial society, and that the proportion without such skills was nearly as high as that in hospital.

This finding has two major implications for policy. First, it is often said that many hospital patients cannot be discharged to the community because they lack such skills; many of the trainees lack them, too. Second, while the training centres are primarily concerned with the development of industrial skills as such, many of their trainees require social skills as well. As we shall show later, comparatively little is done to teach these skills, since the centres are outside the orbit of the education services.

The qualification for training centre staff is the Diploma of the Training Council for Teachers of the Mentally Handicapped. In fact, only 30 per cent of all staff were qualified, and of the ten authorities with training centres, three had no qualified staff at all. (Since some authorities had several centres, the employment of qualified staff does not necessarily mean that they were available for the work of all centres.) There was an acute shortage of staff, whether trained or untrained. The official staff-trainee ratio is 1:15, but few managers thought it possible to attain this. In most of the centres, the ratio was 1:18 or 1:20.

In most of the centres, the daily timetable was highly structured in order to meet the work demands of contracts. Most opened at 8.45 a.m. or 9.00 a.m. and some still had a public roll-call and assembly. There was a fifteen minute tea break mid-morning and mid-afternoon, and an hour and a half for lunch. Work ended at 4.30 p.m.

The official working week was thirty hours. However, in some training centres, notably in authorities 3 and 11, trainees had so far to travel that they often did not start until after 9.30 a.m., and they left work at 3.30 p.m. Trainees had the normal working holidays, working 242 days each year.

It is unlikely that any of the centres was sited with the convenience of transport for trainees as the main consideration. Sites are chosen because they happen to be available at the time, because the local population does not object too strongly, because they are close to industrial plants. It was not unusual for trainees to live ten or twelve miles from their centre. Most were brought in by transport provided by the local authority, some local authorities having their own coaches and others paying local firms or using voluntary services.

Some authorities saw the question of transport as a major problem in development. In authority 6 it was said that a further 90 trainees could be admitted to existing training centres if the necessary transport were available. Others saw the lack of transport facilities as a challenge, and were trying to teach trainees how to travel by bus, count money and recognise signs (fares being reimbursed by the manager).

Staff–trainee relationships, except in the few social training units, were often of a very limited kind, based on staff authoritarianism and the maintenance of social distance.[7] Male trainees often addressed staff as 'sir', and staff clearly saw their role as a supervisory one, based on the need for increased productivity, rather than as a therapeutic or educational one. Trainees who were unable to work consistently were often segregated in a corner of one of the huge industrial work-rooms, and left to fiddle about on their own; the completion of contracts took precedence over the development of skills.

The type of work done in the centres was largely industrial, and of an elementary and mechanical kind. About three-quarters of the total trainee population were engaged on such tasks as assembling telephone connectors, and assembling and packaging other simple pieces of equipment. Contract work was often not easy to obtain – it had to be of a type which provided some remuneration, but not enough to make it attractive to outside workers. Such work is necessarily dull and repetitive, and provides little or no opportunity of developing skills or moving trainees from simple tasks to more complex ones.

At the same time, there had been considerable efforts to develop some social activities during breaks or scheduled periods in the working day. Five or six of the centres provided darts, billiards and sessions for physical training and dancing. More than half of the centres had a social club (though the manager of one confirmed our views about social distance when he said that he kept away from the club because 'the moment a member of staff enters, things immediately go quieter'). Some centres had developed sports interests – tennis, football and cricket.

Social training was often thought of as more appropriate to female trainees than to male trainees. The women were often not kept to a rigid work schedule, and might be taught personal hygiene, dancing or how to lay a table. The men were taught only how to work under a fairly rigid schedule. Once a trainee had been taught a task, he remained on that task until the work ran out. It was noticeable that male and female staff had very little contact, and that the male and female sides of centres usually operated on highly differentiated concepts of male and female roles in society.

A good deal of lip-service was paid to the need for contact with trainees' parents, and some centres had a Parent-Teacher Association. However, meetings of such associations tended to be formal in character, and heavily controlled by the staff – there was little opportunity for parents to discuss the progress and handling of their own children. The bridge between home and work environment was a very slender one. Not more than six or seven centres at most had really worked at this problem – the others often expressed a need for contact with trainees' homes, but distance from the centre or lack of time or both, meant that nothing had been done.

Pay was related in almost all centres to production. It was determined by the amount of work done, not by the amount of effort which went into it. At the time of the survey (1972), the maximum rate of pay was £2 per week and the minimum 25p, most trainees earning between 50p and 75p. A trainee's pay could not be raised by good behaviour and effort, but it could be lowered by misbehaviour or lack of concentration. This system cannot be other than detrimental to the trainee. All his efforts cannot add a penny to his pay-packet, but if he expresses his frustration, his pay is reduced.

Some training centres had machinery for woodwork, metalwork and laundry work. It was often of an obsolete type, and its use was nearly always confined to the staff. Staff contended that the use of equipment was beyond the capacities of trainees, and that the pressure of contracts did not allow enough time to teach patients how to use machines. So the teachers did not teach and the trainees were not trained – both groups being caught up in the pressure to meet contract deadlines. Staff can scarcely be blamed for this, since they were often subjected to pressures to make the centres financially self-supporting. Managers who turned down contracts in order to have time to develop social training believed, rightly or wrongly, that this would be very unpopular with the local authority. The result was a system which sometimes bears more relation to the nineteenth-century concept of 'setting the poor to work' than to modern ideas of social development. Social Services Departments will have to give a very clear lead as to whether the main aims of training centres are social or economic; the two are very often antithetical.

Some managers in training centres were acutely aware of the deficiencies of their service, and of their isolation both from the patients' home backgrounds and from the health and social services. The transfer to the jurisdiction of the Social Services Department has raised their expectations and exacerbated their dissatisfactions. They look to the reorganised Social Services Departments for positive assistance in formulating goals and modes of practice.

Hostels

There were 15 hostels for the adult mentally handicapped and 5 for children in the eleven local authorities at the time of the survey; four hostels were for males only, 5 for females only, and 6 were mixed.

Our main impression was one of extreme variety. Hostels varied from an institution for 40 males with dormitories containing hospital beds and low standards of furnishing to small, cheerful establishments with a homely atmosphere. There were three main types of accommodation: converted mansions (4), purpose-built hostels (7) and council houses (4). While this was a small sample on which to base generalisation, certain facts stood out very clearly.

The converted mansions – large old houses which had formerly belonged to merchants or mill-owners – were in many ways the least suitable. They tended to be dark and gloomy, ill-adapted for communal life or for the needs of mentally handicapped people, and set apart in extensive grounds. Some had acquired an institutional air, beds were often four or six to a large room. The cost of upkeep must have been considerable. Their advantages were that they seldom suffered from overcrowding, and there were very pleasant grounds with lawns and flower-beds. One had a lake, which had caused problems from time to time. Patients were able to do some gardening, but few were required to do so.

The purpose-built hostels generally had small bedrooms for two patients – one hostel containing 24 residents had single bedrooms for all patients – and they were usually light and airy, with modern furniture and bright décor. They had the advantage of large kitchens and dining rooms, extensive laundries, and a sufficiency of toilets and bathrooms. There was space for different kinds of activity – a television room and a quiet room, a games room with darts, table-tennis or billiards and a piano, and in one hostel for women a hair-dressing salon complete with wash-basins, hair-dryers and a cupboard full of wigs. Despite, or perhaps because of, these facilities, the purpose-built hostels were often rather clinical in character, and on the whole the social life seemed less satisfactory than in either the converted mansions, which had once sustained a family existence, or the council houses, which were designed for one. A deputy warden was heard to say on one occasion that 'if all the patients were as good as X, and stayed in their rooms all evening, there would be no trouble'. The influence of architecture on patterns of social interaction is something of which we know very little, but the effects are often clear to see.

The council houses scored because they were small and homely. Two had only five residents each, and we got a strong impression of an approximation to family life in which residents were able to receive a good deal of individual attention. In one small hostel, the warden was known as 'Mum', and her children mixed quite happily with the residents. Yet, though the council houses provided a good setting for social life, they had considerable limitation in physical plant. They lacked the facilities needed for dealing with incontinent patients, there was usually only one sitting-room (which meant television every night) and social closeness could be abrasive as well as supportive.

All the hostels, of whatever type, had television, radio, a record player and books. The majority had pets, and there was some kind of garden. No one pattern of hostel accommodation could be described as ideal for all types of patients – a good deal depended on the matching of patients to the facilities available, and even more on the personalities and attitudes of the wardens.

The total number of residents in the twenty hostels was 304.[8] Their distribution by age and sex, as shown in Table 7.10, is very even.

Table 7.10   Hostel residents, by age and sex

	Male	Female	Total
Under 10	7	4	11
10–19	27	28	55
20–29	35	26	61
30–39	27	30	57
40–49	20	34	54
50–59	28	21	49
60–69	9	8	17
70+	—	—	—
Total	153	151	304

$\chi^2 = 28.5562$, P < 0.001.

Hostel numbers do not seem to have been affected by the tendency to place more males outside the domestic circle (noted both in hospital in-patient figures and in training centre figures) or by the breakdown of parental care in middle age. However, the numbers are very small, and the even distribution may be fortuitous. The small number of residents over the age of 60 is explained by the policy of local authorities in placing older residents in old people's homes.

A census of hostel patients was carried out on the same criteria as the DHSS census of hospital patients reported in chapter 3. Figures are given in Tables 7.11–7.16.

Incontinence is rare in hostel patients, though it is a problem affecting about one-third of hospital patients.

Table 7.11   Hostel residents and hospital patients: incontinence

	Hostel patients (%)	Hospital patients (%)
Wetting nights: frequently	3·6	20·8
occasionally	9·5	18·9
never	86·9	60·3
$\chi^2 = 81\cdot9634$, P < 0·001		
Soiling nights: frequently	1·6	16·2
occasionally	3·0	14·7
never	95·4	69·1
$\chi^2 = 90\cdot0833$, P < 0·001		
Wetting days: frequently	1·3	17·6
occasionally	4·6	16·5
never	94·1	65·9
$\chi^2 = 98\cdot3888$, P < 0·001		
Soiling days: frequently	1·0	15·5
occasionally	3·3	12·1
never	95·7	72·4
$\chi^2 = 77\cdot228$, P < 0·001		

Note. For this and Tables 7.12–7.16, N = 308 hostel patients (direct survey based on hostel wardens' opinions, January–March 1974); N = 1,541 hospital patients

Table 7.12   Hostel residents and hospital patients: physical mobility

	Hostel patients (%)	Hospital patients (%)
Immobile	0·3	8·5
Partially mobile	5·6	19·3
Fully mobile	94·1	72·2
$\chi^2 = 66\cdot2702$, P < 0·001		

There was in fact only one case of a totally bedfast patient in a hostel, and problems with mobility were rare.

Hostel patients are very largely able to feed, wash and dress themselves, and in this respect they differ considerably from the hospital sample.

Table 7.13 Hostel residents and hospital patients: feeding, washing and dressing

	Hostel patients (%)	Hospital patients (%)
Able to feed self: not at all	0·6	10·6
with help	2·7	6·4
without help	96·7	83·0
$\chi^2 = 39\cdot8528$, P < 0·001		
Able to wash self: not at all	1·6	26·9
with help	11·9	16·5
without help	86·5	56·6
$\chi^2 = 111\cdot705$, P < 0·001		
Able to dress self: not at all	2·0	22·8
with help	11·2	20·3
without help	86·8	56·9
$\chi^2 = 104\cdot797$, P < 0·001		

Table 7.14 Hostel residents and hospital patients: vision, hearing and speech

	Hostel patients (%)	Hospital patients (%)
Vision: blind (or almost)	0·3	4·5
poor sight	26·3	12·3
normal	73·4	83·2
Hearing: deaf (or almost)	2·6	3·8
poor hearing	4·6	8·3
normal	92·8	87·9
$\chi^2 = 6\cdot01908$, P < 0·05		
Speech: none	2·3	18·9
odd words only	16·8	20·7
can talk – does not	2·6	2·1
normal	78·2	58·3
$\chi^2 = 61\cdot9551$, P < 0·001		

Vision cannot be statistically tested, as the number with poor vision is too small.

Hearing and speech were significantly better in the hostel patients, though there was a surprisingly large proportion with poor sight.

Table 7.15 *Hostel residents and hospital patients: reading, writing and counting*

	Hostel patients (%)	Hospital patients (%)
Reads: nothing	52·6	71·3
little	23·4	15·7
newspapers/books	24·0	13·0
$x^2 = 42·7386$, P < 0·001		
Writes: nothing	42·4	75·0
little	37·5	16·0
own correspondence	20·1	9·0
$x^2 = 127·878$, P < 0·001		
Counts: nothing	26·6	62·5
a little	22·7	19·7
understands money value	50·7	17·8
$x^2 = 177·335$, P < 0·001		

Hostel patients have markedly better educational abilities, though the high proportions unable to read, write or count and the need for educational services should be noted. In particular, they have a much greater ability to handle money.

In most respects, there is no significant difference between the hostel group and the hospital sample in reported behaviour. It is possible that a higher standard of behaviour is expected in hostels, and that behaviour which would pass unnoticed in hospital is noted and regarded as unusual in the small group setting of the hostel. Also hostel patients probably have more opportunities for committing petty offences than hospital patients. Figures can be misleading unless interpreted in terms of the setting (Table 7.16).

The 308 patients in the hostel sample included only 35 who had been in the hospitals of the Gateshire Region three years earlier. These patients are further considered in chapter 8. Of the total group of patients, 14·5 per cent had been in the hostel for less than a year, 77·6 per cent for between one and ten years, and 7·9 per cent for ten years or more.

These figures cannot be compared with hospital length of stay figures – only three of the hostels have been open for ten years or more and some are comparatively recent, so the records could not show long-stay residents.

Table 7.16   *Hostel residents and hospital patients: behaviour*
              problems

		Hostel patients (%)	Hospital patients (%)
a. Hits out or attacks others:	marked	2·6	9·3
	lesser	21·4	19·4
	no	76·0	71·3
$\chi^2 = 14·8945$, P < 0·001			
b. Tears up papers, magazines, clothing, or damages furniture:	marked	3·6	6·3
	lesser	4·6	11·6
	no	91·8	82·1
$\chi^2 = 17·7229$, P < 0·001			
c. Extremely overactive, paces up and down restlessly:	marked	8·2	10·9
	lesser	4·0	11·0
	no	87·8	78·1
$\chi^2 = 17·5244$, P < 0·001			
d. Constantly seeking attention – will not leave adults:	marked	14·1	9·9
	lesser	13·2	15·1
	no	72·7	75·0
$\chi^2 = 5·14329$, P < 0·1			
e. Continuously injuring himself/herself:	marked	2·3	5·5
	lesser	2·6	6·7
	no	95·1	87·8
$\chi^2 = 13·5855$, P < 0·01			
f. Anti-social, irresponsible, given to petty offences:	yes	12·2	16·3
	no	87·8	83·7
$\chi^2 = 3·2708$, P < 0·1			

It is unlikely in any case that length of stay figures yield much in the way of useful information. In 1972 185 residents (60 per cent) entered hospital direct from another form of institutional care, so their actual length of stay in public accommodation of one kind or another was much longer than the records suggested. In the same year, 77 patients left hostels, and their destinations were as shown in Table 7.17.

Forty-eight discharges, nearly two-thirds of the total, were illusory discharges in that, although they are discharges *from the hostel*, the resident remained in some form of public care. Cmnd 4683 stresses (para. 161) that 'residential homes for the mentally handi-

*Table 7.17   Destination of residents leaving hostels during 1972,
            by sex*

	Male	Female	Total	
Living alone	—	4	4	
Family home	5	9	14	23
Friend or relative	2	3	5	
Other hostel	7	1	8	
Other LA care*	1	12	13	48
Hospital†	10	17	27	
Not known	1	5	6	
Total	26	51	77	

* Includes group homes and fostering.
† Includes hospitals for the mentally handicapped, mental hospitals and general hospitals.

capped are a permanent substitute family home for most of the residents'.

Most of the adult residents in hostels had some form of employment, 89 being in outside employment full-time or (more rarely) part-time, and 190 attending training centres. It should be noted that the separate listing of training centre and hostel populations in official documents as well as in this survey involves substantial double counting, since many people appear under both headings. Jobs tended to be of a manual kind for both sexes – sweeping and cleaning in the local mental hospital, factory work, gardening and domestic work. The warden was usually responsible for finding employment for those who were capable of working, and many found this increasingly difficult in an adverse employment situation.

Compared to hospitals for the mentally handicapped, hostels had a remarkably unregulated social life. Rules were comparatively few, and routine capable of being varied. Most had rules about the time residents were expected to be in at night, usually about 10 p.m., but there were often extensions if residents had a special night out, and one hostel allowed a late pass once a week. Twelve of the fifteen adult hostels had rules about personal hygiene, insisting on regular bathing and haircuts and shaving before breakfast in the case of the men. All had rules about smoking which was generally forbidden in the bedrooms and sometimes in kitchens and dining-rooms, though some wardens said that they turned a blind eye. Eight hostels had no ruling at all about the consumption of alcohol. The four wardens who forbade it completely said that they did so because most of their residents were on medication. No hostels laid down any rules about the possession of potentially dangerous items such as matches, razor blades or scissors. The only other rules discovered were a ban on the playing of transistor radios upstairs in one hostel and the forbidding of male friends in an all-women hostel. Most hostels had rotas for washing-up, bed-making and cleaning, though in three of the purpose-built hostels outside domestic staff were employed for these tasks. Rotas seemed to be fairly flexible, and were only enforced where it was felt that someone was not doing his fair share. In two hostels, residents were explicitly consulted about the menu, and in most of the others, individual likes and dislikes were taken into account. In six hostels, residents were able to have some choice in the decoration of their bedrooms.

In all the hostels an effort was made to keep rules to the minimum necessary in a small community. One warden thought that few rules were necessary because many residents, having been in hospital for long periods, had been socialised into a highly regimented system. The problem was to combat regimentation, not to create it.

There were two quite distinct attitudes to the organisation of social activities. Some wardens organised birthday parties, games and competitions, Bingo, hobbies classes, keep-fit sessions, fashion shows, coffee evenings and day trips to the pantomime or the seaside. Others took the view that this kind of organisation bore the marks of institutionalism, and that residents were far happier to spend their spare time as they pleased, watching television, chatting, or going to their own rooms. Wardens' attitudes polarised between 'Keep them occupied' and 'Let them be apathetic if they want to – this is their home'.

Much of the social organisation of the hostels, the interaction between residents and the quality of the life they lived depended on the personalities and attitudes of the wardens. Ten of them were women and four men, the remaining hostel having a joint appointment of a married couple. The youngest was a man in his late thirties and the oldest a woman of 64, the majority being in their forties or early fifties. There were two single women wardens and two widows, and one single male warden. Of the ten hostels headed by a married warden, only three also employed the spouse: one case was the joint

G

appointment already referred to, one male warden and his wife as deputy warden, and one warden's wife was acting temporarily as a relief warden. Three married wardens, all women, had children living in the hostel. The most common form of housing provision was a self-contained flat in the hostel. The two wardens of council house hostels lived in the council house next door, and one male warden lived with his family in a house in the hostel grounds.

Most had been in their present post for several years – often since the hostel was opened. Seven had nursing qualifications: one was doubly qualified (SRN, RMN), two had SRN only, one had RNMS only, one had RMN only and two were SENs. The others had no qualifications, though several were attending or had attended short courses. Most had institutional experience of some kind, mostly in hospitals or hostels, often in unskilled or semi-skilled posts. Two were housewives without previous experience, and one had been a secretary in a mill. Salaries were low, ranging from about £1,150 p.a. to a maximum of £1,600, with a reduction for residential accommodation.

Some worked a forty-hour week, and had adequate arrangements for relief. One said she worked 74 hours a week, and three said they were on call from early morning to 11.00 or 11.30 at night. It was very clear that the wardens were not doing the job purely for money. The majority gave the impression that they obtained real job satisfaction from 'helping people to feel wanted'. Nearly all complained about the lack of privacy and the lack of time off, but they also stressed the rewards – seeing residents in their first job, getting them to perform simple tasks such as cleaning or shopping, creating a real home. Because of the obvious care and concern for the well-being of the residents, the impression received of the majority of hostels was that they were warm, friendly places in which residents could soon feel at home.

Only in three hostels did the atmosphere seem formal and cold. In the first, the deputy warden, an ex-prison officer, wore a white coat, and spent part of his time while on duty sitting at the reception desk in the hall. Rooms were formally labelled 'lounge', 'library', 'sewing room' and 'hobbies room' – this last being superfluous since none of the residents had been encouraged to develop hobbies – and there were no social activities. In the second, the warden, formerly a hospital sister, insisted on being called 'matron', and the hospital image persisted. In the third, the problem was largely one of size and décor – it looked like an outdated hospital, the corridors being badly lit and in need of a coat of paint, while the chilly lounge had shabby armchairs arranged in rows. These three were a considerable contrast to the warm and cheerful environments provided by the others.

Community relations were easiest for the council houses. They were small, and tended to be quite readily accepted by the neighbours. The larger converted or purpose-built hostels had to work at community contacts: they organised fund-raising activities such as coffee evenings and fashion shows which were quite generously supported, but the help tended to stop at money, and there was little spontaneous interaction. The wardens complained quite bitterly about the lack of community support, and it seemed evident that it was a common experience to be physically in the community without being part of it. Only one of the fifteen hostels had contact with any voluntary workers, and they came once a month.

Contacts with the Social Services Departments were good on the whole: ten wardens felt that they received adequate support, and six stated categorically that they were receiving considerably more support than had been forthcoming from the Health Departments before the transfer in 1971. Some wardens gave the impression that they did not want social workers to visit 'their' residents too often, and regarded them as liable to 'interfere'. This may have been partly the reaction of a closely organised social group to people seen as outsiders. It may also have reflected the wardens' lack of social work expertise, and a certain anxiety about the extension of the powers of qualified social workers. As in other fields of residential care, social workers have some way to go before their knowledge and skills are fully accepted.

A particular point of difficulty related to referral procedures. It was often by no means easy to discover from the wardens who was responsible for referring the residents for admission. Some talked of 'some kind of social worker' and others of referrals 'from the office'. In three hostels, new residents were referred by the psychiatrist, matron at the mental subnormality hospital, social worker and warden working together, and in one, the warden handled referrals directly; but in the other eleven there was little contact with the policy-makers, and there was a distinct sense of grievance at having no share in the making of hostel policy.

Other forms of residential care

As Table 7.8 shows, four of the eleven local authorities had no provision for residential care other than hostel care, and the other seven had very limited provision at the time of the survey. There were only 92 places in the whole Region.

Better Services for the Mentally Handicapped (para. 159) mentions 'lodgings, ordinary housing or a group home, or flatlets with social work support' and goes on to suggest that each local authority should be able to provide a range of choice. We found little range of choice, but a very wide range of quality. One authority had two purpose-built units of eight flatlets each, and had plans for more. These were attractive and modern in external and internal appearance. Each resident's flatlet was kept tidy and clean, with ample room and facilities for clothing and personal possessions. The balance between necessary care and privacy for the residents seemed to be a very good one.

At the other end of the scale, the authority which had the largest number of mentally handicapped housed in a non-institutional setting accommodated all of them in a large rented lodging house, which is worth detailed description in the interviewer's own words:

> The situation ... can be described in one word – rough. Here thirty males live together in two large old houses which have been knocked into one. Externally, it has a dirty, derelict appearance. Structurally, it is poor. It stands three stories high. The bottom floor is used for dining and heating facilities, the landlady using the remaining area for her own private living quarters. There is no carpet, only linoleum and bare boards. The bottom floor has recently been decorated, but as one moves up the stairs, conditions become worse. This may reflect the land-lady's inability to climb the stairs, but it also reflects the laissez-faire attitude of the local authority. By the time the top floor has been reached, conditions have become very poor. The bedrooms are dirty, having only bare boards and old beds. Curtains hang here and there in a dirty and torn state. As the week progresses, things usually become worse as some males frequently sleep with their boots on.

For most authorities, 'non-institutional community care' meant lodgings, though none of the others was as poor in quality as this example. Lodgings were used mainly for middle-aged patients who were in manual employment or attended training centres. In some authorities, contact with the Social Services Department was minimal or non-existent, and the following story records the consequences for one woman patient:

> A middle-aged female patient, after having been discharged in June 1971, was placed in lodgings and referred to the local authority. She was not visited. During the winter of 1971/2, she fell ill, and the landlady informed her general practitioner. On visiting her, he discovered that she had a foul body odour, and that her clothes had not been washed or changed for weeks. She was readmitted to the hospital.

In authorities where the former mental welfare officer still visited, he or she had become a trusted friend and adviser. Residents needed help in knowing how to deal with money, when to buy clothes (and what to buy), how and when to contact a general practitioner, what to do about official forms. Modern urban living requires a high degree of social competence, and even where the mentally handicapped were deemed fit to live independent lives, they were seldom able to cope with the quite complex network of personal decisions which most of us take for granted.

Social workers in the field, and their superiors, tended to see lodgings as a means of offloading the demand on hostels rather than as part of a range of choice. Lodgings were often used as a dumping-ground for those for whom hostel places were not available, or who did not fit into the fairly middle-class ethos of hostel life. It may be administratively convenient and currently fashionable to talk of 'non-institutional forms of care' as though they were superior to hostel care. The reality suggests that a few genuinely are superior: the rest are much worse.

Social work services

Mental health social work has been one of the major casualties in social service reorganisation. Systems of care which had become quite highly developed in some areas have been destroyed, and as yet there is little to take their place. But even where the Mental Health Services were well developed before the Social Services Act, 1970, they tended to concentrate on specific areas of the mental health field: child guidance and the urgent problems of the adult mentally ill absorbed much of their energies. Few authorities developed a really viable casework service to cover the problems of mothers with young children. Even fewer have ever seen the provision of care for the adult mentally handicapped as an important part of their work. Casework is heavily dependent on verbal skills, and social workers with whom the problem was discussed were doubtful as to whether it was even possible for 'these types', as one social worker described them.

What many mentally handicapped people in the community need is perhaps less orthodox casework than what Dr Michael Bayley has recently described as 'a structure for coping'[9] – the deliberate creation and maintenance of networks of support which might include neighbours and friends, local clergy and voluntary workers. Lodging houses, like hostels, tended to be in the community but not of it; and one suspects that many patients in their own homes suffer a similar isolation.

Relations with the health services

The expansion of local authority social services for the mentally handicapped foreshadowed by the White Paper is a result of two factors: the growth in demand consequent on a growing population in which more mentally handicapped people survive, and survive for longer; and the shift in supply from a mainly hospital-based to a mainly community-based service.

In 1972 and 1973 the Regional Hospital Board took the initiative in approaching Directors of Social Services, drawing their attention to the White Paper proposals and calling meetings for discussion; but the response so far has been less than enthusiastic. Examples are given later of situations in which conflict has already occurred between hospitals anxious to discharge patients and local authorities equally anxious not to receive them. A situation in which government puts some pressure on one sector to contract without providing the other with either the means or the will to expand can only be productive of tension.

Problems of referral

A small exercise undertaken by the research team sheds some light on the actual mechanics of referral on discharge. We found examples of excellent co-operation – in one authority which had a large hospital within its boundaries, a social worker from the local authority usually visited the hospital before discharge took place, conferring with the consultant, the hospital social worker and the patient. Some hospitals organised case conferences to which local authority social workers were invited. However, the hospital authorities' eagerness to discharge and the local authorities' reluctance to accept led to some difficult situations:

> The physician superintendent gave the local authority a reasonably free hand to select patients for discharge. After an extensive assessment had been carried out, the number presented to the physician superintendent was ten. From the latter's point of view this was abominably low, since he felt that many more could be discharged given the necessary help and guidance.

> A severely subnormal woman, aged 38, was discharged to a voluntary hostel about twenty miles from the hospital. The Social Services Department were completely ignorant of her discharge. The patient presented problems of incontinence, and was difficult to control. She continually maintained a loud shouting noise, refused to stay in bed at night, and upset the other residents. The hostel staff were totally unable to cope. A social worker approached the physician superintendent about the matter, but the physician superintendent refused even to discuss the issue.

Such conflicts were common. Both sides had grievances born of the reorganisation process and the contradictions in central government policy.

To provide a spot-check on this situation, twenty patients who had been in hospital for at least two years continuously, and who were discharged in the period 1 July 1971 to 31 January 1972 were followed through the referral process to see how much co-operation in fact took place at the operational level.[10]

In only three cases was there any contact between the hospital and the local authority prior to discharge.

Thirteen of the twenty were referred to the local authority at the time of discharge, eleven by letter from the consultant and two by means of a routine form. Seven were not referred at all.

In twelve cases out of thirteen, the information sent to the local authority was a copy of that sent to the general practitioner, i.e. it contained a note of the patient's diagnosis and medication but nothing about his social history or social capacity.

In only three cases out of the thirteen was the local authority invited to contact the psychiatrist if more information was needed.

In no case was a referral made by a hospital social worker to her colleague in the community services. The hospital consultants interviewed were highly resistant to the suggestion that this might be a useful procedure.

In only two cases where referral was made was the patient visited by a local authority social worker within a week. In four cases, the period between discharge and contact with the local authority was over six weeks.

Even this small sample gives ample evidence of mistrust and lack of co-operation on both sides.

Problems of liaison

Another area of concern is that of the health care of patients in hostels and training centres. While these were the responsibility of the Health Departments, some medical and nursing support was usually available to wardens and managers, who often required advice on general health matters or the special problems of mental handicap. Since the transfer to the Social Services Departments, the loss of this support has in many cases been total. When patients are discharged from hospital, the hospital authorities are no longer involved in their care, and many patients do not even have a general practitioner. Wardens often have to register a patient with their own general practitioner to obtain any medical advice at all. There is a clear case for linking health and social services here. The mere fact that a patient is discharged from a health agency to a social service agency does not mean that his medical problems disappear overnight. Assistance could be given either by regular visits to hostels and training centres by a community nurse, or by the extension of hospital out-patient work to provide regular contacts with ex-patients. There would be a good deal to be said for a combination of the two.

We have instanced two examples of ways in which communication between health and social service authorities is failing at the operational level. It is at this level that we need to spell out the currently fashionable phrases about the value of co-operation and co-ordination in realistic terms.

Conclusion

Work with the mentally handicapped forms only a small part of the total responsibilities now facing Social Services Departments; and the present emphasis on genericism in social work has created a certain resistance to planning for special groups. But the problems of this group are acute, and are likely to become more so. The Social Services Departments whose work has been described in this survey have been reorganised from 1 April 1974. Between them, they took over the care of some 320 residents in hostels for the mentally handicapped, about 100 in lodgings, over 2,000 attending training centres, and many mentally handicapped people living in their own homes, plus the social care of mentally handicapped children. And this is only a beginning. As plans now in existence are implemented, and plans outlined in *Better Services for the Mentally Handicapped* acquire more administrative bite, the numbers involved in hostels, lodgings and training centres alone will soar to over 10,000.

We therefore summarise our findings and make some suggestions for future action in the hope that the new Social Services Departments, with their larger areas and (hopefully) greater resources will find them of assistance in the period of extended planning which they now face.

Summary of findings

1 Local authority plans for the mentally handicapped in this Region for the period 1962–72 were unevenly implemented. Some authorities' targets were set very low, and it was clear that this was not regarded as a priority area for development.

2 Plans for the next ten years involve a considerable expansion, but in most cases fall short of the guidelines laid down in *Better Services for the Mentally Handicapped*.

3 There are signs of a tendency to look for cheap solutions (more training places for hospital-based patients, more lodgings), rather than for those solutions which involve a real assumption of extra responsibility.

4 We were impressed by the level of hostel care available; in our opinion it offers a better quality of life than hospital care, except for those patients requiring medical or nursing facilities or continuous process care.

G*

5   Hostel patients are significantly less dependent than hospital patients. The transfer of any proportion of patients from hospital to hostel will, as indicated in chapter 3, mean more intensive staffing.
6   Training centre staff and hostel staff need more and better training. The extension of training programmes now under discussion by the Department of Health and Social Security and the Central Council for Education and Training in Social Work, offers the best hope of raising the quality of service. Local authority members may need encouragement to put their resources into people rather than into bricks and mortar.
7   Training centre staff and hostel staff require help with the community aspects of their work. Local authority community workers should have the skill and knowledge to help them build up networks of statutory and voluntary support to combat the isolation which many experience.
8   Training centre staff and hostel staff face basic dilemmas about the aims and nature of their work. They may be out of date and out of touch in thinking that their superiors expect them to secure rapid turnover and (in the case of the training centres) an economic output; but they will go on thinking in this way until more enlightened aims are explained to them. Central and local government policy with regard to the mentally handicapped has changed a great deal in a short time, and the new thinking requires transmission and translation.
9   Except in certain outstanding cases, accommodation in lodgings was very often unimpressive and sometimes of a very poor quality. The placing of mentally handicapped patients in lodgings often requires a good deal of continuing time and perseverance from a social worker. It is not a cheap and easy alternative to hostel care, and it should only be undertaken when it is genuinely better for the patient.
10   Social work services for the adult mentally handicapped living in their own homes require considerable extension; they might be better developed in terms of creating 'a structure for coping' than in more orthodox casework terms.
11   Relations with the health authorities were at a very low level in some areas. We have pointed to three particular problems: conflict over individual discharges, failures in the referral process and lack of medical and nursing support for patients in hostels and training centres. These issues can only be resolved through local co-operation.

8   The idea and the reality

The problems of hospitals and community services for the mentally handicapped are well known. Though the administrative context has changed and the emphasis on segregation has gone, they have been spelled out in much the same terms – shortage of staff, shortage of training, shortage of suitable accommodation, shortage of money – for many years. Behind these economic factors lies an attitudinal factor: the mentally handicapped rate a low priority in the eyes of the general public, and despite the repeated pressures of the voluntary organisations and the reformers, despite the good intentions of successive governments, the situation is slow to change.

The 1971 White Paper was intended to open the door: to produce a new situation in which hospitals for the mentally handicapped were no longer custodial institutions, and all the varied resources of the health and social services could be brought to bear on the needs of an isolated and underprivileged group of people; but if the door has been opened, it is only by a crack. Our evidence suggests that in one Region at least, despite a great deal of effort and a great deal of goodwill, the problems seem as intractable as ever.

The Wood Committee of 1929, getting its metaphors slightly mixed, attacked the static nature of much institutional care, recommending that a residential institution for the mentally handicapped should be 'not a stagnant pool, but a flowing lake'.[1] We still have our stagnant pools.

There have been some gains – the small 'Crossman units' and the injection of money into furnishings and ward decoration; a spirit of determination and goodwill among some nurses, which has improved the living conditions of many 'high-grade' patients. These advances, however, have been offset by a declining morale among many hospital staff, born of the belief that nursing the mentally handicapped is 'not really nursing'; that the traditional leadership has gone and left a vacuum; and that, in the event of a public inquiry, it is the ward staff who will be left to carry the blame for situations largely beyond their control.

The idea has been laid down by the White Paper. The reality

falls far short, and there is little sign of movement from one to the other. Reactions to this situation vary considerably, and it may be helpful to list some of those which we commonly encountered in the course of this survey:

1 *Total optimism* The past is irrelevant. Let's start from the present and build a good service (a-historical model, employed by some politicians, civil servants and Directors of Social Services).

2 *Modified optimism* Progress may seem very slow, but if one looks back, we have really come a long way in the past twenty (thirty, forty) years. We have forgotten what the bad old days were like, and conditions are gradually improving all the time (millennial model, held by most voluntary society spokesmen and some older doctors and nurses, involving the use of the past as a frame of reference).

3 *Modified pessimism* All these changes are profoundly un-settling, and do little to bring about real improvements for the patients (anti-change model, held by many doctors and nurses).

4 *Total pessimism* Things are getting worse instead of better. All these so-called new ideas have been tried before, and at the end of the day, the staff are left dealing with the same old problems in the same old way (rejection model, held by many ward and hostel staff).

Some of these attitudes are expressed more openly than others. In the National Health Service, optimism is the order of the day, and it is officially unacceptable to express cynicism and despair; but the denial of emotionally-charged attitudes carries its own perils, and we can only say that we have found in our inquiries a degree of despondency among some ward staff which it is dangerous to ignore and which cannot be abolished by merely talking success. The un-comfortable fact is that sheer optimism has not produced the expected changes; and that the gap between official attitudes and the day-to-day reality of the ward or hostel situation is now danger-ously wide in many cases.

The problems of violence

Reactions to violence on hospital wards provide a case in point: the Farleigh Committee printed on the back of their report a state-ment from the nursing staff of Farleigh Hospital, in which they asked for official guidance on how they should handle the occasional violent patient, pointing out that to restrain such a patient laid them open to a possible charge of assault, while to refrain from doing so might lead to a charge of neglect if the patient hurt himself or others.[2] While violence is not frequent, it does occur on 'low-grade' wards. It is not a matter of 'nurse strikes patient' or 'patient strikes nurse', but of a sudden explosion born of tension, frustration and boredom in which either or both can happen. Nor is it confined to the male wards, though it is on these wards that the most damage gets done.

The Farleigh Committee made two recommendations: one for a research project, which is still in progress, and the other for a set of guidelines to be drawn up by an expert committee. A committee was set up, consisting of representatives from the National Association for Mental Health, the British Medical Association, the Royal College of Nursing and other bodies. Eventually it issued a four-page document, couched in generalities so bland as to make many nurses – particularly those at Farleigh – despair. Nurses were told: 'Violence may be forestalled if steps are taken to relieve the patients' feelings ... the use of restraint should be therapeutic, never punitive.'[3] Such statements serve to reinforce the feelings of isolation among ward staff, who take the view that senior staff simply do not understand their problems or the conditions of their daily life. When patients become violent, nurses have been known to walk away and count the linen or engage in some other routine task, rather than get involved in a situation where their intervention may be misunderstood.

A further example comes from our own survey. We have made it clear in chapter 5 that we encountered no open violence in the Gateshire Region, nor were we told of any. However, we observed on a number of occasions that nurses used physical methods of control, including 'a clip round the ear', and that they were quite open in discussing this. When our report was discussed at a senior level, some officials were reluctant to accept that this was the case, or that it could ever occur. To their credit, once they were convinced that this was reportage of hard fact and not mere hearsay, they withdrew their objections: but the gap between what was supposed to happen and what actually happened was sufficiently wide to excite our apprehensions about communication and the value of monitoring and supervisory systems run from within the service. One of the services which an outside research team can render is to tell those in authority what they find unacceptable.

The economic formulation

Lack of progress may arise from the fact that we have been looking for it with the wrong aims and in the wrong way. All the views outlined earlier depend on a simple linear view of development (things are 'getting better' or 'getting worse'), coupled with a belief that the listing of problems will in time automatically lead to their solution.

The problems have repeatedly been conceived of as problems of *shortage*. The answer, inevitably, is 'more': given enough staff, enough training facilities, enough suitable accommodation, enough money, we can build a satisfactory service. But we shall never have 'enough' resources. In a time of economic recession, we may have to fight hard to maintain the limited standards we already have. Even in times of comparative national prosperity, the needs of the mentally handicapped have to be ranked against those of many other groups – the old, the physically handicapped, the mentally ill, battered babies, battered wives – the list is endless and new categories of needs are constantly being added to it. We are up against the old problem of priorities in the health and social services, the basic economic tenet that wants are unlimited and resources always scarce. The battle for a fair share of what resources there are must go on, but it is unrealistic to suppose that it will solve all the problems.

Even if resources were virtually unlimited, many of the problems would probably still exist. Let us suppose that an economic miracle (North Sea oil?) made Britain a very wealthy country, or that a sudden change of heart in the general public promoted the mentally handicapped to the top of the list. Would the removal of economic restraint really solve all the problems? We have never tried a model scheme (the provision of substantial numbers of trained staff and substantial sums of money to assess the effects) in the field of mental handicap. The chances are that if we did, we would uncover a range of more fundamental problems.

It may be that 'shortage' is a smokescreen, and that we shall not achieve much in the way of progress until we get at the problems behind the economic problems. A more radical kind of thinking is required.

The eugenic formulation

The eugenic school of the earlier part of this century tried to short-circuit the cycle of repeated economic demand and repeated frustration by recommending selective breeding. 'Positive eugenics' would encourage the fit and intelligent to have large families. 'Negative eugenics' would ensure that the unfit and unintelligent did not breed. Two conditions were recognised – 'primary amentia', thought to be due largely to genetic variation, and 'secondary amentia', due to pre-natal, peri-natal or post-natal accident. 'Primary amentia' was seen to be the main problem because it was thought to be directly transmissible, and was held to be a major cause (if not *the* major cause) of delinquency, illegitimacy, drunkenness and pauperism. The answer was simple: 'primary aments' must be prevented from having children. This view was presented strongly to the Radnor Commission of 1904–8 by the Eugenics Education Society.[4] Mrs Hume Pinsent, one of its leading members, and later (as Dame Ellen Pinsent) a Commissioner of the Board of Control, outlined in 1910 in a paper on 'Social Responsibility and Heredity' one of the family studies then much in vogue: a 'normal' father and a mentally defective mother had had nine children, of whom one was 'normal'. Three were at a special school, three had died, and two were 'physically frail and verminous'. The family was constantly visited by a variety of officials, and Mrs Pinsent lamented the 'tragic waste of time and money' involved.[5]

Though the Brock Committee of 1934 made some tentative recommendations for the voluntary sterilisation of mental defectives, among other groups with 'morbid heredity',[6] the subject proved too explosive for the House of Commons and never reached the stage of legislation.[7]

More recent work in genetics has modified the simple view of inheritance on which such thinking was based. We now know too much about the complexities of genetic modification and the aetiology of mental handicap to be confident that a policy of 'negative eugenics' would wipe out the problem.

Any reduction in the numbers of the mentally handicapped due to the spread of birth control has been offset by the greater survival rate of mentally handicapped children due to improved obstetric and child-rearing practices; but the eugenic view has never died out. Though for a long period it was not intellectually respectable, many Medical Officers of Health, general practitioners and social workers have echoed Mrs Pinsent's lament; and it is interesting to see that something akin to the eugenic view has been restored to at least partial respectability in the last year or two in the form of the theory of transmitted deprivation, which rests on the view that poverty, linked to mental defect among other factors, is an inter-generational phenomenon.

'Normalisation' as the answer

This policy, which has its origin in Professor Tizard's Brooklands study, is probably the most successful to date. It has transformed the work of some 'high-grade' wards, altered the thinking of many members of nursing staff, and has been a powerful factor in the pro-jected shift of the less handicapped patients to community care. However, there are two sets of difficulties. The first is that the original work at Brooklands was done with children, and there is no experimental base for extending the work to adults. It may be argued that this is common sense, and that it works, but Professor Tizard's original findings were very carefully delimited, and the principles have been applied far beyond the boundaries he set. We know very little about what happens to adult mentally handicapped people when they are treated as 'normal', and it is time we found out. The second is that, as we have seen in chapter 5, the process of normalisation throws an extra strain on the 'back wards', by concentrating patients who do not fit the policy; by concentrating staff whose attitudes make them unfit to operate it; and then by applying to both expectations which are manifestly unrealistic. The policy is a sound and humane one. Unfortunately, like so many sound policies, it has been applied with more enthusiasm than com-mon sense, and the strains are showing.

Deviancy theory as the answer

A basic tenet in deviancy theory is the belief that stigmatised groups owe their status primarily to the way in which society defines them. Thus, a criminal is someone who has broken a rather arbitrary criminal code; a mentally ill patient is someone who has been defined as such by his family or by the wider society for their own purposes.[8] The supposed condition has no objective reality. Similarly, some people get labelled 'subnormal' and treated in a special way; but there is in fact no clear distinction between the group which gets labelled and people who are living normal lives in the community. We cannot point to any factor of intelligence or social maladjust-ment which precisely demarcates this group. On the whole, the labelling is dysfunctional – segregation and low expectations create low standards of performance. It is like putting a 'B'-stream child in a 'D'-stream class.

This view has obvious affinities with 'normalisation', though its roots are different, being in sociology rather than in psychology. The results are similar – it is of considerable benefit to people who are able to live something approaching a normal life, but it fails in application to those with more severe forms of handicap. It is reasonable enough (and not even new) to maintain that there is no clear dividing line between 'normality' and 'subnormality'; but it is not reasonable to push the argument to the length of denying the existence of the 'subnormal' group. The needs and capacities of Paddy or Mr Pelham on Ward 99 are not identical or in most respects similar to those of, say, a university vice-chancellor. They need special help and protection in some form. The point is a very obvious one, and it is astonishing that so many deviancy theorists cannot see it. The problems of mental handicap arise partly from societal definition, but to abolish the labels will not entirely eliminate the problem. In a world without labels, we should still be left with a group of people who needed special assistance because, in the words of the Radnor Commission, they were 'incapable of taking part in the struggle of life'.

A fresh assessment

If we are to move out of administrative stalemate, we need fresh insights, and these can only be found by going back to first principles.

What is mental handicap? Tizard has this to say: 'The term *mentally subnormal* (or mentally retarded or mentally deficient or defective) is applied to persons who are seriously lacking in intelligence and who, because of their subnormal mental functioning, require special educational and social services.'[9]

So much for the excesses of 'normalisation'. 'Frequently, especially among the most seriously retarded cases, they have special medical or nursing problems also.'

He goes on to say that classification by grade is 'crude' but 'remarkably useful especially for administrative purposes'. It is based on the International Classification of Diseases (World Health Organisation, 1957) which specifies that 'idiocy' corresponds to an IQ of 0–19, imbecility to an IQ of 20–49 and moronity or feeble-mindedness to an IQ of 50–70. However, there is a qualification:[10]

In England, dull and backward children of IQs in the range of
50–70 points are only called feeble-minded if *in addition to*
their intellectual subnormality they present problems of
management and behaviour ... the great majority of children
of this grade of intelligence do not present such problems, and
are not therefore called feeble-minded or mentally deficient.

He adds that diagnosis 'cannot in the nature of things be very
precise'.[11]

This is a good, up-to-date definition, but it is easy to see why
the deviancy theorists have found grounds for doubt. The deficiencies of intelligence tests (particularly when administered to people
above or below the 'normal' range) are by now widely acknowledged.
In any case, many patients now in subnormality hospitals have never
had such a test, and others had one crudely administered so long
ago that little reliance could be placed on the findings.

The criteria of assessment change sharply from the first two
categories to the third. For idiocy and imbecility, it is intelligence;
for the feeble-minded, it is intelligence plus psycho-social mal-
adaptation; and there is no clear differentiation between innate
incapacity and acquired incapacity. Itard's study of the Wild Boy
of Aveyron (1799)[12] rested on the assumption that acquired incapacity could be identified and overcome, though he never proved
his case.

Nor do the definitions allow for the interaction between the
individual and society, or the differential pressures which particular
societies bring to bear on individuals. Dr Stanley Powell Davies
wrote in 1923 that feeble-mindedness was a relative condition and
quoted the case of a boy reported by a French alienist to be 'feeble-
minded in Paris and normal at home'.[13]

To add to the confusion, mental handicap has not always included
subnormality of intelligence. The Mental Deficiency Act, 1913, included a category called 'moral imbeciles',[14] and patients with IQs
of 120 or more could be certified on the grounds that their moral or
emotional development was retarded. The Mental Health Act, 1959,
dealt firmly with this problem by defining such people as psycho-
paths (a form of mental illness) and specifying two grades of subnormality, both of which must include subnormality of intelligence;[15]
but 'subnormality' was never a very appealing word, and the 1971
White Paper has introduced ambiguity again by talking of 'mental

handicap', which may in some cases be due to disabilities of hearing, vision or language, resulting in an inability to communicate.[16] So a deaf, blind or dyslexic child who did not respond readily to treatment could still be categorised as mentally handicapped.

We are left with a bundle of conditions of multiple causation, imprecise definition and, in some cases, uncertain outcome. The only connecting thread is subnormality of intelligence, and even that fails at times. All that can be said is that this group of people do not have 'normal' intellectual development, and need special assistance.

What kind of assistance do they need? A major problem is that needs tend to get formulated in terms of resources available rather than vice versa. We have to attempt to free our minds from the constraints of what we have, and to think in terms of what the patients themselves require, avoiding the familiar division of needs into 'medical' and 'social'.

1   Because they are to some extent 'unfitted for the struggle of life', they need some kind of *continuous social care.* The best means of achieving this is in family life, where the family is secure enough and strong enough to offer good, unobtrusive support to all its members, including the handicapped one. Where there is no family, or where the strain on family resources is too great (either because of the severity of handicap or the slenderness of resources), we have to find other means. At one end of the continuum is the hostel, where support can be given by a warden and to some extent by the group, one resident supporting another. At the other end of the continuum is the hospital patient who needs continuous nursing care, twenty-four hours a day. There is no obvious break in the continuum. The shape of our services forces an artificial discontinuity.

2   Some of the mentally handicapped need *medical treatment,* but this takes many forms. All need the basic medical care for minor or chronic physical ailments which is normally provided for most citizens by the general practitioner service. Some need specialist care, e.g. in orthopaedics or genito-urinary services. Those with behaviour problems need the help of a psychiatrist. Some need the specialist knowledge of consultants in metabolic disorders or neurology. While there is a case for a small number of specialists engaged in research and practice specifically concerned with mental handicap, there is no longer a case for treating the medical needs of the mentally handicapped as a separate service. To do so is to deny specialism, not to create it. Cmnd 4683 recognises this position in

bringing consultants formerly specialising in mental handicap into closer relationship with their colleagues in general medicine.[17] The problem is that the withdrawal of a specialised category of medical care may leave a vacuum, since in a hard-pressed service, consultants in other specialisms may not give much priority to the needs of mentally handicapped patients – and they may not even be brought to their attention.

3   The mentally handicapped require *teaching* to make the best of their limited educational potential. This should include a number of forms of education which are normally regarded as the right of every child – education in literacy, numeracy and such basic social competences as handling money or eating at table; spatial and temporal orientation; expression in drama, singing and dance; physical education; education in societal values (whether in the form of simple religious teaching or some other approach). The administrative decision behind the Education (Handicapped Children) Act, 1970 – that no child is now to be regarded as 'ineducable'[18] – is a step forward. Unfortunately – for administrative reasons – the Education Department's responsibility ends at sixteen. Yet all mentally handicapped people need ongoing education. The services of higher and further and adult education are not for them, and the limited and industrially-oriented work of training centres does not fill the need. There is a sound case for extending the responsibility of the Education Department to all the mentally handicapped, whether at home, in hospital or in hostels.

4   The mentally handicapped need *habilitating* (for want of a better word). The specialist services of the physiotherapist, occupational therapist, speech therapist and the remedial gymnast can help them to make the best of educational opportunity and increase their general personal and social competence. A patient who 'can talk but does not', or who is losing the use of his limbs through inaction, needs special help before he can take part in a lesson or dance or go on a visit. Behind these four basic needs of caring, treating, teaching, habilitating, lie two other needs: assessing and enabling.

5   *Assessing* means judging the requirements of an individual patient in terms of the four basic needs and the capacity of the appropriate services to meet them. It is a complex task which requires three kinds of knowledge; knowledge of the patient, knowledge of the area of need and knowledge of the services. Traditionally this has been left to the medical profession – either the general practitioner or the hospital-based specialist in mental handicap; but their know-

ledge of the patients has often been impressionistic, their knowledge of areas of need (other than the purely medical) seriously deficient and their knowledge of the developing social and educational services almost nil. A proper assessment system needs to be multi-professional – it should certainly involve the skills of an educational psychologist and a social worker as well as those of a medical practitioner – and it needs to be invoked at regular intervals throughout a patient's life. Too many patients have been pigeon-holed on the basis of a once-for-all medical assessment, without even the benefit of an intelligence test.

6 *Enabling* means bringing the services into operation to meet the need. Ideally, there should follow from assessment a therapy plan for each patient. Someone has to operate it and see that it is put into effect. In the case of the hospitalised patient, this might be the community services officer, working in liaison with ward staff and the social services. In the case of a patient in the community, it is a task for the social worker, who can help with personal and family problems as well as acting in a liaison capacity.

Professional lack of fit

Once the problems are stated in this form, it is evident that there is a quite appalling 'lack of fit' between the professional personnel we have and the professional personnel we need. The persistence of the 'medical' model of treatment means that we have large numbers of people called 'doctors' and 'nurses' whose work does not primarily involve medical and nursing skills, and who are called on daily for the exercise of skills in which they have not been trained. Other people who have the necessary skills are either not employed at all or employed in very small numbers and relegated to a subordinate position where their work is only minimally effective. It is small wonder that many of them become frustrated and leave for more active fields of employment.

Dr Pauline Morris tried to meet this situation by recommending that hospitals for the mentally handicapped should set up a 'training arm', composed of social workers, physiotherapists and other non-medical specialists equal in influence and capacity to the medical/nursing service. She foresaw that the implementation of such a proposal would mean a good deal of intra-professional conflict, but took the orthodox conflict theory view – that conflict could be a fruitful preliminary to growth.[19] The proposal is an interesting one, but has been widely recognised to be unrealistic. The constraints are simply too great. The hospitals have a staff establishment almost exclusively composed, apart from the administration, of nurses. These staff have contracts. They cannot be arbitrarily dismissed, nor can the hospitals afford to double their treatment costs by introducing a parallel 'training' staff. Even if they could find the means for employing such staff, they could not find the staff. Social workers now have to be seconded from (and paid by) the local authority Social Services Department. Their numbers in hospitals are scarcely likely to increase. Occupational therapists, physiotherapists, speech therapists and remedial gymnasts are in very short supply for a number of reasons:

1   Training school places are limited.
2   Salaries are low.
3   Most entrants are women (partly because of the identification of these specialisms as feminine occupations, partly because of low pay; as so often, the two factors interact), and the wastage rate due to marriage and expanding job opportunities elsewhere is high.
4   There are more attractive opportunities even within the Health Service for such staff. We saw in chapter 3 how they tended to gravitate to the acute general hospitals.
5   Neither the health authorities nor the professions concerned regard work with the mentally handicapped as a priority.

In the long term, a very active government-sponsored training programme, allied to higher salaries, better working conditions and a higher professional status, might improve the position of these neglected specialisms, but it is still unlikely that there would be large numbers available for work in hospitals for the mentally handicapped.

We have a large number of people (over 1,500 in this Region alone) who are categorised as nurses, but who feel that their link with general nursing is tenuous in the extreme. The best of them are reaching out for other skills – those of other practitioners who are very few in numbers. A realistic answer is not the replacement of nursing staff or the creation of a second army of 'training staff', but the retraining of the staff we have.

The Briggs Committee recognised this with the recommendation that nursing for the mentally handicapped should evolve into a separate 'caring profession',[20] but they did not spell out the administrative process by which this evolution was to be achieved.

A new 'caring profession'

The case for a common training of ward staff and hostel staff is a strong one, but it is considerably affected by recent developments in the training of hostel staff. The Social Services Act, 1970, transferred all hostels for the mentally handicapped *inter alia* to the care of the local authority Social Services Department. The Central Council for Education and Training in Social Work has published two documents, in which work in hostels is seen as part of residential social work and residential social work is firmly proclaimed to be 'part of social work'.[21] The plans for training in the new sphere of residential social work have some interesting elements – there is an attempt to apply the techniques of group work and community work, as well as case work, to the residential setting; a proposal to upgrade residential work, giving it a status equivalent to that of field social work and facilitating transfers from one to the other; and a proposal for two levels of qualification – CQSW (the present national social work qualification) and CPSW (a new Certificate of Proficiency in Social Work, which it is proposed should be 'equal in status' to the CQSW though reached by a less academic and more practical route.[22]

These plans represent a considerable step forward in residential care; but it is clear from what we know of the needs of the mentally handicapped in hospital that the evolution of a 'separate caring profession' cannot be achieved simply by the substitution of a social work qualification for a nursing qualification. There is a continuum of need from those who can be best helped by residential social work techniques (either in hostels or likely to be transferred to hostels) to those who need full nursing care. Many of those between the two extremes need elements of both, and all need other skills as well. In training terms, there are five main possibilities:

1   A course carrying a full double qualification – RNMS and CQSW.
2   A course carrying a double qualification at a more practical level – SEN and CPSW.
3   A short post-qualification course in one specialism for those holding a full qualification in the other, i.e. a short course in residential social work for staff holding RNMS and a short course in nursing the mentally handicapped for staff holding CQSW.
4   Separate trainings but mixed deployment – staff holding RNMS and staff holding CQSW as members of a single team.

5   A new specialist qualification with elements of both.

Of these, only the first and the last seem to offer practical possibilities. Possibility 2 would be difficult to organise. SEN and CPSW (the latter is as yet largely an unknown quantity, since no training programmes have been worked out) would both depend on extensive experience with concurrent training. It would take a very long time to acquire both qualifications by experience, and the staff who are suitable for this type of training are almost by definition unsuitable for lengthy training involving problems of double orientation. Possibility 3 (a short post-qualification course) would be almost impossible to frame: both the CCETSW and the GNC would have strong objections to reducing their professional skills and knowledge to the scope of a short course for staff with a different basic qualification. Possibility 4 (mixed deployment) sounds attractive (most of all because it involves no training problems), but it is difficult to see who would head a mixed team, or how they could be deployed in the hospital setting.

It is also necessary to bear in mind the fact that many nursing staff and some social work staff have no qualification at all. Often the only fully-qualified nurse on a ward is the charge nurse, and qualified social workers are in painfully short supply. Our choice, therefore, is either to train a cadre of staff who are RNMS/CQSW (a formidable combination), or to invent a new qualification.

RNMS/CQSW has the merit of fitting in easily with current training patterns and offering students a double qualification. The problems are, first, that the syllabus would have to be acceptable to both the GNC and the CCETSW. RNMS is a three-year qualification and CQSW at minimum a two-year qualification. Some CQSW courses involve up to five years' university training. The minimum period of training (two years in a Polytechnic or College of Commerce) is usually only possible for candidates with social work experience. Though there is some overlap between the two syllabuses, it is unlikely that a joint course lasting less than five years could be made acceptable. Second, the chances of the doubly-qualified staff staying in hospital work are not very great. Local authority Social Services Departments can often offer better salaries, quicker promotion and better hours and conditions of work.

We are left, then, with the possibility of a special course for a new 'caring profession' working exclusively with the mentally handicapped. This proposal is totally against the current trends to genericism in nursing and social work. It will please neither the

GNC nor the CCETSW. It will produce a hybrid capable only of employment in the field of mental handicap and will require a special training body at national level (which will not please the DHSS, either). Nevertheless, we are convinced that this is the only training possibility which offers real hope for a breakthrough, and that the obstacles in the form of professional status, professional pride and professional prejudice ought to be vigorously tackled.

These obstacles do not only exist in the ranks of nurses and social workers. They are equally strong among teachers, occupational therapists, physiotherapists, speech therapists and remedial gymnasts, each professional body being convinced that its skills can only be acquired by a long and arduous training. One accepts the whole professional package or none at all. Mrs Eda Topliss, writing of a successful ward experiment in a geriatric hospital (where the problems of intraprofessional relations are in some respects very similar), describes how 'bed care of the patients was not regarded as the most important form of nursing':[23]

> The nurses were thus denied many of the satisfactions that came from the scrupulous discharge of traditional nursing roles ... they were asked instead to involve themselves more fully in the work of the physiotherapist and the occupational therapist who taught simple basic principles of physiotherapy and occupational therapy respectively to the nurses and nursing auxiliaries.

The nurses took to this new routine without difficulty. Only one insisted at interview that the formal nursing traditions were better for patients. The rest 'derived a new source of satisfaction from their work'. However, two major factors contributed to the success of this scheme. The first was strong and united leadership – 'the combined charismatic influence of hospital secretary's office, of the matron's position and of the hospital status and professional skills of consultants'. The second was the unusual position of the physiotherapist and the occupational therapist. Both:

> expressed clearly at a meeting the awareness that in teaching the simple techniques of their respective skills to the nursing personnel, who then carried them out with the patients, they were infringing the professional codes of their respective associations. In neither case was there any attempt at the meeting to deny the conflict, but both practitioners were assured that what they were doing in the hospital was in the best interests of

the patients. The implications of this assurance was clearly that the professional codes, on this particular point at least, were *not* in the best interests of the patients, and every encouragement was given the practitioners to take sides with the hospital in this conflict.

Neither the occupational therapist nor the physiotherapist was in close touch with other members of her professional association. Both were in fact married women – perhaps with limited career aspirations, and certainly more closely identified with the work of the hospital than with the restrictive stance of the professional organisations.

If professional codes are, as Mrs Topliss suggests, '*not* in the best interests of the patients', one wonders what possible justification there can be for calling them professional. While sociologists argue endlessly about the hallmarks of a profession, and whether this or that occupation can be properly called 'professional', there is at least common agreement that a profession has a code of ethics which puts the patient or client first. If the 'professions supplementary to medicine'[24] have lost this basic understanding, we might as well call them trade unions and have done with it.

However, we do not feel that this is the case. The desire of a professional or sub-professional group to safeguard its own skills is understandable, and the risk of having them diluted and applied inadequately by a more numerous and powerful professional group (in this case nurses) is real. The battle between nurses and occupational therapists in particular has raged in many a hospital, and it is possible to sympathise both with the nurses, who ask to be allowed to practise simple OT skills and complain that occupational therapists 'take all the interesting work away from us', and with the occupational therapists, who fear that their skills will be wrongly applied and that hospitals will cease to employ qualified occupational therapists altogether. What is needed is a new intraprofessional contact, in which occupational therapists and other specialists are recognised as advisers and consultants (a better status than the one they often have now) and they in return teach simple skills to be practised under their supervision.

As long as the ward task of caring for the mentally handicapped is recognised as 'nursing', this is a counsel of perfection. The evolution of a 'new caring profession' might make it possible. A special course for the care of the mentally handicapped (let us follow the fashion for initials, and call it the CMH course) could include elements of teaching by occupational therapists, physiotherapists, speech therapists and remedial gymnasts; these specialists would have the opportunity of separating out those simple elements in their own work which could be safely trusted to the CMH student; and there would be opportunities for post-qualification supervision and consultation.

We have no hesitation in departing from the Briggs recommendations in saying that much of the teaching for the CMH group should be done on the wards and in the hostels. A qualified CMH student would need a thorough understanding of both hospital and community care, and while some of this can be imparted in the lecture room, there is a need for patient-centred teaching backed by tutorials. This does not necessarily mean that ward charge nurses or hostel wardens must be able to teach: it does mean that tutors must be prepared to take part in the job in order to make their teaching relevant. This may be revolutionary. We think it is vital if students are to avoid the disjunction between theory and practice which so often occurs.

Our ideal course, then, would be one in which the elements of the main bodies of knowledge and skill relevant to the care of the mentally handicapped were taught by members of the professions concerned at least partly in the ward situation, with an emphasis on practice tutorials and a 'link' tutor able to relate the disparate elements into a coherent experience.

Since the number of qualified tutors is minimal, there would be a good case for a special tutor's course, and it may be at this level that the proposal for a joint qualification would be of most value. The National Institute for Social Work would possibly be the proper body to run an advanced course for suitable staff with RNMS, who would study both the elements of social work (on a multimethod basis, i.e. case work, group work and community work) together with teaching technique and the work of rehabilitation staff. Such a course would take not less than one year – preferably two – and include field work and teaching practice. It sounds expensive; but if each Region were to send one advanced student to a course per year for five years, the Regions would have the nucleus of a staff capable of operating CMH courses.

The worst method of approach would be to base the CMH courses or the tutor's course on existing educational institutions. Neither universities nor polytechnics are geared to provide training in practitioner skills which are genuinely based on practice, and the tendency to graft a new course on to existing courses, to extend the work of existing staff, is almost irresistible, particularly in a time of financial stringency. The proper place for university input is in research of the kind outlined in chapter 5 (and comparable studies mounted in community agencies) to provide material which can be fed into teaching. A paper by Derek Thomas, Senior Psychologist at Northgate and District Hospital, Morpeth, Northumberland, draws attention to the 'remarkable absence of detailed research' and the need to assess afresh the skills required in care.[25]

The problem of inertia

Behind all the problems which have been discussed in this study lies one fundamental problem: that the field of mental handicap is one which very few people in the National Health Service rate a priority, and in which efforts at reform are at best sporadic. A new approach is popular for a time, but soon loses momentum; but the Ely and Farleigh Reports, *Put Away* and other literature abound with evidence of the fact that nobody cares very much – at least not for very long.

There are reasons for this: some are societal reasons manifested as residual stigma and a low social priority. We have found that when the cause of the mentally handicapped is urged on a politician or a senior civil servant, the response is frequently on the lines of 'Yes, I appreciate what you say; but who is to be left out if we divert resources to the mentally handicapped – the old, the mentally ill, the blind, the physically handicapped?'

In this form, the question is unanswerable. One does not want to urge the care of one neglected and underprivileged group at the expense of another; but the input required is in national terms so tiny, and the effect on a particularly neglected and underprivileged group could be so great that the question really need not be argued in economic terms. The blockages to progress are not primarily economic. They arise from the fact that the mentally handicapped are a relatively small group in society; they cannot compete for resources on their own behalf (like, for example, retirement pensioners and the physically handicapped – two groups both large in numbers and politically active), and there appears to be no urgency about their problems. If action is not taken for a mentally ill person immediately, his condition may worsen considerably, with consequences both to himself and to others; but the mentally handicapped child or adult will still be there in much the same condition next month, next year or the year after.

Behind these societal reasons for inertia lie another set of reasons which are particular to mental handicap itself. It is necessary to face these honestly; and we cannot subscribe either to the optimism of the labelling theorists, who insist that the mentally handicapped are not a definable group in any way, or to the sentimentality of some voluntary organisations, which focus their appeals on mentally handicapped children rather than adults and lay great stress on their 'lovability'. Some are 'lovable' – that is, they elicit an easy response of protectiveness and affection. Some are harder to love, and it is perhaps necessary to rescue a word tarnished by popular associations and to remind ourselves that mature love or affection is an affair of the will as well as of the emotions.

Some mentally handicapped people (though not all) are unattractive in appearance. They induce in the casual onlooker an instinctive revulsion, a wish to look elsewhere, a desire not to know. This can be confirmed on any bus or railway station when a mentally-handicapped person is travelling, in any holiday camp where a group from the neighbouring hospital is taken for a day out. Conversations stop, eyes are averted, and a sort of invisible glass wall goes up between them and the 'normal' world. They may be refused admission to restaurants (on the grounds that 'the customers would not like it') and be spoken to by bus conductors and railway clerks with a sort of rough jocularity which is meant to be kind, but conceals a basic unease.

Those who work with them constantly soon forget oddities of appearance or gesture. It is one of the curious factors of residential work in the health or social services that the common denominator, whether it be mental handicap or deafness or blindness or epilepsy, is very quickly taken for granted. People with these problems (like Chinese or Arabs) cease to 'look alike' as soon as one knows a few of them really well as individuals; but the first reaction (and most of our society never gets beyond the first reaction) is one of unease and even outrage – 'This ought not to happen. It's not normal. It must be somebody's fault'. Parents of mentally handicapped children suffer acutely from this, often at three levels: there is the stigma of having a handicapped child; the assumption (even in these comparatively enlightened days) that they are somehow to blame, either through heredity or child-rearing methods; and the even deeper assumption that there must be something 'wrong' with them too. Many people are too civilised to express these assumptions in words; but they are expressed no less effectively in tones of voice, careful avoidance of eye contact and lacunae in conversation. Such prejudice, like colour prejudice or sex prejudice, runs deep; and it is by no means certain that the best way to get rid of it is to ignore its existence.

Even for those who work daily with the mentally handicapped and get to know them as individuals, there are further difficulties. Most of the mentally handicapped have a very limited capacity for social interaction. Getting to know them is hard work. They are often not 'grateful' for services, and do not easily reciprocate gestures of friendship. Affection, if aroused, may take embarrassing and demanding forms. Their response to teaching is inevitably slow – there are no easy rewards in terms of improved capacity. It may be a major breakthrough to teach a 54-year-old man to tie his own shoelaces, but an appreciation of this fact requires a considerable social adjustment on the part of the teacher.

Together, these factors are productive of an in-built tendency to inertia unless active measures are taken to counteract it. There is a need for a continuous input of energy into the service for the mentally handicapped. The most enlightened scheme will sink back into routine unless it is monitored and evaluated at regular intervals. This input can best come at ward or hostel level from training and research of the kinds we have outlined. It will be the responsibility of the Mental Health Care Planning Teams to see that a similar input of energy devoted to the mentally handicapped is generated right through the administrative system, if we are to prevent the recurrence of the situation in which 'nobody was batting for Ely'.

9   Summary and conclusions

There are two long-standing problems in the services for the mentally handicapped: stigma and inertia. These are linked and they underlie all the other problems. They do not get any less, though they perhaps take less overt forms than in the past.

They can only be fought by energy and imagination – employed at many levels from the ward situation through the machinery of the health and social services to the corridors of Westminster and the Elephant and Castle. One of the major limitations to progress has been the fact that we have tended to work at only one level in the administrative process: but a White Paper or a research report does not of itself achieve changes in the ward situation, and a good ward experiment will die of inanition and staff changes unless it is backed by support from higher up the system.

Our survey covered only one of the fourteen Regions of England and Wales. However, we have made comparisons with national statistics, compared our findings with those of Dr Pauline Morris's national survey, and made a number of visits to hospitals and research teams in other parts of the country. All the general evidence we have is that the problem is a national one and that the Gateshire Region is not in any way atypical.

We summarise below the main problems in terms of their origin, and then follow with recommendations grouped in terms of which authority or organisation is in a position to implement them.

1   *Problems arising from earlier – and now outdated – policies for the mentally handicapped:*
- isolation of hospitals;
- poor and often forbidding architecture;
- poor internal provision, e.g. in the lack of sanitary facilities and the size of wards;
- custodial attitudes;
- poor staff morale;
- patient passivity;
- predominance of routine;

205

- lack of community contacts;
- lack of community facilities.

2 *Problems arising from current societal attitudes to the mentally handicapped:*
- low priority in the health and social services: lack of economic resources of all kinds;
- poor staff recruitment;
- limited opportunities for socialisation;
- lack of research.

3 *Problems arising from the nature of the mentally handicapped as a group:*
- no political pressure;
- no public appeal;
- often unattractive appearance and behaviour;
- very slow progress;
- poor personal interaction.

4 *Problems created by recent Health Service policy measures:*
- a split service, 'medical' and 'social';
- lack of fit between patients' needs and available staff skills resulting from:
  a increasing genericism in medicine, nursing and social work;
  b failure to utilise other relevant skills;
- loss of medical leadership (probably not needed in terms of skill, but a great loss in terms of status and prestige).
- lack of support from senior staff due to:
  a failure of the tripartite system in hospitals;
  b lack of specialist representation at a sufficiently high level in the new managerial hierarchies of health and social services;
- worsening of staff morale due to:
  a the factors quoted above;
  b (in hospitals) the projected run-down of beds and discharge of the 'better' patients;
  c uncritical application of 'normalisation' which sets up unresolvable tensions for staff;
  d effect of public criticism (Ely, Farleigh, etc.).

This is a formidable list, particularly in section 4. We do not imply that the effect of recent policy measures is wholly or even mainly adverse; but as Professor and Mrs Somers once noted, 'All creative achievement is disruptive. Every partial solution promptly explodes open a new series of problems.'[1] The side-effects of administrative policies are at least as worthy of attention as the side-effects of new drugs. They may have been particularly destructive in this small backwater of the health and social services.

Recommendations

These are given in three sections: those directed to the health authorities (Regional Health Authorities, Area Health Authorities and District Management Teams, with the detailed work seen as the responsibility of the Health Care Planning Team for mental health); those directed to social service authorities (the Social Services Committees and Social Services Departments of local authorities); and those directed to national bodies, notably the Department of Health and Social Security and the National voluntary societies. It is in this last section that the innovatory recommendations occur.

(A) Health authorities

1 *Large, old hospitals in rural areas should continue to be replaced by small hospital units in or near towns.* Although this may mean increased costs, we think the case for such a policy is overwhelming in terms of staff recruitment, community contacts and benefit to patients and their relatives.

2 *Small hospital units should be run on a 'federal' principle:* that is, efforts should be made to develop a style of administration which would combine the advantages of large units (economies of scale, a career structure for staff, joint appointments, specialist facilities) with the advantages of small ones (homeliness, face-to-face interaction, a sense of belonging, flexibility). Small units should not be allowed to become isolated, and schemes should be drawn up to ensure that they have full professional support and a fair share of the scarce skills of non-medical specialists such as social workers and physiotherapists.

3 *A review should be made of hospital signposting and transport services.* Where transport services are inadequate and hospitals isolated, the provision of a hospital bus or minibus to transport relatives at cost should be explored.

4 *All patients, particularly those assumed to be severely sub-*

H

normal, should be subject to regular assessment by an independent team. This might take place every three years, the team consisting of a clinical psychologist, an educational psychologist and a psychiatrist. This should not be allowed to degenerate into a paper procedure by those in daily contact with the patients.

5   *A programme of minor works should be set up for each hospital,* involving the imaginative assessment, in consultation with ward staff, of such matters as partitioning, the provision of additional sanitary facilities and other modifiable features. Ward staff should not merely be asked by the architect or works officer what they want; they may not know. They should be drawn into a conscious exercise of team planning.

6   *Community Services Organisers* (CSOs) should be appointed for each large hospital or group of small hospitals, whose task it would be to create and maintain relationships for patients (rather than for hospitals as organisations) with the local community, with the social services both statutory and voluntary and with patients' families. This post would replace the more limited post of Voluntary Services Organiser (VSO) now developing in some hospitals, and would require a special training programme (see recommendation 15).

(B) Social services authorities

7   *Hostel accommodation should be reviewed* and a coherent policy for the use of hostels should be developed in view of the recommendations of the 1971 White Paper.

8   *Conferences and training days should be initiated for hostel staff* to acquaint them with the recent policy changes and to help them to think constructively about the creation of a more professional service. Where possible, study groups should be set up to consider hostel problems and to make recommendations.

9   *Efforts should be made to create a network of medical, nursing and ancillary support for hostels.* It is recognised that this would take much goodwill and some ingenuity on both sides of the newly-established 'health' and 'social services' frontiers. We think that every hostel for the mentally handicapped should have the benefit of regular visits and support from a doctor with experience in the field of mental handicap (not necessarily a consultant), a qualified nurse, and where necessary a physiotherapist, an occupational therapist and a speech therapist.

10 *Training centres should be assessed* with two principles in mind: the development of progressive training which would extend the trainees' capacities, and the development of social and educational skills.

11 *Regular social work support should be made available to both hostel staff and training centre staff.* Where possible this should be linked to training schemes through case discussions and other teaching methods.

12 *Regular visits by social workers should be made to mentally handicapped persons in lodgings* and other relatively unstructured domestic situations.

13 We make no recommendations concerning mentally handicapped persons living in their own homes, since these did not form part of our survey. We endorse Dr Michael Bayley's concept of the creation of 'a structure for coping', involving the creation of a network of family, neighbourhood and social service support.[2] The principle of combining skills and resources to create a network of support for individuals is very similar to that underlying a number of our own recommendations.

(C) National authorities and organisations

14 *The Education (Handicapped Children) Act, 1971, should be amended to permit the extension of services of the Local Education Authority to mentally handicapped persons over the age of sixteen,* whether in hospital, in hostels or training centres, or in their own home.

15 *A national training course for Community Services Organisers (CSOs)* should be set up under the aegis of either the National Association for Mental Health or the British Association for the Retarded. The course should be full-time and last at least three months. Entrants need not be social workers, but they should have experience of working in the health or social services, and preferably a diploma in either social administration or community work. Salaries and conditions of work should be commensurate with the importance of the work and should ensure a status at least equivalent to that of a ward charge nurse.

16 *Every effort should be made through consultation with the training organisations and employing bodies to secure a considerable increase in the employment of psychologists, physiotherapists, occupational therapists, speech therapists and remedial gymnasts*

in services for the mentally handicapped. These workers should be available to local authority hostels as well as to hospitals. Where possible, they should work as advisers and consultants rather than 'competing' with the nursing staff.

17 Pending the outcome of long-term discussions on a 'caring profession', *pilot schemes should be set up for training for the care of the mentally handicapped*. The first step would be to work out an acceptable syllabus, including the following elements:

 i the social needs of the mentally handicapped;
 ii basic nursing;
 iii co-operation with specialist workers (including some simple skills where these can be taught and delegated);
 iv policy changes in the health and social services;
 v the sociology of institutions and agencies in the health and social services;
 vi small group behaviour.

The course should last at least two years and include about 50 per cent of time spent on field work in both hospital and community settings. Field work should be linked to regular practice tutorials. Training and professional support should be seen as parts of a continuing process – contact with specialist staff should start in training and be continued in the work situation.

18 *Major research projects should be mounted on both hospital ward care and hostel care*. These should involve the skills of psychologists, sociologists and social administrators, and there should be at least one nurse with RNMS on each team. The focus would be on the development of new technologies of patient management aimed at minimising routine and maximising the individual potential of patients through the application of the principles of modelling theory, learning theory, group dynamics or behaviour modification. (We are divided on the application of behaviour modification techniques, some members of the team regarding this as the best possibility of a major breakthrough while others stress the dangers involved in a mechanistic approach.

19 *The voluntary associations concerned with the care of the mentally handicapped should consider the formation of joint committees at Area Health Authority/Social Services Department level*. Apart from the Department of Health and Social Security itself, this is the only point in the administrative structures at which health and social services are in direct correspondence with one another. It is

at this point that voluntary organisations have the greatest chance of influencing local policy, and it would be a pity if their own disorganisation prevented it. This should lead to the more effective use of the considerable resources which the voluntary services are able to command.

20 *Whatever practical steps are taken should be repeatedly monitored and evaluated.* The tendency to inertia is the greatest barrier to improvement, and its onset can be insidious.

To the ancient Greeks, *idiōtēs* meant a person who took no part in public affairs, and hence was subject to contempt. If the mentally handicapped are to be brought into the life of our own society, we need an advance on a broad front, with no short cuts and no easy solutions. We are conscious that in asking for a specialist service with a multiskill basis, we are opposing current policies and trends which are based on genericism, and which offer many advantages to the professionals. Present policies are consistent, administratively tidy and acceptable. We are asking for inconsistency and administrative untidiness; but the problems of the mentally handicapped are acute. They have been, so to speak, acute for a long time; and we hope we offer a means of improvement.

H*

Postscript

This project began operation in September 1971. The first reaction in the hospitals was hesitant. There had been so many surveys and so many visiting experts; but when the staff found that members of the team were prepared to stay with them for some months in order to find out the nature of the work, and that they genuinely wanted to know what the staff members thought, the attitude changed to co-operation and some enthusiasm. Members of the team were repeatedly asked to 'let them [i.e. Authority] know what it's really like' and hopes were expressed that 'something might really happen this time'.

In view of the urgency of the problems, we had promised the Regional Hospital Board an interim report in fifteen months (by Christmas 1972). This was actually delivered (personally, because of a tight schedule and Christmas mail delays) on Christmas Eve. Much detailed work remained to be done, but the gist of the main findings and recommendations was there. In view of our comments on the gap between idea and action, it may be of interest to record the fate of the interim document.

Several discussions were held with senior officials of the Board, and all the recommendations (which included specific details on physical provision, though not on individual members of staff, since we held the latter to be confidential) were carefully checked through. Copies of the interim report, interleaved with comments from Board staff, were circulated to all members of the mental health sub-committee, including the Board's chairman. A full meeting of the chairman, the sub-committee, senior Board officials and members of the team took place on 25 May 1973.

The general reaction was very favourable. The sub-committee was reassured to find that there were no open abuses, and very much aware that a predominantly young team of social scientists, well versed in the 'protest' literature of the 1960s, would not have hesitated to bring abuse to their notice if it had been found. They readily accepted the view that the services, like those in most other parts of the country, were in some ways sub-standard, and were anxious to take such action as they could to improve them.

There was a lengthy discussion about ward standards. Official returns to the Board indicated that both bed-space and the provision of sanitary facilities were up to DHSS standards. Our evidence indicated a number of instances in which this was not the case in terms of actual use of space and facilities. It was easy to see how the discrepancy could occur. A ward charge nurse short of day space could have beds pushed closer together to provide it. Sanitary facilities might be sufficient in overall number, but in the wrong place for use by particular groups of patients. The Board agreed to send out a directive to Hospital Management Committees, asking them to look at these matters again and, where necessary, to plan minor works programmes.

Plans were already approved for upgrading of four wards which we named as being particularly sub-standard, and there were long-term plans for the gradual replacement of large rural hospitals by small urban ones, for the development of 'federal' administration and for the extension of day-places, though it was made clear that 'all this will take years to do'.

Recommendations on signposting were readily accepted. This was an obvious need which had not occurred to people in the service (who knew their way). It could be done readily without controversy and without great expense. The suggestion of a bus or minibus service for visiting relatives was more difficult, since there were problems of insurance. However, the Board finally agreed to ask HMCs to review both signposting and transport facilities.

There was further discussion over the question of involving ward staff in physical planning, the Board representatives contending that this was already done, and the research workers replying that if this were so, ward staff were not consulted in a way which made it possible to express their own expertise. We suggested that they might be involved to a greater extent in team planning and discussions of an ongoing kind, since they did not readily think in architectural terms, and often needed some help in relating ward activities to spatial and other constraints.

The three major innovatory recommendations – for a research scheme on ward management, the appointment of community services officers and a pilot training programme for a 'caring profession' – were welcomed. It was agreed that a research scheme should be worked out between the university and the Board and that the

Research Division of the Department of Health and Social Security should be asked to fund it. Money was set aside for the appointment of two Community Services Organisers, one in each of the two largest hospitals. The research team agreed to draft a job description (see Appendix 4) and to provide some pre-service training. A joint sub-committee on a curriculum for a 'caring profession' was appointed and a date was set in September 1973 for its first meeting.

But by September, the effects of the National Health Service (Re-organisation) Act, 1973, were being felt. Both the Regional Hospital Board and the Hospital Management Committees were in their last six months of existence.

The research scheme was sent to DHSS, which was then under-going its own internal reorganisation. Some months elapsed and much negotiation took place before we received a cautious agree-ment to pay the salaries of existing members of the team for one year in the first instance. By that time, the team had broken up and its members had found other posts.

The meeting of the sub-committee on a 'caring profession' had to be postponed. Staff changes and the pressure of reorganisation made it impossible to find another date, and there have been no further proposals for a meeting. The two posts for community ser-vices officers were advertised twice and there was no response. They have not been advertised again. The chairman of the Regional Hos-pital Board and the secretary to the Board, both of whom took a considerable personal interest in the proposals, have now retired and hold no office in the reorganised structure.

When chapter 7, on community care, was fully written up, we sent a detailed and specific version to the directors-designate of the three main Social Services Departments in the new local govern-ment structure, asking whether they would be interested in a joint day conference at the university on the findings. Two replied with enthusiasm, but the actual holding of the conference has been post-poned by reorganisation. The third took a different view, stating emphatically that none of our strictures applied to his service, and that mentally handicapped people in his authority would be assisted primarily through a general family care service, rather than through special services. Some correspondence ensued. A meeting was offered but refused; and a final letter from the director requested that his views should be recorded in our report. (In fact, none of the information given in chapter 7 is specific to the authority in question, except the statistical material given in tables and taken from published sources; and even this does not name the authority.) However, we have now carried out his request.

In the winter of 1973–4 the economic position worsened and plans for expenditure on the health and social services were cut back. In February 1974 there was a General Election which resulted in a minority government. It looks at the time of writing as though a period of economic uncertainty may be matched by political uncertainty for some time to come.

In May 1974 Mrs Castle, as Secretary of State for the Social Services, announced her intention to press for loan consents so that 'the pace of development could be *restored to the level*'[1] envisaged in Cmnd 4683 (emphasis added).

Appendix 1: a case conference at Maple Grange

Maple Grange has had little psychiatric support for some years. On paper, a consultant is allocated to the hospital, but his visits are infrequent. Staff at Maple are conscious of the inadequacy of medical coverage, and point to the fact that some of the medical records have not been kept up to date and that medication cards have not been regularly re-assessed. However, there is widespread recognition that this is not the consultant's fault – he is responsible for about a thousand beds scattered over a wide area, and much extra-mural work besides.

However, staff feel that when he does appear, he is seldom willing to become involved in patient problems. As one charge nurse put it:

> He doesn't seem to have the least bit of interest in the patients that are here now. He came here only yesterday and I asked him if he would review George Pollit's medicines because I think they aren't doing him any good, and he told me he didn't have time. It's always the same with him, he never has time ... he's just so airy-fairy ... you can never tie him down to anything.

On another occasion in the office of a new charge nurse, his superior (No. 7) came in and said that the consultant would be coming round that day. He told the charge nurse not to bother unduly because the doctor wouldn't want to spend much time on the ward.

Into this general situation a new ingredient was introduced early in 1971 when the junior partner of the local GP accepted the appointment of part-time consultant in psychiatry at Maple Grange. The GP, Dr Dexter, had served as locum for the senior partner, who is also a medical officer at the hospital, and had acquired an interest in both the patients and the field of mental handicap. Unlike the full-time consultant, Dr Dexter had no training in the treatment of either mental illness or mental handicap and was in consequence 'feeling his way'.

At the time that Dr Dexter took up this appointment, which occupies one morning a week, Mr Newbolt arrived at Maple as the

217

new senior nursing officer under the Salmon scheme. As newcomers and outsiders with ideas about what was needed at the hospital, they came together to discuss possible programmes they could implement. Dr Dexter said:

> Up until recently we have just been talking about things we could try . . . so we have got together to find ways of cutting the size of the wards down and at the moment we have plans for splitting Smith ward into two smaller units. But this idea for the case conference is a little bit different because we wanted to do something for the patients and for the nurses. We wanted to show them that someone was prepared to do something practical, that someone was interested in their patients. I think this is important for their morale as much as anything.

The meeting was held one morning and no one, not even Dr Dexter, had very clear ideas of what they would do. The outline plan was to have the charge nurses on the two main wards present two patients of their own choice. These would be discussed and recommendations would be made for treatment or special action. Present at the meeting were Dr Dexter, Mr Newbolt, a nursing officer, and the two charge nurses.

Dr Dexter started the meeting by saying that they would have to play it by ear since he was not an expert on mental handicap and would in consequence have to find things out as they went along. He outlined the procedure they would follow and said that he wanted the charge nurses to give brief histories of their patients and that a general discussion would ensue. The first patient was brought in by a charge nurse who gave a history on the basis of what was in the charts and his own knowledge of the patient. Dr Dexter and the others asked several questions, and it was noted that there were certain inaccuracies in the patient's medical record. For example, it was written in the chart that the patient was hemiplegic, but simple tests performed in the meeting by Dr Dexter indicated that he was not paralysed on his left side as the record suggested. The meeting also recommended that the patient, who came into the meeting shoeless, should be fitted out with some type of footwear and be referred to an orthopaedic surgeon.

The second patient, a young man of about thirty, was brought in and his brief history given. During this and the previous presentation, Dr Dexter had read passages out from the medical records and asked for corroboration from the charge nurses. When medical terms arose that were not known by the group, Dr Dexter asked the charge nurses to look them up and give a short presentation on them at the next case conference. One charge nurse pointed out that the patient, John Pringle, was difficult to motivate and was interested only in guns and violence and cigarettes. John, he pointed out, could be something of a nuisance, because he would force other patients to give him cigarettes and would become quite aggressive if they failed to comply. He continued by saying that John appeared to have a psychiatric condition as well, because he would often walk around conversing with an invisible partner:

> He sometimes comes into the office saying things like – 'Do you want to kill yourself, John?' 'Yes I'm going to kill myself now.' 'But if you kill yourself now you won't get any supper.' 'Well I'll wait until supper.' He goes around talking like this and it's more like some of the mental illnesses than subnormality. I feel that he may be schizophrenic rather than subnormal because he's quite intelligent.

The other charge nurse agreed with these observations and Dr Dexter asked for John to be brought in. Dr Dexter and Mr Newbolt asked him some questions, and the former gave him a simple IQ test to perform, involving fitting coloured wooden shapes into equivalent slots in a board. He appeared to grasp this quite quickly and on the second and third trials performed it very fast. Some more questions were asked and, even though he could not answer them all (e.g. 'Who is the Prime Minister?'), John seemed to be highly aware of his environment.

After the patient left, Dr Dexter commented that he was inclined to agree with the charge nurses' judgment and went back through his case notes and read out passages that were pertinent to his being diagnosed as mentally handicapped in his teens. The notes stated that he was 'troublesome' in school at the age of nine and was diagnosed as epileptic and withdrawn from school for that reason. One charge nurse was surprised by this and said, 'John isn't epileptic is he?' The other replied that he had known John for the nine years he had been at Maple Grange and had never seen any sign of his being epileptic. Dr Dexter said that they would put him down to have an EEG and this would throw some light on the matter, although he said it did look as though his record was not accurate.

There was some conversation about this and the point was made that if the stigma of epilepsy was attached to a person it would isolate him from other people. The discussion was drawn together by Dr Dexter, who said that it looked as though there was some evidence to suggest that John had had some form of mental illness as a child which had caused him to be somewhat withdrawn and aggressive at school. He pointed out that there was no evidence to suggest that he had been unable to keep up with the school work. The statement about epilepsy in the record was the first indication that there was some form of trouble, and Dr Dexter found there was some likelihood that the term 'epileptic' was applied to him by teachers who were unable to handle him. The subsequent diagnosis of mental handicap would derive support because of his early withdrawal from school and his isolation in hospital where he received little opportunity to develop intellectually.

The reconstruction of John's history challenged some fifteen years of medical and social assumptions about his condition. The meeting recommended that he be seen by a consultant psychiatrist at the neighbouring general hospital and that his mental state be assessed by someone competent in the field of mental illness. A charge nurse commented, 'If he'd had a decent environment in the first place instead of being in one of these hospitals he might have developed intellectually.' Dr Dexter replied that to live in such a hospital was enough to make anyone mentally handicapped.

As the meeting ended a charge nurse said:

> You see how it is with these case notes? Dr Dampier copied them from Dr Donaldson and he just copied them from Dr Darke ... and no one bothered to find out if they were correct or not.... This is the first sign that any doctor is going to do anything for the patients here.

Had the present consultant ever held case conferences? He replied:

> Oh yes, he held them on the ward and all the staff had to listen while he gave lectures on medical theories and things like that. It was all very interesting but it had nothing to do with the patients. As I say, today's meeting was the first sign that a doctor is going to do more than talk about patients and do something instead. I'm only sorry I had to wait so long to see it.

Appendix 2: time schedule for the project

July 1971	Project agreed between university and Regional Hospital Board. Preliminary contacts made with hospitals. Basic team appointed.
July–August 1971	Team split: i preparation of lecture notes for September; ii basic documentation; iii basic bibliography; iv experience as nursing assistant; v experience as social work assistant; vi visits to Geele (Belgium), Farleigh and other hospitals. Contacts with other research teams.
September 1971	Stage I: Intensive lectures and discussions. Reports on experience. Analysis of policy documents. Discussion on methodology. Formulation of checklist.
October 1971–early 1972	Stage II: Members of team atached to hospitals on a territorial basis, each taking one or two HMCs. Personal contact with senior staff. Every ward visited, discussions with staff. Items on checklist covered. Ward schedules completed. Stage II reports submitted. Weekly full-day team discussions throughout this period.
February/March–December 1972	Stage III: Plans for detailed investigations completed. Change of direction, each team member (plus one diploma student) taking responsibility for one aspect of study throughout the Region. Personal introductions where necessary by team member responsible for Stage II in particular hospitals. Weekly team discussions continued. Basic statistical work. Finding and draft reports discussed. Submission of interim report.

January 1973–
March 1974

Additional statistical work and subsidiary investigations. Discussions with Regional Hospital Board. Formulation of research plan on ward management. Negotiations with DHSS. Checking and updating of material. Writing-up.

Appendix 3: checklist on hospitals for the mentally handicapped as social sub-systems

Stage I of the project required members of the research team each to take one group of hospitals and to study it in depth for a period of three to five months. In our preliminary discussions we were divided between the 'rigorists', who wanted to work out a detailed research instrument which could be administered by any member of the team and would ensure comparable results, and the 'intuitionists', who contended that to draw up such an instrument would mean pre-judging situations of which we then had little knowledge and that the right approach was to 'go in, get to know the people, and sniff around'.

In the end, we compromised, and drew up from our existing knowledge of hospitals in general and hospitals for the mentally handicapped in particular a checklist of areas to be covered by each research worker in his report. This was made as value-free as possible, and it left the individual worker with considerable freedom to evaluate what he found.

The reports formed the basis for the general picture of the hospitals given in chapter 2. It was not possible to get fully comparable material for every section of the checklist, but we think that the approach was generally successful in providing a lively picture of the hospitals in operation, where a more rigorous questionnaire might merely have confirmed our own prejudices. Material on the committee structure (HMCs) has been omitted from this study since the HMCs have now gone out of existence.

Checklist

Physical setting and facilities	History of building
	Architectural plan (sketch)
	Physical location
	Distribution of accommodation
	Local name

Statistics	Patients: numbers, sex, age, diagnosis, social, physical and educational capacities Admission, discharge, length of stay Resident population as at 31 December Staff: medical, nursing, administration, rehabilitation (speech therapists, teachers, physiotherapists, etc.) Costs per bed
Committee structure (HMC)	Age, sex, social background, length of service, extent of involvement, relations with chief officers
Senior staff structure	Authority patterns Working of 'tripartite system' Consultant, PNO, senior administrator, (?)rehabilitation officer Formalised staff meetings Informal staff groupings Staff handovers
Ward system	Patient classification, physical facilities (heating, furnishing, decoration, lockers, use of space), staffing, ward organisation, formal and informal routines (bathing, shaving, standardised medical procedures) Sanctions (including use of restraint and seclusion) and privileges Food Patients' clothing Ward meetings
Staff relations	Who eats with whom? Who joins the staff club? Role allocation Personal relations
Staff–patient relations	Do patients work for staff: (a) in the hospital; (b) in staff homes? 'Trusties' Special roles

Patient–patient relations	Patterns of help and dependency Personal friendships Group formation
External relations	With local community With other hospitals With local authority Voluntary organisations Patients' families
Objectives and ideology	Manifest objectives (journals, magazines, speeches, annual reports) Assumed objectives Extant objectives Sectional and personal objectives
Culture	Official culture: rules, regulations, standards of conduct, uniforms Ritual: Sports Day, Open Day, ward parties, etc.; official religious observance: (q.v. ward system) Sanctions on patients and staff Ward staff culture: positive and negative aspects Jokes Myths Jargon Speech patterns
Patient activities outside the ward	Entertainments and outings Education OT/IT/working out Games and remedial gymnastics
Specialist facilities in hospital	Psychology Pathology laboratory Speech therapy Physiotherapy Chiropody Social work

Other factors (possibly specific to hospital)

Appendix 4: job description for community service organisers

The work of a Community Service Organiser (CSO) would involve liaison between the hospital and the community in three main ways:

i   the development and strengthening of links between patients and their families during hospitalisation, including the provision of transport and other facilities to assist relatives to visit the hospital and patients to spend periods at home;

ii   the recruitment, training and deployment of volunteers for work in the hospital, and for work with individual patients or patient groups which involves visits to or placements in the community;

iii   the development of links with statutory and voluntary agencies to create and maintain a broad network of support for patients and their relatives.

These proposals involve a more comprehensive approach than that usually required of a Voluntary Service Organiser,[1] whose concern is primarily with volunteers and voluntary agencies, since family, voluntary and statutory care are seen as parts of a total complex of potential support. The focus of the work would be on organisation and co-ordination from a hospital base, and it is seen as complementary to the work of the medical social worker. A suitable qualification for a CSO would be a degree or diploma in social administration or a diploma in community work.

The first task of a newly-appointed CSO would be to make a survey of the needs of patients and the ways in which they might be met in consultation with hospital staff. In an acute general hospital, this might be mainly concerned with the provision of facilities in the hospital and visiting services. In a hospital for the mentally ill or the mentally handicapped, it would involve the exploration of facilities for some individual patients during a pre-discharge period (the patient being transferred to the care of the local authority Social Services Department on discharge) together with the creation of more permanent hospital–community contacts for long-stay patients.

It is important that new ways of meeting needs should be developed, and that the service should not be stereotyped in terms of known channels of assistance such as the WRVS trolley service or the Rotarians' annual party, valuable though these are. Such services should form the baseline for new and more individualised services.

The initial assessment period might take from one to six months. It is important that it should involve the full co-operation and understanding of hospital staff, relatives and community agencies, and that it should result in the creation of a web of contacts between individuals and groups at different levels.

Once this has been achieved, the ongoing work would be expected to include:

i   attendance at staff meetings; interviews and consultations with senior staff;

ii   the maintenance of liaison with ward staff;

iii   consultation with voluntary and statutory agencies in the area;

iv   public speaking at clubs, schools, societies and firms in the area;

v   writing memoranda, information handouts and Press articles;

vi   interviews with patients and their relatives;

vii   selection, training and deployment of volunteers;

viii   administrative duties.

The CSO would need to maintain an office, and also get about the hospital and out in the community. A separate office should be provided, and a half-time secretary would be necessary to man the office and to carry out routine clerical work (telephone calls, correspondence, making up rotas, dealing with callers). A mileage allowance for the use of a car would be necessary.

Appendix 5: notes on the methodology of the attitude survey

1 The Treatment Orientation Scale

Attitude statements for the scale were based on discussions with nursing staff in Stage II of the project and piloted on nurses in two hospitals in a neighbouring Regional Hospital Board area. Special attention was paid to the vernacular used by nurses in framing the statements.

A five-point Likert scale was used[1] in preference to a cumulative or discriminative scale, because of the relative ease of construction and the ease with which it is possible to administer the scale, the method of response being readily apparent. This was of importance owing to the diversity of interview situations in which the scale was applied. At one extreme there was the relative tranquility of the Sister's office, at the other extreme the clamour of a corner in a day room of a disturbed children's ward. Obviously, in the latter situation the scale format could not be too complex or too difficult to convey in more than a few words. It has to be easy for the respondent to grasp the mechanics of reply, and simple for the interviewer to administer. These two principles determined not only the choice of the Likert scale, but also guided the overall design and structure of the interview schedule.

2 The interview schedule

From the outset it was decided that the interview schedule would be tightly structured to standardise for the differences between the four interviewers employed in the main study and for the diversity of interview situations that were encountered. The schedule eventually used reflected this, and only three questions at the end were left open and unstructured. This was a deliberate tactic as during the course of Stage II it had been found that one problem was to stop people talking. It was, therefore, decided that careful consideration should be given to 'phasing out' respondents from the interview situation. This is an area given scant attention by textbooks on methodology, which concentrates on the 'phasing in' of the respondent – the implication being that once rapport has been established, then the ending will largely take care of itself.

Obviously the 'phasing in' of respondents is of crucial importance, but it was felt that in the context of the overall organisation of the project two assumptions could be made about approaching the interview situation. First, that during Stage II, respondents had got to know about the project and its aims, either from personally meeting the members of the research team attached to their hospitals or by talking to friends who had. Second, respondents had been assured that the project was confidential. Members of the team reported that staff often tested them by attempting to make them reveal confidential information in, for example, the relaxed atmosphere of the canteen.

On the basis of these two assumptions – that knowledge about the aims of the study and the guarantee of confidentiality could be taken as given – the following framework for the interview schedule was decided upon; a brief introductory statement that repeated the purpose and confidentiality of the study, to be immediately followed by the attitude statements; the final section of the schedule consisting of the questions relating to the demographic data. In this final section, all questions were structured and precoded with the exception of the last three.

Although the area of study is especially sensitive at present, this 'both-feet-in-at-the-beginning' approach worked well in the field situation, the interviews flowing smoothly in the varied situations in which the schedule was applied. Further, the assumptions on which the framework had been based proved valid, as queries related predominantly to the selection procedure by which the respondent had been picked rather than to what we were doing or whether the schedule was confidential.

The questions in the final section which were structured and precoded, were filled in during the course of the interview so that the data were ready to be transferred directly on to punch-cards once it had been checked. The attitude statements, however, were scored in the office. This was because the scoring on some of the statements was reversed, as favourable and unfavourable statements had been randomly ordered to help prevent the creation of a response set.[2] To have had to score the statements in the field, either by remembering the direction of scoring or by a separate sheet indicating the scores, would have added considerably to the task of the interviewer. A ribbon layout for recording the responses to the attitude statements, adopted because it was easy for the eye to follow, also helped prevent a response set as it resulted in only a few statements on each page. This offset the disadvantage of an increase in bulk of the schedule that would have been avoided if a matrix had been used to record the responses.

In any research project there is a degree of suspicion about the motives of the research worker. This has understandably increased in subnormality hospitals as a result of recent criticism, and the opening paragraph of the statement of the nurses at Farleigh Hospital indicates the concern that is felt:[3]

> We, the nurses of Farleigh Hospital, feel strongly that we are now in a position which leaves us defenceless against, and wide open to, unfair criticism from people who are inexperienced in the care of subnormal people, and who are also hypersensitive and prone to exaggeration.

It was decided not to ask questions in three areas which have proved contentious in previous projects and which were not essential for analysis in this study. These areas relate to father's occupation, political affiliation and religious beliefs. In fact, the latter two areas have proved so inflammatory in a study of student nurses in general hospitals that the GNC felt obliged in their annual report for 1970–1 to offer an explanation as to why such questions were asked.[4] These three areas were, therefore, excluded.

Not one person who was contacted refused either to co-operate or to fill in all items in the schedule. This may be regarded as an informal indicator of the effectiveness of the ground-work of Stage II, referred to above.

3　Sample error

The basis of sampling is described in chapter 4. With a stratified sample, as used in this study, there were two possible sources of error:

1　discrepancy in the proportion of ward grades within the sample compared to the population from which the sample was drawn; and

2　discrepancy in the characteristics of staff within each ward grade of the sample compared to the population from which the sample was drawn.

Table A.1 presents the figures relating to the first possibility.

As the figures for the two groups are approximately the same,

Table A.1 Total ward grade percentage figures for the Gateshire Region compared to sample percentage figures

Ward grade	Total (N = 1,167) (%)	Sample (N = 227) (%)
Registered	20	21
Enrolled	26	25
Training	13	14
Assistant	41	41
Total	100	100

Note. All percentages have been rounded off.

it was not felt necessary to weight the respondent figures to ensure that each ward grade was represented in the correct proportion. However, there is a possibility of error in the characteristics of staff within each ward grade.

From experience in the field it was felt that the sample would be deficient in the numbers of part-time staff represented. This was because they were the hardest group of staff to contact, owing to the wide variation in the number of hours and the times at which they were worked. To test this Table 3.21 was consulted.[5] Data for part-time staff in this table is presented in the form of whole-time equivalents, and this was reworked on the assumption that one part-time nurse contributes two-thirds of a working week. Table A.2 compares the percentage figures for part-time staff within each ward grade that were obtained from this method to those in the sample.

Table A.2 indicates that part-time staff are underrepresented in

Table A.2 Ward grade, staff working part-time in the total and sample populations in the Gateshire Region (percentage)

Ward grade	Total	Sample
Registered	18	11
Enrolled	35	9
Training	3	—
Assistant	43	20

I

the sample. It is doubtful that a substantial proportion of those missed are either male or on the night shift. There is only a small number of part-time male staff and the night shift were easily contacted. Those underrepresented will therefore tend to be female staff working part-time on the day shift.

The sample respondent figures, however, were not adjusted to acount for this underrepresented category, as the numbers of ward staff on which the percentage figures have been based differ considerably. For example, after Table 3.21 was reworked, the total number of ward staff came to 1,246 compared to 1,169 in the sampling frame. Differences were also found in the numbers in each ward grade. The differences in percentage are therefore only suggestive of the deficiency, and could not be used to provide appropriate weights. However, the qualification that part-time female day staff are underrepresented must be borne in mind.

4 Attitude and behaviour

'Attitude' has been used in this study as referring to a person's feelings either for or against a psychological object,[6] in this case the treatment of mentally handicapped patients. Textbooks on social psychology, however, introduce two further dimensions into their discussions on attitude – what a person believes about the psychological object (cognition) and their behavioural intentions towards that psychological object (conation).[7]

In an attempt to predict behaviour, frameworks are then constructed on the basis of various permutations of these three dimensions. Such frameworks are often elaborate and conceptually intricate. The problem they have to cope with, however, is basically simple: what people say does not necessarily accord with what they do. The reason for this can be found both in the nature of the attitude scale to which the person responds and in the nature of behaviour.

First, the nature of the attitude scale. This often measures a person's feelings towards a class of people or objects and not to a specific person or object. An example is given by Fishbein:[8]

> One frequently measures a subject's attitudes toward 'Negroes' and then attempts to predict his behaviour with respect to a particular Negro individual. However, it is unlikely that the subject's beliefs about this particular Negro individual are even

similar to his beliefs about 'Negroes in general'. Clearly if a subject were asked to describe a 'Negro' he would give a very different set of responses than if he were asked to describe Martin Luther King or Cassius Clay.

It is misleading to infer from a person's responses to the general his responses to the particular. The attitude statements used in this study, therefore, show a nurse's feelings towards the treatment of mentally handicapped patients in general, but not feelings towards the treatment of any particular patient.

Second, the nature of behaviour. This is concisely presented in Kurt Lewin's formula:

$$B = F (P, E).$$

Here behaviour (B) is a function (F) of the interaction between the person (P) and his environment (E).[9] The complex and intricate nature of the environmental part of the formula (E) when applied to a hospital is shown by the checklist in Appendix 3. This checklist conveys the multiple factors that may impinge upon the nurse in the hospital environment. The behaviour of the nurse on the ward is often a compromise between conflicting constraints.

A nurse may take, and say he has, great pride in the patients looking neat and respectable. But if there are no clean shirts, and the laundry cannot supply any more, then pyjama jackets might have to be used as an alternative. Although what the nurse said about liking patients to be respectably dressed does not accord with how he dressed them, this does not mean what he said was invalid. The possibility of situations such as this means that responses to attitude statements are assumed valid and qualified by the statement 'other things being equal' when an attempt to predict behaviour from such responses is made.

This often tenuous link between expressed attitude and actual behaviour, especially in a specific situation, means that proposals forwarded on the basis of responses to attitude statements have to be concerned with creating an environment which facilitates not only the adoption, but also the application, of such proposals. These two considerations have guided the recommendations outlined. There is, however, a further point that must be raised.

Throughout this report an attempt has been made to prevent value judgments from colouring the discussion. However, in forwarding recommendations on staff attitudes to the treatment of patients, it is necessary to state what is considered the 'best' and 'most desirable' attitude for staff to hold. King, Raynes and Tizard were faced with a similar decision when discussing the implications of their study on patterns of residential care. In deciding the 'best' residential environment, the criteria they used was 'where we would prefer that we ourselves or our children might be brought up'.[10] A similar rule-of-thumb criterion has been used in deciding that an optimistic orientation to the treatment of mentally handicapped patients is 'better' than a pessimistic orientation. The rationalisation for this is that an optimistic orientation is more likely to encourage a flexible approach to the needs of patients, thus enabling patients to realise their potential.

5 Tables showing responses of trained and untrained ward staff to the individual attitude statements

Two χ^2 statistics are quoted in the tables. The first, χ_1^2, distinguishes between certainty and uncertainty. The second, χ_2^2, between agreement and disagreement. An estimate of χ^2 for the whole table may be obtained by adding the two separate statistics and their degrees of freedom.

1 Over the years the type of patient has become more difficult to care for:

	Disagree	Uncertain	Agree	No.
Trained	23	5	32	60
Untrained	64	14	58	136
Total	87	19	90	196

$\chi_1^2 = 0 \cdot 18$, N.S.; $\chi_2^2 = 1 \cdot 72$, N.S.

2 Doctors in this hospital just don't know what it is like on the ward first thing in the morning:

	Disagree	Uncertain	Agree	No.
Trained	13	2	45	60
Untrained	12	21	103	136
Total	25	23	148	196

$\chi_1^2 = 5 \cdot 89$, P < $0 \cdot 02$;
$\chi_2^2 = 4 \cdot 48$, P < $0 \cdot 05$.

3 Therapy can achieve little with low-grade patients:

	Disagree	Uncertain	Agree	No.
Trained	38	9	13	60
Untrained	57	13	66	136
Total	95	22	79	196

$\chi_1^2 = 1\cdot24$, N.S.
$\chi_2^2 = 11\cdot54$, P < 0·001.

4 Promiscuity and mental subnormality go hand in hand:

	Disagree	Uncertain	Agree	No.
Trained	26	17	17	60
Untrained	40	32	64	136
Total	66	49	81	196

$\chi_1^2 = 0\cdot51$, N.S.
$\chi_2^2 = 5\cdot95$, P < 0·02.

5 Once a nurse has been trained in mental subnormality, he has all the knowledge he needs for the care of patients:

	Disagree	Uncertain	Agree	No.
Trained	50	1	9	60
Untrained	74	11	51	136
Total	124	12	60	196

$\chi_1^2 = 2\cdot99$, P < 0·1.
$\chi_2^2 = 11\cdot90$, P < 0·001.

6 Patients in this hospital can respond to care:

	Disagree	Uncertain	Agree	No.
Trained	1	1	58	60
Untrained	4	5	127	136
Total	5	6	185	196

$\chi_1^2 = 0\cdot56$, N.S.
$\chi_2^2 = 0\cdot29$, N.S.

7 Nursing experience should be appreciated by doctors:

	Disagree	Uncertain	Agree	No.
Trained	0	3	57	60
Untrained	0	2	134	136
Total	0	5	191	196

$\chi_1^2 = 2·09$, N.S.
χ_2^2 not possible.

8 Routine habit-training is essential for patients:

	Disagree	Uncertain	Agree	No.
Trained	1	2	57	60
Untrained	1	4	131	136
Total	2	6	188	196

$\chi_1^2 = 0·02$, N.S.
$\chi_2^2 = 0·36$, N.S.

9 No one really knows why patients improve:

	Disagree	Uncertain	Agree	No.
Trained	36	9	15	60
Untrained	36	37	63	136
Total	72	46	78	196

$\chi_1^2 = 3·45$, P < 0·1.
$\chi_2^2 = 15·79$, P < 0·001.

10 When looking after patients, ability and common sense are more important than formal training:

	Disagree	Uncertain	Agree	No.
Trained	11	10	39	60
Untrained	5	4	127	136
Total	16	14	166	196

$\chi_1^2 = 11·83$, P < 0·001.
$\chi_2^2 = 15·00$, P < 0·001.

11   Patients should be sterilised:

	Disagree	Uncertain	Agree	No.
Trained	34	7	19	60
Untrained	55	26	55	136
Total	89	33	74	196

$\chi_1^2 = 1\cdot65$, N.S.
$\chi_2^2 = 2\cdot89$, P $< 0\cdot1$.

12   It is best to isolate low-grade patients from those who are not so bad:

	Disagree	Uncertain	Agree	No.
Trained	18	9	33	60
Untrained	36	19	81	136
Total	54	28	114	196

$\chi_1^2 = 0\cdot04$, N.S.
$\chi_2^2 = 0\cdot33$, N.S.

13   Patients should not be treated like young children:

	Disagree	Uncertain	Agree	No.
Trained	13	9	38	60
Untrained	33	27	76	136
Total	46	36	114	196

$\chi_1^2 = 0\cdot65$, N.S.
$\chi_2^2 = 0\cdot39$, N.S.

14   The conditions of hospital wards are as good as they can be with the type of patient living there:

	Disagree	Uncertain	Agree	No.
Trained	32	0	28	60
Untrained	32	8	96	136
Total	64	8	124	196

$\chi_1^2 = 29\cdot02$, P $< 0\cdot001$.
$\chi_2^2 = 14\cdot61$, P $< 0\cdot001$.

15   Kindness is more important than a therapeutic programme for patients:

	Disagree	Uncertain	Agree	No.
Trained	20	6	34	60
Untrained	12	14	110	136
Total	32	20	144	196

$x_1^2 = 3.93$, N.S.
$x_2^2 = 18.62$, P < 0.001.

16   Mental subnormality often leads to mental illness:

	Disagree	Uncertain	Agree	No.
Trained	38	7	15	60
Untrained	29	47	60	136
Total	67	54	75	196

$x_1^2 = 10.93$, P < 0.001.
$x_2^2 = 20.39$, P < 0.001.

17   We cannot expect to understand the odd behaviour of patients:

	Disagree	Uncertain	Agree	No.
Trained	31	9	20	60
Untrained	47	11	78	136
Total	78	20	98	196

$x_1^2 = 2.17$, P < 0.01.
$x_2^2 = 7.89$, P < 0.01.

18   Most patients will never know right from wrong:

	Disagree	Uncertain	Agree	No.
Trained	32	6	22	60
Untrained	57	9	70	136
Total	89	15	92	196

$x_1^2 = 0.67$, N.S.
$x_2^2 = 3.13$, P < 0.1.

19 Little can be done to help low-grade patients to improve:

	Disagree	Uncertain	Agree	No.
Trained	47	2	11	60
Untrained	65	13	58	136
Total	112	15	69	196

$\chi_1^2 = 2\cdot29$, N.S.
$\chi_2^2 = 13\cdot27$, P < 0·001.

20 There is a sharp dividing line between 'normal' and 'mentally subnormal':

	Disagree	Uncertain	Agree	No.
Trained	28	6	26	60
Untrained	23	17	96	136
Total	51	23	122	196

$\chi_1^2 = 0\cdot25$, N.S.
$\chi_2^2 = 18\cdot90$, P < 0·001.

21 It is not right to expect untrained staff to help patients with therapy:

	Disagree	Uncertain	Agree	No.
Trained	42	1	17	60
Untrained	83	10	43	136
Total	125	11	60	196

$\chi_1^2 = 2\cdot54$, N.S.
$\chi_2^2 = 0\cdot52$, N.S.

22 Patients can often lead a life which is just as valuable as anyone else's:

	Disagree	Uncertain	Agree	No.
Trained	8	6	46	60
Untrained	20	15	101	136
Total	28	21	147	196

$\chi_1^2 = 4\cdot61$, N.S.
$\chi_2^2 = 8\cdot16$, N.S.

I*

6 Discriminatory power value

The total score range on the Treatment Orientation Scale, containing twenty-two statements each scored from one to five, is from 22 to 110. These two extremes reflect the 'ideal' optimist and pessimist

Table A.3   *Discriminatory power ranking of attitude statements in the Treatment Orientation Scale*

Statement	Order	DP*
Therapy can achieve little with low-grade patients	1=	2·5
It is best to isolate low-grade patients from those who are not so bad	1=	2·5
Little can be done to help low-grade patients to improve	1=	2·5
Most patients will never know right from wrong	4	2·4
Promiscuity and mental subnormality go hand in hand	5	2·3
The conditions of hospital wards are as good as they can be with the type of patient living there	6	2·2
Patients should be sterilised	7=	2·1
There is a sharp dividing line between 'normal' and 'mentally subnormal'	7=	2·1
Mental subnormality often leads to mental illness	9	1·9
We cannot expect to understand the odd behaviour of patients	10	1·8
Once a nurse has been trained in mental subnormality, he has all the knowledge he needs for the care of patients	11	1·7
When looking after patients, ability and common sense are more important than formal training	12=	1·6
Kindness is more important than a therapeutic programme for patients	12=	1·6
It is not right to expect untrained staff to help patients with therapy	14	1·4
No one really knows why patients improve	15	1·3
Patients should not be treated like young children	16	0·9
Over the years the type of patient has become more difficult to care for	17	0·6
Patients in this hospital can respond to care	18	0·5
Patients can often lead a life which is just as valuable as anyone else's	19	0·3
Nursing experience should be appreciated by doctors	20=	0
Routine habit-training is essential for patients	20=	0
Doctors in this hospital just don't know what it is like on the ward first thing in the morning	22	−0·3

* Discriminatory power statistic.

respectively. It is possible, however, to obtain a score of 66 by checking the Uncertain box, scored three, for all statements, and this introduces an element of reservation in analysis. This is emphasised by the discriminatory power statistic obtained for each statement.

Table A.3 shows the discriminatory value[11] obtained for each statement, and ranks each statement relative to others in the scale in terms of their ability to discriminate between high and low scorers. Ideally, what is required is a value of four, for this shows that high and low scorers responded to a statement at opposite ends of the response categories, i.e. one group strongly agreed and the other strongly disagreed depending on the phrasing of the question. To obtain a value of four for a statement is rare, but it is important that the value is as high as possible, for it indicates that persons of different attitude complexion are responding differently to the statement. A low value, on the other hand, shows that a statement is not particularly good at discriminating between such persons. From Table A.3 it can be seen that approximately one-third of the statements in the Treatment Orientation Scale (7 out of 22) have a discriminatory power value that is less than one. This, allied to the mean score value of 64·2 for the total sample, indicates that results obtained from the scale must be treated with caution.

Such a qualification does not apply when statements are looked at out of the context of a scale, i.e. when responses to individual statements become the focus of interest.

Notes

Chapter 1 The policy background

1 *Better Services for the Mentally Handicapped*, Department of Health and Social Security/Welsh Office, Cmnd 4683, HMSO, June 1971.
2 See *Management Arrangements for the Reorganised National Health Service*, HMSO, 1972.
3 *Report of the Royal Commission on Mental Illness and Mental Deficiency*, Cmnd 169, HMSO, 1957.
4 The Mental Health Act subsequently added the classification of 'subnormality' to 'severe subnormality'.
5 This pamphlet is undated, but to the writer's recollection, it was current during the sitting of the Royal Commission. Internal references make it clear that it was published after 1950 and before the Mental Health Act.
6 J. Tizard, *Community Services for the Mentally Handicapped*, Oxford University Press, 1964, pp. 89–90.
7 Tizard, op. cit., pp. 133–4.
8 *Report of the Committee of Inquiry into Allegations of Ill-treatment of Patients and other Irregularities at the Ely Hospital, Cardiff*, Cmnd 3795, HMSO, March 1969.
9 P. Morris, *Put Away: A Sociological Study of Institutions for the Mentally Retarded*, Routledge & Kegan Paul, 1969.
10 Morris, op. cit., pp. 216–20.
11 Morris, op. cit., p. 307.
12 Morris, op. cit., p. xxi (introduction by Professor Peter Townsend).
13 See correspondence in *The Times* and the *Guardian* in May 1972.
14 *Report of the Farleigh Committee of Inquiry*, Cmnd 4557, HMSO, 1971.
15 *MIND Report No. 1*, National Association for Mental Health, 1971.
16 *Sunday Times*, 26 June 1971.
17 The Briggs Report, *Report of Committee on Nursing*, Cmnd 5115, HMSO, October 1972; Summary of Recommendations.
18 A. Kushlick, 'A Comprehensive Service for the Mentally Subnormal', in H. Freeman and J. Farndale (eds), *New Aspects of the Mental Health Services*, Pergamon Press, 1967.
19 Sir Keith Joseph, 'Some Mental Health Needs', Hargreaves Memorial Lecture, 1972 (taken down verbatim).
20 *Report of the Care of Patients at South Ockenden Hospital*, HMSO, May 1974.
21 *The Times*, 16 May 1974.

Chapter 2   The hospitals

1 See Appendix 3.
2 For an outline of the stages of the project, see Appendix 2.
3 Actual bed occupation figure was somewhat lower. See chapter 3.
4 See Circular HM (60) 66.

Chapter 3   Life on the wards: needs and resources

1 See P. Morris, *Put Away: A Sociological Study of Institutions for the Mentally Retarded*, Routledge & Kegan Paul, 1969, chapter 5, pp. 84–95.
2 Two such cases were, however, observed at times not recorded on the schedules.
3 See V. B. Barkers and D. Johnson, 'The presentation of acute hospital in-patient statistics', *Hospital and Health Services Review*, January 1973, pp. 11–14.
4 *Health and Personal Social Services Statistics for England and Wales, 1972*, HMSO, 1973, table 4.2.
5 See further evidence on pp. 180–2.
6 The sample also included mentally subnormal patients in hospitals for the mentally ill. These were counted on a 100 per cent basis because of the small numbers. In the Survey Region there were 315 such patients.
7 *Health and Personal Social Services Statistics for England and Wales, 1972*, HMSO, 1973, table 1.2.
8 See B. Ward, K. Jones, W. Taylor and C. P. Gore, *Census of Psychiatric Patients in the Leeds Regional Hospital Board Area*, 28 May 1963, para. 39 (obtainable from the Yorkshire Regional Health Authority).
9 See K. Jones and A. Tillotson, *The Adult Population of Epileptic Colonies*, Social Studies in Epilepsy No. 3, British Epilepsy Association, 1965, table X and following discussion on 'domestic difficulties'.
10 See p. 103 for a case of incontinence actually provoked by the behaviour of nursing staff in a hospital in another Region.
11 In view of the transfer of educational functions in hospitals for the mentally handicapped to Local Education Authorities in April 1970, it is curious that the census form puts the word 'school' in inverted commas.
12 This calculation is based on the following data: 77 children were under the age of 10; 218 were aged 10–19; assuming half the latter group to be aged 10–14, this gives a total of 186 children to be subtracted.
13 *Health and Personal Social Services Statistics, for England and Wales, 1972*, HMSO, 1973, tables 3.13 and 9.2. 'Psychiatric nurses' include nurses in mental hospitals and hospitals for the mentally handicapped. Part-time staff rendered in whole-time equivalents (WTE).
14 See Table 4.13.

Chapter 4 Nursing attitudes

1 Department of Health and Social Security, *National Health Service Hospital Advisory Service: Annual Report for 1969–70*, HMSO, 1971, p. 16.
2 Cmnd 4683, p. 1.
3 Cmnd 4683, p. 9.
4 An account of the research design for the Treatment Orientation Scale, together with a note on some methodological problems is given in Appendix 5.
5 P. Morris, *Put Away: A Sociological Study of Institutions for the Mentally Retarded*, Routledge & Kegan Paul, 1969, p. 50.
6 R. D. King, N. Raynes and J. Tizard, *Patterns of Residential Care*, Routledge & Kegan Paul, 1971, p. 177.
7 J. Tizard, *Community Services for the Mentally Handicapped*, Oxford University Press, 1964, pp. 135–6; A. Kushlick, 'Evaluating Residential Services for Mentally Handicapped Children', unpublished paper.
8 Morris, op. cit., p. 116.
9 Maureen Oswin, *The Empty Hours*, Allen Lane, 1971, pp. 162–9.
10 Morris, op. cit., pp. 116–18.
11 Oswin, op. cit., p. 161.
12 A. V. Cicourel, *Method and Measurement in Sociology*, Free Press, New York, 1964, p. 114.
13 For a fuller discussion of the points raised here, see Appendix 5.
14 See Table 3.20.
15 All nurses in training, whether student or pupil, spend at least six weeks of their course working on the night shift. As the majority of their time, however, is spent working the various day shifts, they have all been classified as day shift.
16 The Salmon Report, *Report of the Committee on Senior Nursing Staff Structure*, HMSO, 1966.
17 Although both student and pupil nurses were coded together as 'nurses in training' for purposes of punching, it was possible to go back to the interview schedules to differentiate between the two groups.
18 Some of the 'untrained' group had received short induction courses or in-service training, but the term 'trained' as used here refers only to a formal and systematic training leading to registration or enrolment by examination.
19 Kathleen Jones, *Mental Health and Social Policy, 1845–1959*, Routledge & Kegan Paul, 1967, pp. 43–90; and N. O'Connor and J. Tizard, *The Social Problem of Mental Deficiency*, Pergamon Press, 1956, pp. 1–11.
20 Morris, op. cit., p. 21.

Chapter 5 Problems of the 'back wards'

1 'Ward 99', by John Brown, was published in an extended form in *Nursing Times*, vol. 68, no. 7, 7 February 1972.

2 Where practical, night staff dressed patients in the same clothes they had worn the previous day, and these were changed for freshly-laundered items after breakfast.

3 Or believed to be tough. A consultant dermatologist assures us that modes of shaving, in fact, have no effect on hair growth.

4 See N. R. Bartel and S. L. Guskin, 'A Handicap as a Social Phenomenon', in W. Cruikshank (ed.), *Psychology of Exceptional Children and Youth*, Prentice-Hall, Englewood Cliffs, New Jersey, 1971, p. 82.

5 J. Castell and P. Mittler, 'Intelligence of patients in subnormality hospitals: a survey of admissions, 1961', *British Journal of Psychiatry*, vol. 3, 1965, pp. 219–25.

6 Bartel and Guskin, op. cit.; and S. L. Guskin, 'The influence of labelling upon the perception of subnormality in mentally defective children', *American Journal of Mental Deficiency*, vol. 67, 1962, pp. 402–6.

7 The limitations of intelligence testing and other problems of labelling in relation to mentally handicapped people are discussed by Peter Townsend in the foreword to P. Morris, *Put Away: A Sociological Study of Institutions for the Mentally Retarded*, Routledge & Kegan Paul, 1969.

8 See E. Spradtin and F. L. Giradeau, 'The Behaviour of Moderately and Severely Retarded Persons', in N. R. Ellis, *International Review of Research into Mental Retardation*, vol. 1, Academic Press, New York, 1966, p. 286.

9 G. Plowman, 'The Structure and Dynamics of Institutions', in *New Thinking about Institutional Care*, Report of the Oxford Conference of the Association of Social Workers, Association of Social Workers, 1967, p. 17.

10 See M. Kohn, *Class and Conformity: a Study of Values*, Dorsey Press, Homewood, Illinois, 1969, where it is argued that working-class parents are more likely to evolve authoritarian patterns of child management than middle-class parents.

11 The use of models connected with animal behaviour is confirmed by a research worker from another university, who cited examples of their use by medical as well as nursing staff. A consultant asserted that patients had to be 'broken in like horses' before they became docile and tractable; and an older charge nurse could remember a medical superintendent who contended that patients had to be 'tamed' like wild animals.

12 Cf. R. J. Capobianco and D. Cole, 'Social behaviour of mentally retarded children', *American Journal of Mental Deficiency*, vol. 64, 1960, pp. 638–51; and J. Tizard, *Community Services for the Mentally Handicapped*, Oxford University Press, 1964, pp. 121–2.

13 Cf. M. N. Carol, 'Junk collection among mentally retarded patients', *American Journal of Mental Deficiency*, vol. 72, no. 6, 1968, pp. 308–14; and Erving Goffman's description of 'stashing' by mental patients in *Asylums*, Anchor Books ed., Doubleday, New York, 1961, pp. 248–54.

14 On exchange as a generalised social process, see P. Blau, *Exchange and Power in Social Life*, Wiley, New York, 1964.

15 Cf. Morris, op. cit., pp. 117–18.

16 Goffman, op. cit., p. 9.

17 R. L. Coser, 'Alienation and Social Structure', in E. Friedson (ed.), *The Hospital in Modern Society*, Free Press, New York, 1963.

18 See J. Tizard, 'The Role of Social Institutions in the Causation, Prevention and Alleviation of Mental Retardation', unpublished paper, pp. 57–8; and K. Jones, 'The Development of Institutional Care', in *New Thinking about Institutions*, ASW Conference Report, 1967; the latter suggests that the emphasis on order and submissiveness in institutional inmates may have a political origin.

19 For a discussion of the concept of 'ward intruders' in general hospitals, see K. Jones, 'Society as the client', *Medical Social Work Conference Supplement*, vol. 19, no. 3, June 1966. The problems of introducing voluntary workers are further discussed in chapter 6.

20 C. Perrow, *et al.*, *Organisation for Treatment*, Tavistock, 1970, see technology as a major variable in treatment and distinguish between restrictive technologies and those allowing for growth.

21 J. Tizard, *Community Services for the Mentally Handicapped*, Oxford University Press, 1964, part IV.

22 R. D. King, N. Raynes and J. Tizard, *Patterns of Residential Care*, Routledge & Kegan Paul, 1971.

23 A. Bandura, 'Social Learning and Identification Process', in D. A. Goslin and D. C. Glass (eds), *Handbook of Socialization Theory and Research*, Rand McNally, Chicago, 1967.

24 For an introduction, see W. R. Bion, 'Experiences in groups', *Human Relations*, vols 1–2, 1948–50; A. P. Hare, E. Borgatta and R. F. Bales, *Small Groups: Studies in Social Interaction*, Knopf, 1955; E. A. Shils, 'The Study of the Primary Group', in D. Lerner and H. Lasswell (eds), *The Policy Sciences*, Stanford University Press, 1951.

25 S. Bijou, 'A Functional Analysis of Retarded Development', in N. R. Ellis, *International Review of Research into Mental Retardation*, vol. 1, Academic Press, New York, 1966, p. 2.

26 See, e.g., E. Estes, *Learning Theory and Mental Retardation*, Academic Press, New York, 1970, pp. 39–41; and E. Spradkin and F. L. Giradeau, 'The Behaviour of Moderately and Severely Retarded Persons', in Ellis, op. cit., vol. 1, p. 286. For discussion of the application of behaviour modification principles, see L. P. Ullman and L. Krasner, *Case Studies in Behaviour Modification*, Holt, Rinehart & Winston, 1965; L. P. Ullman and L. Krasner, *Research in Behaviour Modification: New Developments and Implications*, Holt, Rinehart & Winston, 1965; F. Kanfer and J. Phillips, *Learning Foundations of Behaviour Therapy*, Wiley, 1970, especially chapters 6 and 7.

27 T. Ayllon and N. Azrin, *The Token Economy*, Appleton-Century-Crofts, 1968; and T. Ayllon and J. Mitheal, 'The psychiatric nurse as a behavioural engineer', *Journal of Experimental Analysis of Behaviour*, vol. 3, 1959, pp. 323–4.

28 R. Tharp and R. Wetzel, *Behaviour Modification in the Natural Environment*, Academic Press, New York, 1970.

29 J. S. Birnbrauer and J. Lawler, 'Token reinforcement for learning', *Mental Retardation*, vol. 2, 1964, pp. 275–9.

30 R. Gray and J. Kasteller, 'The effects of social reinforcement and training on institutionalised mentally retarded children', *American Journal of Mental Deficiency*, vol. 74, 1969, pp. 50–6.

Chapter 6 Hospital and community

1 *The Voluntary Worker in the Social Services*, Allen & Unwin, 1969. Report of Committee of the National Council for Social Service and the National Institute for Social Work Training; chairman, Geraldine M. Aves.

2 See 'The National Community Development Project: Inter-project Report, 1974' (obtainable from the Centre for Environmental Studies, London).

3 HM (62) 29, *Voluntary Help in Hospitals*; HM (68) 22, *Voluntary Service in Hospitals for Young People*; HM (69) 58, *Voluntary Help in Hospitals*.

4 HM (65) 104, para. 10.

5 Cmnd 4683, HMSO, 1971, para. 188.

6 Cmnd 3995, HMSO, 1969, para. 555.

7 P. Morris, *Put Away: A Sociological Study of Institutions for the Mentally Retarded*, Routledge & Kegan Paul, 1969, p. 314.

8 Morris, op. cit., p. 194.

9 'Parole' is an inappropriate term in days of informal admission. However, it is retained here because most hospitals still use it.

10 For Table 6.6 and all subsequent usage:
   UL = urban large   US = urban small
   RL = rural large   RS = rural small
   UM = urban medium-sized
   RM = rural medium-sized

11 Milan has 62 per cent of its patients over 40 years old; Laker has 39 per cent of its patients over 40 years old.

12 At Milan 39 per cent of patients' homes are 31 + miles distant; at Laker 29 per cent of patients' homes are 31 + miles distant.

13 This figure refers to Laker, Lamprey and Marathon only. The Milan Grange League of Friends was still in its early stages at the time of the survey.

14 Except for the effects on the two small units, South House and Sycamore House, noted on p. 150.

15 Some women from the local village have recently been drawn in as domestic staff.

16 'Parole' patients here refers not to those patients with staff sanction to leave the hospital alone, but to those who actually do. The numerical difference can be large.

17 An urban/social equivalent of Outward Bound.

18 The existence of a physician superintendent with offices in the

hospital, and of a nurses' training school, seem particularly important.

19 The two small hospitals are excluded from this table. See p. 150.

20 Cf. the Aves Report, which specifies that 'except in an emergency, volunteers should not be used, in public services, to undertake manual or domestic work for which paid workers are normally employed' (p. 195).

21 Morris, op. cit., p. 208.

22 Morris, op. cit., p. 208.

23 The phrase comes from Gresham Sykes's *Society of Captives*, Princeton University Press, 1958, where it relates to prisons; but it is equally applicable to hospitals.

24 From 1974 all hospital social work posts were transferred to the local authority Social Services Departments, though the rights of social workers now in post are safeguarded.

Chapter 7 Community care

1 The Association of Psychiatric Social Workers and the Association of Mental Welfare Officers were merged in the new British Association of Social Workers in 1971.

2 See *Health and Welfare: The Development of Community Care*, Ministry of Health, Cmnd 1973, HMSO, 1963.

3 *Better Services for the Mentally Handicapped* (Cmnd 4683, HMSO, 1971) asks for 'homes, not hostels', but the older term is retained in this discussion for clarity.

4 Cmnd 4683, paras 159–60 and table 5.

5 *Better Services for the Mentally Handicapped*, op. cit., p. 43.

6 The hospital sample reported in Table 7.9 is dealt with more fully in chapter 3.

7 Our observations confirmed the findings of N. O'Connor and J. Tizard, *The Social Problem of Mental Deficiency*, Pergamon Press, 1956, pp. 91 ff.

8 These figures exclude one new hostel for 15 children, for which records were not available.

9 M. J. Bayley, *Mental Handicap and Community Care*, Routledge & Kegan Paul, 1973, pp. 228–35, 316–17, 320–1, 328.

10 The total number of discharges from all the hospitals in the survey area during this period was 57. The 20 cases followed up were a random sample taken from this group.

Chapter 8 The idea and the reality

1 Board of Education and Board of Control, *Report of Joint Committee on Mental Deficiency*, 1929.

2 *Report of the Farleigh Hospital Committee of Inquiry*, Cmnd 4557, HMSO, 1971, appendix 5.

3 For a fuller discussion of this issue, see K. Jones, 'Violence and the mentally handicapped', *New Society*, 31 January 1974.

4 *Report of the Royal Commission on the Care of the Feeble-minded*, HMSO, 1908.

5 Personal papers of Dame Ellen Pinsent (lent by her daughter, the late Lady Adrian).

6 Ministry of Health, *Departmental Committee on Sterilisation*, HMSO, 1934.

7 Hansard, 20 June 1934; Speech by Sir Hilton Young, Minister of Health.

8 See R. A. Scott and J. D. Douglas, *Theoretical Perspectives on Deviancy*, Basic Books, New York, 1972; H. Becker, *Outsiders: Studies in the Sociology of Deviance*, Free Press, New York, 1963; D. Matza, *Becoming Deviant*, Prentice-Hall, Englewood Cliffs, New Jersey, 1969; E. M. Lemert, *Human Deviance, Social Problems and Social Control*, Prentice-Hall, Englewood Cliffs, New Jersey, 1967.

9 J. Tizard, *Community Care of the Mentally Handicapped*, Oxford University Press, 1964, p. 5.

10 Tizard, op. cit., p. 6.

11 Tizard, op. cit., p. 7.

12 J. H. G. Itard, *L'Éducation du Sauvage d'Aveyron*, 1799.

13 S. Powell Davies, *The Social Control of the Mentally Deficient*, Constable, 1930 (English edition).

14 Mental Deficiency Act, 1913, section 1(d).

15 Mental Health Act, 1959, section 4.

16 Cmnd 4683, para. 10.

17 Cmnd 4683, paras 125–38.

18 Education (Handicapped Children) Act, 1970, section 1.

19 P. Morris, *Put Away: A Sociological Study of Institutions for the Mentally Retarded*, Routledge & Kegan Paul, 1969, p. 307.

20 *Report of the Committee on Nursing*, chairman, Professor Asa Briggs, Cmnd 5115, HMSO, 1972, paras 557–65 and recommendation 74.

21 Central Council for Education and Training in Social Work, *Discussion Document on Residential Care*, February 1973; CCETSW Paper 3, *Residential Work is Part of Social Work*, November 1973. Both obtainable from CCETSW, Clifton House, Euston Road, London NW1 2RS.

22 *Residential Work is Part of Social Work*, op. cit., paras 99–106.

23 E. M. Topliss, 'Staff Communications, Relationships and Deployment in a Geriatric Hospital', paper presented to the Medical Sociology Section of the British Sociological Association, York, November 1972.

24 M. Martin, *Colleagues or Competitors: the Supplementary Professions to Medicine*, Occasional Papers in Social Administration, G. Bell, 1965.

25 D. Thomas 'A new caring profession—is it necessary?', *Nursing Times*, 26 July 1973, pp. 969–72.

Chapter 9 Summary and conclusions

1 H. Somers and A. Somers, *Doctors, Patients and Health Insurance*, Brookings Institution, Washington, DC, 1961, p. 12.
2 M. J. Bayley, *Mental Handicap and Community Care*, Routledge & Kegan Paul, 1973, pp. 228–35, 316–17, 320–1, 328.

Postscript

1 *The Times*, 15 May 1975.

Appendix 4: job description for community service organisers

1 See *Organisers of Voluntary Services in Hospitals*, King's Fund, 1968; *Volunteers in Hospitals*, King's Fund, 1971.

Appendix 5: notes on the methodology of the attitude survey

1 See Allen L. Edwards, *Techniques of Attitude Scale Construction*, Appleton-Century-Crofts, Century Psychology Series, New York, 1957, pp. 13–14.
2 A. N. Oppenheim, *Questionnaire Design and Attitude Measurement*, Heinemann, 1966, pp. 117–18.
3 *Report of the Farleigh Hospital Committee of Inquiry*, Cmnd 4557, HMSO, 1967, p. 38.
4 *Annual Report* of the General Nursing Council, 1970–1, pp. 31–2.
5 See p. 63.
6 L. L. Thurstone, 'The Measurement of Social Attitudes', in K. Thomas (ed.), *Attitudes and Behaviour*, Penguin, 1971, p. 21.
7 See, e.g., P. F. Secord and C. W. Backman, *Social Psychology*, McGraw-Hill, New York, 1964, pp. 97–100; D. Krech, R. S. Crutchfield and E. L. Ballachey, *Individual in Society*, McGraw-Hill, New York, 1962.
8 M. Fishbein, 'Attitude and the Prediction of Behaviour', in K. Thomas (ed.), *Attitudes and Behaviour*, Penguin, 1971, p. 58.
9 For a discussion of the relevance of Lewin's formula to attitude theory, see N. C. Weisberg's commentary on M. L. DeFleur and F. R. Westie's 'Attitude as a Scientific Concept', in Thomas (ed.), op. cit., pp. 312–16.
10 R. D. King, N. Raynes and J. Tizard, *Patterns of Residential Care*, Routledge & Kegan Paul, 1971, p. 199.
11 Rensis Likert, 'The Method of Constructing an Attitude Scale', in M. Fishbein (ed.), *Attitude Theory and Measurement*, Wiley, New York, 1967, p. 95.

Index

Admission and discharge, 47–9
Ahmad, Ajmal, xviii
Alienation, 117–19
Ambivalence, 23
Animals, image of patients as, 109, 246
Architecture, hospital, 6, 8, 20, 205
Ashman, Sally, xviii
Assessment, 105–6, 207–8, 217–20
Asylums, see Goffman, Erving
Attitude and behaviour, relationship between, 232–4
Attitude survey, nursing staff, chapter 4 and appendix 5 *passim*
  methodology, 229–41, 251
  sample error, 230–2
  statement responses, 234–9
Aves Report, 131, 248, 249
Ayllon, T. and Azrin, N.,129, 247

'Back wards', Back Ward Syndrome, 24–5, 26–7, chapter 5 *passim*
Baker, A. A., *see* Hospital Advisory Service
Bandura, Albert, 126, 247
Barkers, V. B. and Johnson, D., 244
Barr, Pamela, xviii
Bartel, N. R. and Guskin, S. L., 246
Barton, W. Russell, 5
Bayley, Michael, 180, 184, 209, 249, 251
Becker, Howard, 250
Bedding in hospital wards, 43
Beddington, John, xviii
Bed-space, 43, 214
Behaviour modification, *see*

Learning theory
Behaviour problems, 57–9
Better Services for the Mentally Handicapped, xv, xvi, 1–3, 6, 13–16, 18, 28, 32–3, 67–8, 131, 155, 157–62, 180, 185, 193–4, 243, 245, 249, 250
Bijou, Sidney, 127, 247
Bion, Wilfred, 247
Birnbrauer, J. S. and Lawler, J., 129, 248
Blau, Peter, 247
Briggs Committee, 196, 201, 215, 243, 250
British Association for the Retarded, 209
Brock Committee, *see* Sterilisation
Brooklands Study, 4–5, 13, 69, 126, *see also* Normalisation
Brown, John, 245, *see also* 'Ward 99'
Burt, Cyril, 10

Capobianco, R. J. and Cole, D., 246
'Caring profession', *see* Briggs Committee
Carol, M. N., 246
Case conference at Maple Grange, appendix 1 *passim*
Castell, J., 246
Castle, Barbara, 15, 216
Central Council for Education and Training in Social Work, 197, 250
Chronically Sick and Disabled Persons Act, 1970, 154
Cicourel, A. V., 70, 245
Circular HM(62)29, 248

Circular HM(65)104, 6, 9, 131, 248
Circular HM(68)22, 248
Circular HM(69)58, 248
Clinical model of mental handicap, 10
Clothing, *see* Patients' clothing
CMH course, 200–2, 210, 214–15
'Colonial' defence, 21–2, 28
Community Care, 1, 4, 8, 10, 13–15, 24, 33, 40, 96, 131, chapter 7 *passim*, 183, 215–16
Community Care Blue Book, 1963, *see Health and Welfare*
Community Development Projects, 131, 248
Community Liaison Officers, *see* Community Service Organisers
Community, problems of definition, 152–3
Community relations hospitals, chapter 6 *passim* hostels, 177 training centres, 166–7
Community Service Organisers, 153, 208, 209, 214–15, 226–7, 251
Community services, *see* Community Care, Social Services Departments
Community Services for the Mentally Handicapped, 6, 243, 247, 250, *see also* Brooklands Study
Conflict, conflict theory, 10, 14, 195–6
Consultants, *see* Medical staff
Continuous process care, 60–2, 193
Coser, Rose Laub, 118, 247
Crossman, R. H. S., xv, 11, 20, 185

Davies, Stanley Powell, 192, 250
Day care, 1, 2, 6, 157–9, *see also* Training centres

Definition of mental handicap, 10–11, 105–6, 191–5, *see also* Assessment, Nursing staff
Department of Health and Social Security (DHSS), 41, 49–50, 131, 207, 209–11
Dependency survey, 59–62
Deviancy theory, 10–11, 190–1, 192
Deviant behaviour, 23, 109–10
Discharge, *see* Admission and discharge
Discriminatory power statistic, 240–1
Doctors, *see* Medical staff

Economic formulation, 188, 202
Educational standards
of hospital patients, 55–6
of hostel residents, 172
of trainees, 163–4
Education (Handicapped Children) Act, 1970, 194, 209, 250
Education, meaning of in activity classification, 56
Edwards, A. L., 251
Eliot, T. S., xvii
Ely Hospital inquiry, xv, 6–9, 24, 25, 37, 122, 132, 243
Estes, E., 247
Eugenic formulation, 188–9

Family contacts, family networks of patients, *see* Relatives of patients
Family model of care, *see* Parental role
Farleigh Hospital inquiry, xv, 12, 24, 25, 37, 186–7, 230, 243, 249, 251
'Federal' administration of hospitals, 207, 214
Finance, 1, 13–14, 188, 216, *see also* Economic formulation
Fishbein, Martin, 232, 251
Follett, Hilary, xviii

Food in hospitals, 26, 29–30, 41, 98, 104
Foster care, 1
Furnishing and decoration
finance for, 185
in hospitals, 162
in hostels, 168–9
in training centres, 162

Gateshire survey
initiation of, xv, xvii, xviii
organisation of, 16–17, 221–2
reaction to, 213–16
see also Methodology
General Election 1970, effects of, 11
General Nursing Council, 230, 251
Goffman, Erving, 5, 117, 152, 246, 247
'Good' wards, 23–5, 96
Gorman, Vincent, xviii
Gray and Kasteller, 129, 248
Grey Document, see Management Arrangements for the Reorganised National Health Service
Group homes, 1
Group roles, 21

Hare, A. P., Borgatta, E. and Bales, R. F., 247
Health and Personal Social Services Statistics for England/England and Wales, 48, 49, 244
Health and Welfare: the Development of Community Care, 156–62, 183, 249
Health Services and Public Health Act, 1968, 154
Homosexuality, 27
Hospital administrators, hospital secretaries, 35–7
Hospital Advisory Service, xv, xvi, 11, 20, 30, 32, 67, 245
Hospital/Community links, chapter 6 *passim*
Hospital Management

Committees, 147, 221, 223, 224
Hospitals, chapters 2–6 *passim*
future plans for, 1, *see also Better Services*
laundry services, 30, *see also* Incontinence
local names for, 19–20
location, 19–20, 205, 207, 248
objectives and ideology, 31–4
outings, *see* Social activities
siting and building, 18–20
size, 18
social sub-systems, 223–5
urban/rural differentiation, 19, 37, 38, 39, 152–3
see also Leadership, Medical staff, Nursing staff, Patients, Rehabilitation, Staff attitudes, Transport, Tripartite administration, Ward conditions
Hostels, 1, 4, 6, 10, 15, 16, 61, 155, 159–61, 167–77, 175–6, 208, 210, 249
Howe, Geoffrey, 11

Idea and reality, xvii, 10, 15, chapter 8 *passim*
Ill-treatment of patients, *see* Violence
Incontinence
in hospitals, 43, 44, 45, 53–4, 59–61, 62, 97, 98–9, 103
in hostels, 169, 170
in training centres, 163
Industrial therapy, *see* Rehabilitation
Inertia, 8, 9, 15, 117, 151–2, 202–4, 211
Inquiries, Government, 23, *see also* Ely, Farleigh, South Ockenden inquiries
Institutional Neurosis, see Barton, W. Russell
Integration, meaning of, 4, *see also* National Health Service Reorganisation Act

Intelligence quotient,
  intelligence testing, 10, 11,
  56, 62, 105–6, 191–2
Isolation of hospitals, *see*
  Hospitals (location),
  Transport
Itard, J. H. G., 192, 250

Jones, Kathleen, xvii, 245, 247,
  249, *see also* Ward, B., *et al.*
Jones, Kathleen and Tillotson,
  Aileen, 244
Joseph, Keith, xv, 11–12, 14,
  243

Kanfer, F. and Phillips, J., 247
King, R. D., Raynes, N. and
  Tizard, J., 5, 69, 126, 234,
  245, 247, 251
Kohn, M., 246
Krech, D., Crutchfield, R. S.
  and Ballanchey, E. L., 251
Kushlick, Albert, 13, 243

Labelling, labelling theory,
  19–20, 23, 106
Labour White Paper (draft,
  1970), xv
Leadership, 34–7, 185, 189, 206,
  see also Tripartite adminis-
  tration
League of Friends, 27, 29, 132,
  135, 139–40, 143–7
Learning opportunities for
  patients, 113–16
Learning theory, 127–9
Lemert, E. M., 250
Length of stay in hospital, 53
Lewin, Kurt, 233
Lewis, John, xviii
Likert, R., Likert Scale, 93, 228,
  251
Lions Club, 145
Local authorities, *see*
  Community Care, Social
  Services Departments
Local Authority Social Services
  Act, 1970, 154, 179–80,
  197

Local Government Act, 1972,
  local government
  reorganisation, 16, 155
Location of hospitals, *see*
  Hospitals (location)
Locked wards, 42
Lodgings, 161, 178–9, 183, 184
Longevity of mentally
  handicapped, 1, 51–2
'Low-grade' patients, *see* 'Back
  wards'

*Management Arrangements for
  the Reorganised National
  Health Service*, 3, 243
Martin, Margaret, 250
Matza, David, 250
Medical care in hostels, 182, 184,
  208
Medical model of patients, 105
Medical Officers of Health,
  attitudes to Social Services
  Departments, 154–6
Medical records at Maple
  Grange, 218–20
Medical staff in hospitals, 1, 2,
  34–7, 62–3, 65–6, 123–4,
  206, 217–20
Medical treatment of mentally
  handicapped, 193–4
Mental Deficiency Act, 1913, 14,
  192, 250
'Mental disorder', meaning of, 3
Mental handicap and mental
  illness, 89, 94, 219–20
Mental Health Act, 1959, 3–4,
  14, 34, 103–4, 243, 250
Mental Health Review Tribunals,
  3
Methodology of Gateshire
  survey, xvii-xviii, 16–17,
  70–1, 132–3, 228–41, 251
MIND, *see* National
  Association for Mental
  Health
Mittler, Peter, 246
Mixed hospital groups, 41
Modelling theory, 126–7

Monitoring and evaluation, need
for, 211
Morris, Dr Pauline, 11, 13, *see
also Put Away*
Multidisciplinary management,
see Leadership, Tripartite
administration

National Association for Mental
Health, 209, 243
National Council for Civil
Liberties, 3
National Health Service Act,
1946, 14, 154–5
National Health Service
Reorganisation Act, 1973,
3, 13–15, 16, 31, 35, 41, 155
National Institute for Social
Work, 201
National Society for Mentally
Handicapped Children, 14,
135, 144, 145
Neighbourhood contacts, 132,
140–7
Normalisation, 23, 31, 190, *see
also* Brooklands Study
Nurses, 20–2, 63–4, 66, chapters
4 and 5 *passim*
assistant nurses, 70–80, 82–3,
103, 110, 231
enrolled nurses, 70–80, 82–3,
118, 119, 231
length of service, 75, 80
on night shift, 72–4, 79, 92,
245
part-time, 72–4, 92, 231–2
qualifications, 75–9, 80
registered nurses, 69, 70–80,
82, 102, 109, 118, 122, 231
training, 70–80, 82, 83, 93,
102, 231, 245
Nursing administration, 34–7
Nursing staff, attitudes of
to case conference, 217–20
to nursing, 115–19, 120–1,
123, 196
to patients, 20–3, 68–9, 80–95,
103, 105–6, 115, *see also*
Staff-patient relationships

to rehabilitation staff, 39–40
to Treatment Orientation
Scale, 81–95

Objectives, ideology, goals of
hospital staff, 31–4
Occupational therapists,
occupational therapy, 27–8,
32, 56, 108, *see also*
Rehabilitation staff
Oppenheim, A. N., 251
Oswin, Maureen, 69, 245
Out-patient services, 1, 2, 47

Parental role, 22, 108–10, 114,
120
Parole, 141, 142, 248
Parsons, Talcott, 69
Paternalism, 22
Patient attitudes, 110–13
Patient census, 1970, 49–59
Patient-patient interaction, 26–7,
113, 225
Patients' clothing, 30–1, 246
Patients' compliance, 110–13
Patterns of Residential Care, see
King, Raynes and Tizard
Pay to trainees, 166–7; for
hospital patients, *see*
Pocket money
Perrow, C., 247
Physical mobility
of hospital patients, 54
of hostel residents, 170
of trainees, 163
Physician superintendents, 9–10,
34–7, 248–9
Physiotherapy, *see* Rehabilitation
Pilot training programme, *see*
CMH course
Pinsent, Mrs Hume (Dame
Ellen Pinsent), 189, 250
Planning for the mentally
handicapped, *see Better
Services*, Ten-year plans
Plowman, Garth, 109, 245
Pocket money for patients, 25,
28–9

Population
  hospitals, 47–62
  hostels, 169–74
  training centres, 163–4
Powell Davies, *see* Davies,
  Stanley Powell
Press attitudes, 11–12, 13
Priorities, 18, 188, 206
Privacy, lack of in hospitals, 43,
  45
Privileges, *see* Sanctions and
  privileges
Professional lack of fit, 195–6
Promiscuity, fears of in mentally
  handicapped, 11, 83–6,
  93–4
Pseudonyms, use of in survey, 17
Psychiatric social workers, 155,
  161
Psychiatrists, *see* Medical staff
Public attitudes, 11, 12, 186,
  203–4
'Public school' defence, 22
Punishment, *see* Sanctions and
  privileges
Put Away, xv, xvi, xviii, 9–11,
  40, 42, 46, 69, 132, 151–2,
  195–6, 205, 243, 244, 245,
  246, 247, 248, 249, 250

Radnor Commission, 1904–8,
  189, 191, 250
Rea, Dr Norman, xviii
Red Cross, 145
Reduction in hospital beds, 1
Referral on discharge, 49–50,
  177, 180–2, 184, 249
Rehabilitation, 32, 194, 225
Rehabilitation staff, 10, 39–40,
  64–6, 122, 124, 129–30, 140,
  195–202, 209–10, 250
Reinforcement, *see* Learning
  theory
Relatives of patients, 132,
  133–40, 166
Reorganisation of National
  Health Service, *see* National
  Health Service,
  Reorganisation Act

Repitition as learning, 107–8,
  see also Treatment
  techniques
Research, future, 210
Research scheme, *see* Gateshire
  survey, Methodology
Resource allocation, 31–2, *see
  also* Finance, Priorities
Revans, R., 11
RNMS, *see* Nurses
Rotary Clubs, 145
Routine, use and abuse of, 21,
  119–24, 125, 205
Royal Commission on Mental
  Illness and Mental
  Deficiency, 1954–7, 3, 4, 6,
  243

Salmon Report, Salmon
  structure, 77, 80, 218, 245
Sanctions and privileges, 25–6,
  127–9
Scapegoating
  patients, 21
  staff, 8
Schoolchildren, use of as
  volunteers, 143–4, 147
Scott, R. A. and Douglas, J. D.,
  250
Secord, P. F. and Backman,
  C. W., 251
Segregation of the mentally
  handicapped, 3
Sexual behaviour of patients,
  83–6, 93–4
Shaving as part of ward ritual,
  98–101, 107, 109–10, 125,
  246
Shils, E. A., 247
Shortage, *see* Economic
  formulation
Signposting, 19, 214
Sladden, Susan, xviii
Smith, Sandra, xviii
Social activities
  in hospitals, 27–8, 147–9
  in hostels, 175
  in training centres, 166

Social policy, process of, xvi–xvii

Social Services Act, *see* Local Authority Social Services Act

Social Services Departments, xviii, 15–16, 68, 153, chapter 7 *passim*, 208–9, 211, *see also* Community Care

Social skills of trainees, 163–4, 166

Social workers, 1, 65, 155, 161–2, 177, 178–80, 196, 197–202, 209, 249

Social work, social workers, in hospitals, 64–5, 180–1, 201, 249, *see also* Rehabilitation staff

Somers, H. and Somers, A., 207, 251

South Ockenden Hospital inquiry, 15, 243

Speech handicaps, 55, 59–62, 65, 171

Speech therapists, speech therapy, 40, 65, 209–10, *see also* Rehabilitation staff

Spradtin, E. and Girardeau, F. L., 246, 247

Staff attitudes, 21–6, 29, 30–4, chapter 4 *passim*, *see also* Medical staff, Nursing staff, Routine, 'Colonial' defence, 'Public school' defence, Parental role, Ambivalence, Objectives

Staff attitudes at Cloverfield and Blackbrick, 9–10

Staff morale, 185, 186, 205

Staff-patient relationships, 224 in hospitals, 20–3, 103–6, 108–13, *see also* Nursing staff in hostels, 168 in training centres, 165

Stage I, Stage II, Stage III, *see* Gateshire survey

State enrolled nurses, *see* Nurses

Sterilisation of mentally handicapped, 83, 85, 109, 250

Stigma, 203–4, *see also* Public attitudes

'Structure for coping', *see* Bayley, Michael

Sykes, Gresham, 249

Ten-year plans, local authority, 156–62

Terman-Merrill tests, 105

Tharp and Wetzel, 129, 248

Thomas, Derek, 202, 250

Thurstone, L. L., 251

Tizard, J., 4–6, 13, 191–2, 245, 247, 249, *see also* Brooklands Study, Normalisation

Topliss, Eda, 199–200, 250

Townsend, Peter, xv, 10–11, 13, 246

Training new proposals for, 200–2, 210, 214–15 nurses' attitude to, *see* Nursing staff present training of nurses, *see* Nurses

Training arm, training branch, 10–13, 40, 195–6, *see also* *Put Away*, Rehabilitation staff

Training centres, 2, 4, 6, 56, 156–8, 162–7, 209

Training centre staff, 164, 165

Transmitted deprivation, theory of, 189–90

Transport to hospitals, 19, 207, 214 to training centres, 165

Treatment Orientation Scale, 68–9, 70, 80–5, 228–41

Treatment techniques, 106–8, 126–30

Tredgold, R. F., 83

Tripartite administration in hospitals, 34–7, 41, 206

Ullman, L. P. and Krasner, L., 247
Urben, Elizabeth, xviii

'Vicious circle', *see* Back Ward Syndrome
Villa-system in hospitals, advantages and disadvantages of, 18–19
Violence, 7, 11, 25, 41, 103, 109, 112, 186–7, 249
Voluntary organisations, 40–1, 144–6, 150–1, *see also* League of Friends, Red Cross, Rotary Clubs, etc
Voluntary Service Organisers, 131, 143, 144, 153, 208, 251, *see also* Community Service Organisers
Voluntary workers in hospitals, 132, 144–7, 151, 152, 248, 251

'Ward 99', 97–104, 125, 191, 245
Ward, B., Jones, K., Taylor, W. and Gore, C. P., 244
Ward conditions, 42–6, 96–7, *see also* 'Back wards'
'Ward intruders', 122, 247
Ward staff, *see* Nursing staff
Weisberg, N. C., 251
White Paper, 1971 (Cmnd 4683), *see Better Services*
Women's Institutes, 145
Wood Report, 1929, 185, 249
Work
  in hostels, 174–5
  in training centres, 165–7
Wrongful detention, alleged, 3, 11–12
WRVS, WVS, 27, 132

Year Book of Social Policy in Britain, xvi

Routledge Social Science Series

Routledge & Kegan Paul   London and Boston

68–74 Carter Lane   London EC4V 5EL
9 Park Street   Boston   Mass 02108

Contents

International Library of Sociology 3
General Sociology 3
Foreign Classics of Sociology 4
Social Structure 4
Sociology and Politics 4
Foreign Affairs 5
Criminology 5
Social Psychology 5
Sociology of the Family 6
Social Services 7
Sociology of Education 7
Sociology of Culture 8
Sociology of Religion 9
Sociology of Art and Literature 9
Sociology of Knowledge 9
Urban Sociology 9
Rural Sociology 10
Sociology of Industry and Distribution 10
Documentary 11
Anthropology 11
Sociology and Philosophy 12
International Library of Anthropology 12
International Library of Social Policy 12
International Library of Welfare and Philosophy 13
Primary Socialization, Language and Education 13
Reports of the Institute of Community Studies 13
Reports of the Institute for Social Studies in Medical Care 14
Medicine, Illness and Society 14
Monographs in Social Theory 14
Routledge Social Science Journals 15

Authors wishing to submit manuscripts for any series in
this catalogue should send them to the Social Science Editor,
Routledge & Kegan Paul Ltd, 68–74 Carter Lane,
London EC4V 5EL

● Books so marked are available in paperback
All books are in Metric Demy 8vo format (216 × 138mm approx.)

International Library of Sociology

General Editor John Rex

GENERAL SOCIOLOGY

Barnsley, J. H. The Social Reality of Ethics. *464 pp.*
Belshaw, Cyril. The Conditions of Social Performance. *An Exploratory Theory. 144 pp.*
Brown, Robert. Explanation in Social Science. *208 pp.*
● Rules and Laws in Sociology. *192 pp.*
Bruford, W. H. Chekhov and His Russia. *A Sociological Study. 244 pp.*
Cain, Maureen E. Society and the Policeman's Role. *326 pp.*
Gibson, Quentin. The Logic of Social Enquiry. *240 pp.*
Glucksmann, M. Structuralist Analysis in Contemporary Social Thought. *212 pp.*
Gurvitch, Georges. Sociology of Law. *Preface by Roscoe Pound. 264 pp.*
Hodge, H. A. Wilhelm Dilthey. *An Introduction. 184 pp.*
Homans, George C. Sentiments and Activities. *336 pp.*
Johnson, Harry M. Sociology: *a Systematic Introduction. Foreword by Robert K. Merton. 710 pp.*
Mannheim, Karl. Essays on Sociology and Social Psychology. *Edited by Paul Keckskemeti. With Editorial Note by Adolph Lowe. 344 pp.*
Systematic Sociology: *An Introduction to the Study of Society. Edited by J. S. Erös and Professor W. A. C. Stewart. 220 pp.*
Martindale, Don. The Nature and Types of Sociological Theory. *292 pp.*
●**Maus, Heinz.** A Short History of Sociology. *234 pp.*
Mey, Harald. Field-Theory. *A Study of its Application in the Social Sciences. 352 pp.*
Myrdal, Gunnar. Value in Social Theory: *A Collection of Essays on Methodology. Edited by Paul Streeten. 332 pp.*
Ogburn, William F., and **Nimkoff, Meyer F.** A Handbook of Sociology. *Preface by Karl Mannheim. 656 pp. 46 figures. 35 tables.*
Parsons, Talcott, and **Smelser, Neil J.** Economy and Society: *A Study in the Integration of Economic and Social Theory. 362 pp.*
●**Rex, John.** Key Problems of Sociological Theory. *220 pp.*
Discovering Sociology. *278 pp.*
Sociology and the Demystification of the Modern World. *282 pp.*
●**Rex, John** (Ed.) Approaches to Sociology. *Contributions by Peter Abell, Frank Bechhofer, Basil Bernstein, Ronald Fletcher, David Frisby, Miriam Glucksmann, Peter Lassman, Herminio Martins, John Rex, Roland Robertson, John Westergaard and Jock Young. 302 pp.*
Rigby, A. Alternative Realities. *352 pp.*
Roche, M. Phenomenology, Language and the Social Sciences. *374 pp.*
Sahay, A. Sociological Analysis. *220 pp.*
Urry, John. Reference Groups and the Theory of Revolution. *244 pp.*
Weinberg, E. Development of Sociology in the Soviet Union. *173 pp.*

FOREIGN CLASSICS OF SOCIOLOGY

●**Durkheim, Emile.** Suicide. *A Study in Sociology. Edited and with an Introduction by George Simpson. 404 pp.*
Professional Ethics and Civic Morals. *Translated by Cornelia Brookfield. 288 pp.*
●**Gerth, H. H.,** and **Mills, C. Wright.** From Max Weber: *Essays in Sociology. 502 pp.*
●**Tönnies, Ferdinand.** Community and Association. *(Gemeinschaft und Gesellschaft.) Translated and Supplemented by Charles P. Loomis. Foreword by Pitirim A. Sorokin. 334 pp.*

SOCIAL STRUCTURE

Andreski, Stanislav. Military Organization and Society. *Foreword by Professor A. R. Radcliffe-Brown. 226 pp. 1 folder.*
Coontz, Sydney H. Population Theories and the Economic Interpretation. *202 pp.*
Coser, Lewis. The Functions of Social Conflict. *204 pp.*
Dickie-Clark, H. F. Marginal Situation: *A Sociological Study of a Coloured Group. 240 pp. 11 tables.*
Glaser, Barney, and **Strauss, Anselm L.** Status Passage. *A Formal Theory. 208 pp.*
Glass, D. V. (Ed.) Social Mobility in Britain. *Contributions by J. Berent, T. Bottomore, R. C. Chambers, J. Floud, D. V. Glass, J. R. Hall, H. T. Himmelweit, R. K. Kelsall, F. M. Martin, C. A. Moser, R. Mukherjee, and W. Ziegel. 420 pp.*
Jones, Garth N. Planned Organizational Change: *An Exploratory Study Using an Empirical Approach. 268 pp.*
Kelsall, R. K. Higher Civil Servants in Britain: *From 1870 to the Present Day. 268 pp. 31 tables.*
König, René. The Community. *232 pp. Illustrated.*
●**Lawton, Denis.** Social Class, Language and Education. *192 pp.*
McLeish, John. The Theory of Social Change: *Four Views Considered. 128 pp.*
Marsh, David C. The Changing Social Structure of England and Wales, 1871-1961. *288 pp.*
Mouzelis, Nicos. Organization and Bureaucracy. *An Analysis of Modern Theories. 240 pp.*
Mulkay, M. J. Functionalism, Exchange and Theoretical Strategy. *272 pp.*
Ossowski, Stanislaw. Class Structure in the Social Consciousness. *210 pp.*
Podgórecki, Adam. Law and Society. *About 300 pp.*

SOCIOLOGY AND POLITICS

Acton, T. A. Gypsy Politics and Social Change. *316 pp.*
Hechter, Michael. Internal Colonialism. *The Celtic Fringe in British National Development, 1536–1966. About 350 pp.*
Hertz, Frederick. Nationality in History and Politics: *A Psychology and Sociology of National Sentiment and Nationalism. 432 pp.*

Kornhauser, William. The Politics of Mass Society. *272 pp. 20 tables.*

Laidler, Harry W. History of Socialism. *Social-Economic Movements: An Historical and Comparative Survey of Socialism, Communism, Co-operation, Utopianism; and other Systems of Reform and Reconstruction. 992 pp.*

Lasswell, H. D. Analysis of Political Behaviour. *324 pp.*

Mannheim, Karl. Freedom, Power and Democratic Planning. *Edited by Hans Gerth and Ernest K. Bramstedt. 424 pp.*

Mansur, Fatma. Process of Independence. *Foreword by A. H. Hanson. 208 pp.*

Martin, David A. Pacifism: *an Historical and Sociological Study. 262 pp.*

Myrdal, Gunnar. The Political Element in the Development of Economic Theory. *Translated from the German by Paul Streeten. 282 pp.*

Wootton, Graham. Workers, Unions and the State. *188 pp.*

FOREIGN AFFAIRS: THEIR SOCIAL, POLITICAL AND ECONOMIC FOUNDATIONS

Mayer, J. P. Political Thought in France from the Revolution to the Fifth Republic. *164 pp.*

CRIMINOLOGY

Ancel, Marc. Social Defence: *A Modern Approach to Criminal Problems. Foreword by Leon Radzinowicz. 240 pp.*

Cain, Maureen E. Society and the Policeman's Role. *326 pp.*

Cloward, Richard A., and **Ohlin, Lloyd E.** Delinquency and Opportunity: *A Theory of Delinquent Gangs. 248 pp.*

Downes, David M. The Delinquent Solution. *A Study in Subcultural Theory. 296 pp.*

Dunlop, A. B., and **McCabe, S.** Young Men in Detention Centres. *192 pp.*

Friedlander, Kate. The Psycho-Analytical Approach to Juvenile Delinquency: *Theory, Case Studies, Treatment. 320 pp.*

Glueck, Sheldon, and **Eleanor.** Family Environment and Delinquency. *With the statistical assistance of Rose W. Kneznek. 340 pp.*

Lopez-Rey, Manuel. Crime. *An Analytical Appraisal. 288 pp.*

Mannheim, Hermann. Comparative Criminology: *a Text Book. Two volumes. 442 pp. and 380 pp.*

Morris, Terence. The Criminal Area: *A Study in Social Ecology. Foreword by Hermann Mannheim. 232 pp. 25 tables. 4 maps.*

Rock, Paul. Making People Pay. *338 pp.*

●**Taylor, Ian, Walton, Paul,** and **Young, Jock.** The New Criminology. *For a Social Theory of Deviance. 325 pp.*

SOCIAL PSYCHOLOGY

Bagley, Christopher. The Social Psychology of the Epileptic Child. *320 pp.*

Barbu, Zevedei. Problems of Historical Psychology. *248 pp.*

Blackburn, Julian. Psychology and the Social Pattern. *184 pp.*

●**Brittan, Arthur.** Meanings and Situations. *224 pp.*

Carroll, J. Break-Out from the Crystal Palace. *200 pp.*

●**Fleming, C. M.** Adolescence: Its Social Psychology. *With an Introduction to recent findings from the fields of Anthropology, Physiology, Medicine, Psychometrics and Sociometry. 288 pp.*

● The Social Psychology of Education: *An Introduction and Guide to Its Study. 136 pp.*

Homans, George C. The Human Group. *Foreword by Bernard DeVoto. Introduction by Robert K. Merton. 526 pp.*

● Social Behaviour: *its Elementary Forms. 416 pp.*

●**Klein, Josephine.** The Study of Groups. *226 pp. 31 figures. 5 tables.*

Linton, Ralph. The Cultural Background of Personality. *132 pp.*

●**Mayo, Elton.** The Social Problems of an Industrial Civilization. *With an appendix on the Political Problem. 180 pp.*

Ottaway, A. K. C. Learning Through Group Experience. *176 pp.*

Ridder, J. C. de. The Personality of the Urban African in South Africa. *A Thematic Apperception Test Study. 196 pp. 12 plates.*

●**Rose, Arnold M.** (Ed.) Human Behaviour and Social Processes: *an Interactionist Approach. Contributions by Arnold M. Rose, Ralph H. Turner, Anselm Strauss, Everett C. Hughes, E. Franklin Frazier, Howard S. Becker, et al. 696 pp.*

Smelser, Neil J. Theory of Collective Behaviour. *448 pp.*

Stephenson, Geoffrey M. The Development of Conscience. *128 pp.*

Young, Kimball. Handbook of Social Psychology. *658 pp. 16 figures. 10 tables.*

SOCIOLOGY OF THE FAMILY

Banks, J. A. Prosperity and Parenthood: *A Study of Family Planning among The Victorian Middle Classes. 262 pp.*

Bell, Colin R. Middle Class Families: *Social and Geographical Mobility. 224 pp.*

Burton, Lindy. Vulnerable Children. *272 pp.*

Gavron, Hannah. The Captive Wife: *Conflicts of Household Mothers. 190 pp.*

George, Victor, and **Wilding, Paul.** Motherless Families. *220 pp.*

Klein, Josephine. Samples from English Cultures.
  1. Three Preliminary Studies and Aspects of Adult Life in England. *447 pp.*
  2. Child-Rearing Practices and Index. *247 pp.*

Klein, Viola. Britain's Married Women Workers. *180 pp.*
  The Feminine Character. *History of an Ideology. 244 pp.*

McWhinnie, Alexina M. Adopted Children. *How They Grow Up. 304 pp.*

● **Myrdal, Alva,** and **Klein, Viola.** Women's Two Roles: *Home and Work. 238 pp. 27 tables.*

Parsons, Talcott, and **Bales, Robert F.** Family: Socialization and Interaction Process. *In collaboration with James Olds, Morris Zelditch and Philip E. Slater. 456 pp. 50 figures and tables.*

SOCIAL SERVICES

Bastide, Roger. The Sociology of Mental Disorder. *Translated from the French by Jean McNeil. 260 pp.*

Carlebach, Julius. Caring For Children in Trouble. *266 pp.*

Forder, R. A. (Ed.) Penelope Hall's Social Services of England and Wales. *352 pp.*

George, Victor. Foster Care. *Theory and Practice. 234 pp.*
  Social Security: *Beveridge and After. 258 pp.*

George, V., and **Wilding, P.** Motherless Families. *248 pp.*

●**Goetschius, George W.** Working with Community Groups. *256 pp.*

Goetschius, George W., and **Tash, Joan.** Working with Unattached Youth. *416 pp.*

Hall, M. P., and **Howes, I. V.** The Church in Social Work. *A Study of Moral Welfare Work undertaken by the Church of England. 320 pp.*

Heywood, Jean S. Children in Care: *the Development of the Service for the Deprived Child. 264 pp.*

Hoenig, J., and **Hamilton, Marian W.** The De-Segregation of the Mentally Ill. *284 pp.*

Jones, Kathleen. Mental Health and Social Policy, 1845-1959. *264 pp.*

King, Roy D., Raynes, Norma V., and **Tizard, Jack.** Patterns of Residential Care. *356 pp.*

Leigh, John. Young People and Leisure. *256 pp.*

Morris, Mary. Voluntary Work and the Welfare State. *300 pp.*

Morris, Pauline. Put Away: *A Sociological Study of Institutions for the Mentally Retarded. 364 pp.*

Nokes, P. L. The Professional Task in Welfare Practice. *152 pp.*

Timms, Noel. Psychiatric Social Work in Great Britain (1939-1962). *280 pp.*

● Social Casework: *Principles and Practice. 256 pp.*

Young, A. F. Social Services in British Industry. *272 pp.*

Young, A. F., and **Ashton, E. T.** British Social Work in the Nineteenth Century. *288 pp.*

SOCIOLOGY OF EDUCATION

Banks, Olive. Parity and Prestige in English Secondary Education: a Study in Educational Sociology. *272 pp.*

Bentwich, Joseph. Education in Israel. *224 pp. 8 pp. plates.*

●**Blyth, W. A. L.** English Primary Education. *A Sociological Description.*
  1. Schools. *232 pp.*
  2. Background. *168 pp.*

Collier, K. G. The Social Purposes of Education: *Personal and Social Values in Education. 268 pp.*

7

Dale, R. R., and **Griffith, S.** Down Stream: *Failure in the Grammar School.* *108 pp.*

Dore, R. P. Education in Tokugawa Japan. *356 pp. 9 pp. plates.*

Evans, K. M. Sociometry and Education. *158 pp.*

● **Ford, Julienne.** Social Class and the Comprehensive School. *192 pp.*

Foster, P. J. Education and Social Change in Ghana. *336 pp. 3 maps.*

Fraser, W. R. Education and Society in Modern France. *150 pp.*

Grace, Gerald R. Role Conflict and the Teacher. *About 200 pp.*

Hans, Nicholas. New Trends in Education in the Eighteenth Century. *278 pp. 19 tables.*

● Comparative Education: *A Study of Educational Factors and Traditions.* *360 pp.*

Hargreaves, David. Interpersonal Relations and Education. *432 pp.*

● Social Relations in a Secondary School. *240 pp.*

Holmes, Brian. Problems in Education. *A Comparative Approach. 336 pp.*

King, Ronald. Values and Involvement in a Grammar School. *164 pp.*

School Organization and Pupil Involvement. *A Study of Secondary Schools.*

● **Mannheim, Karl,** and **Stewart, W. A. C.** An Introduction to the Sociology of Education. *206 pp.*

Morris, Raymond N. The Sixth Form and College Entrance. *231 pp.*

● **Musgrove, F.** Youth and the Social Order. *176 pp.*

● **Ottaway, A. K. C.** Education and Society: An Introduction to the Sociology of Education. *With an Introduction by W. O. Lester Smith. 212 pp.*

Peers, Robert. Adult Education: *A Comparative Study. 398 pp.*

Pritchard, D. G. Education and the Handicapped: *1760 to 1960. 258 pp.*

Richardson, Helen. Adolescent Girls in Approved Schools. *308 pp.*

Stratta, Erica. The Education of Borstal Boys. *A Study of their Educational Experiences prior to, and during, Borstal Training. 256 pp.*

Taylor, P. H., Reid, W. A., and **Holley, B. J.** The English Sixth Form. *A Case Study in Curriculum Research. 200 pp.*

SOCIOLOGY OF CULTURE

Eppel, E. M., and **M.** Adolescents and Morality: *A Study of some Moral Values and Dilemmas of Working Adolescents in the Context of a changing Climate of Opinion. Foreword by W. J. H. Sprott. 268 pp. 39 tables.*

● **Fromm, Erich.** The Fear of Freedom. *286 pp.*

● The Sane Society. *400 pp.*

Mannheim, Karl. Essays on the Sociology of Culture. *Edited by Ernst Mannheim in co-operation with Paul Kecskemeti. Editorial Note by Adolph Lowe. 280 pp.*

Weber, Alfred. Farewell to European History: *or The Conquest of Nihilism. Translated from the German by R. F. C. Hull. 224 pp.*

SOCIOLOGY OF RELIGION

Argyle, Michael and **Beit-Hallahmi, Benjamin.** The Social Psychology of Religion. *About 256 pp.*

Nelson, G. K. Spiritualism and Society. *313 pp.*

Stark, Werner. The Sociology of Religion. *A Study of Christendom.*
  Volume I. *Established Religion. 248 pp.*
  Volume II. *Sectarian Religion. 368 pp.*
  Volume III. *The Universal Church. 464 pp.*
  Volume IV. *Types of Religious Man. 352 pp.*
  Volume V. *Types of Religious Culture. 464 pp.*

Turner, B. S. Weber and Islam. *216 pp.*

Watt, W. Montgomery. Islam and the Integration of Society. *320 pp.*

SOCIOLOGY OF ART AND LITERATURE

Jarvie, Ian C. Towards a Sociology of the Cinema. *A Comparative Essay on the Structure and Functioning of a Major Entertainment Industry. 405 pp.*

Rust, Frances S. Dance in Society. *An Analysis of the Relationships between the Social Dance and Society in England from the Middle Ages to the Present Day. 256 pp. 8 pp. of plates.*

Schücking, L. L. The Sociology of Literary Taste. *112 pp.*

Wolff, Janet. Hermeneutic Philosophy and the Sociology of Art. *About 200 pp.*

SOCIOLOGY OF KNOWLEDGE

Diesing, P. Patterns of Discovery in the Social Sciences. *262 pp.*

●**Douglas, J. D.** (Ed.) Understanding Everyday Life. *370 pp.*

●**Hamilton, P.** Knowledge and Social Structure. *174 pp.*

Jarvie, I. C. Concepts and Society. *232 pp.*

Mannheim, Karl. Essays on the Sociology of Knowledge. *Edited by Paul Kecskemeti. Editorial Note by Adolph Lowe. 353 pp.*

Remmling, Gunter W. (Ed.) Towards the Sociology of Knowledge. *Origin and Development of a Sociological Thought Style. 463 pp.*

Stark, Werner. The Sociology of Knowledge: *An Essay in Aid of a Deeper Understanding of the History of Ideas. 384 pp.*

URBAN SOCIOLOGY

Ashworth, William. The Genesis of Modern British Town Planning: *A Study in Economic and Social History of the Nineteenth and Twentieth Centuries. 288 pp.*

Cullingworth, J. B. Housing Needs and Planning Policy: *A Restatement of the Problems of Housing Need and 'Overspill' in England and Wales. 232 pp. 44 tables. 8 maps.*

9

Dickinson, Robert E. City and Region: *A Geographical Interpretation* *608 pp. 125 figures.*
The West European City: *A Geographical Interpretation. 600 pp. 129 maps. 29 plates.*
● The City Region in Western Europe. *320 pp. Maps.*
Humphreys, Alexander J. New Dubliners: *Urbanization and the Irish Family. Foreword by George C. Homans. 304 pp.*
Jackson, Brian. Working Class Community: *Some General Notions raised by a Series of Studies in Northern England. 192 pp.*
Jennings, Hilda. Societies in the Making: *a Study of Development and Re-development within a County Borough. Foreword by D. A. Clark. 286 pp.*
●**Mann, P. H.** An Approach to Urban Sociology. *240 pp.*
Morris, R. N., and **Mogey, J.** The Sociology of Housing. *Studies at Berinsfield. 232 pp. 4 pp. plates.*
Rosser, C., and **Harris, C.** The Family and Social Change. *A Study of Family and Kinship in a South Wales Town. 352 pp. 8 maps.*

RURAL SOCIOLOGY

Chambers, R. J. H. Settlement Schemes in Tropical Africa: *A Selective Study. 268 pp.*
Haswell, M. R. The Economics of Development in Village India. *120 pp.*
Littlejohn, James. Westrigg: *the Sociology of a Cheviot Parish. 172 pp. 5 figures.*
Mayer, Adrian C. Peasants in the Pacific. *A Study of Fiji Indian Rural Society. 248 pp. 20 plates.*
Williams, W. M. The Sociology of an English Village: *Gosforth. 272 pp. 12 figures. 13 tables.*

SOCIOLOGY OF INDUSTRY AND DISTRIBUTION

Anderson, Nels. Work and Leisure. *280 pp.*
●**Blau, Peter M.,** and **Scott, W. Richard.** Formal Organizations: *a Comparative approach. Introduction and Additional Bibliography by J. H. Smith. 326 pp.*
Eldridge, J. E. T. Industrial Disputes. *Essays in the Sociology of Industrial Relations. 288 pp.*
Hetzler, Stanley. Applied Measures for Promoting Technological Growth. *352 pp.*
Technological Growth and Social Change. *Achieving Modernization. 269 pp.*
Hollowell, Peter G. The Lorry Driver. *272 pp.*
Jefferys, Margot, *with the assistance of Winifred Moss.* Mobility in the Labour Market: *Employment Changes in Battersea and Dagenham. Preface by Barbara Wootton. 186 pp. 51 tables.*

Millerson, Geoffrey. The Qualifying Associations: *a Study in Professionalization. 320 pp.*

Smelser, Neil J. Social Change in the Industrial Revolution: *An Application of Theory to the Lancashire Cotton Industry, 1770-1840. 468 pp. 12 figures. 14 tables.*

Williams, Gertrude. Recruitment to Skilled Trades. *240 pp.*

Young, A. F. Industrial Injuries Insurance: *an Examination of British Policy. 192 pp.*

DOCUMENTARY

Schlesinger, Rudolf (Ed.) Changing Attitudes in Soviet Russia.
2. The Nationalities Problem and Soviet Administration. *Selected Readings on the Development of Soviet Nationalities Policies. Introduced by the editor. Translated by W. W. Gottlieb. 324 pp.*

ANTHROPOLOGY

Ammar, Hamed. Growing up in an Egyptian Village: *Silwa, Province of Aswan. 336 pp.*

Brandel-Syrier, Mia. Reeftown Elite. *A Study of Social Mobility in a Modern African Community on the Reef. 376 pp.*

Crook, David, and **Isabel.** Revolution in a Chinese Village: *Ten Mile Inn. 230 pp. 8 plates. 1 map.*

Dickie-Clark, H. F. The Marginal Situation. *A Sociological Study of a Coloured Group. 236 pp.*

Dube, S. C. Indian Village. *Foreword by Morris Edward Opler. 276 pp. 4 plates.*

India's Changing Villages: *Human Factors in Community Development. 260 pp. 8 plates. 1 map.*

Firth, Raymond. Malay Fishermen. *Their Peasant Economy. 420 pp. 17 pp. plates.*

Firth, R., Hubert, J., and **Forge, A.** Families and their Relatives. *Kinship in a Middle-Class Sector of London: An Anthropological Study. 456 pp.*

Gulliver, P. H. Social Control in an African Society: a Study of the Arusha, Agricultural Masai of Northern Tanganyika. *320 pp. 8 plates. 10 figures.*

Family Herds. *288 pp.*

Ishwaran, K. Shivapur. *A South Indian Village. 216 pp.*

Tradition and Economy in Village India: *An Interactionist Approach. Foreword by Conrad Arensburg. 176 pp.*

Jarvie, Ian C. The Revolution in Anthropology. *268 pp.*

Jarvie, Ian C., and **Agassi, Joseph.** Hong Kong. *A Society in Transition. 396 pp. Illustrated with plates and maps.*

Little, Kenneth L. Mende of Sierra Leone. *308 pp. and folder.*

Negroes in Britain. *With a New Introduction and Contemporary Study by Leonard Bloom. 320 pp.*

11

Lowie, Robert H. Social Organization. *494 pp.*
Mayer, Adrian,C. Caste and Kinship in Central India: *A Village and its Region. 328 pp. 16 plates. 15 figures. 16 tables.*
Peasants in the Pacific. *A Study of Fiji Indian Rural Society. 248 pp.*
Smith, Raymond T. The Negro Family in British Guiana: *Family Structure and Social Status in the Villages. With a Foreword by Meyer Fortes. 314 pp. 8 plates. 1 figure. 4 maps.*

SOCIOLOGY AND PHILOSOPHY

Barnsley, John H. The Social Reality of Ethics. *A Comparative Analysis of Moral Codes. 448 pp.*
Diesing, Paul. Patterns of Discovery in the Social Sciences. *362 pp.*
●**Douglas, Jack D.** (Ed.) Understanding Everyday Life. *Toward the Reconstruction of Sociological Knowledge. Contributions by Alan F. Blum. Aaron W. Cicourel, Norman K. Denzin, Jack D. Douglas, John Heeren, Peter McHugh, Peter K. Manning, Melvin Power, Matthew Speier, Roy Turner, D. Lawrence Wieder, Thomas P. Wilson and Don H. Zimmerman. 370 pp.*
Jarvie, Ian C. Concepts and Society. *216 pp.*
Pelz, Werner. The Scope of Understanding in Sociology. *Towards a more radical reorientation in the social humanistic sciences. 283 pp.*
Roche, Maurice. Phenomenology, Language and the Social Sciences. *371 pp.*
Sahay, Arun. Sociological Analysis. *212 pp.*
Sklair, Leslie. The Sociology of Progress. *320 pp.*

International Library of Anthropology
General Editor Adam Kuper

Brown, Paula. The Chimbu. *A Study of Change in the New Guinea Highlands. 151 pp.*
Lloyd, P. C. Power and Independence. *Urban Africans' Perception of Social Inequality. 264 pp.*
Pettigrew, Joyce. Robber Noblemen. *A Study of the Political System of the Sikh Jats. 284 pp.*
Van Den Berghe, Pierre L. Power and Privilege at an African University. *278 pp.*

International Library of Social Policy
General Editor Kathleen Jones

Bayley, M. Mental Handicap and Community Care. *426 pp.*
Butler, J. R. Family Doctors and Public Policy. *208 pp.*
Holman, Robert. Trading in Children. *A Study of Private Fostering. 355 pp.*

Jones, Kathleen. History of the Mental Health Service. *428 pp.*

Thomas, J. E. The English Prison Officer since 1850: *A Study in Conflict. 258 pp.*

Woodward, J. To Do the Sick No Harm. *A Study of the British Voluntary Hospital System to 1875. About 220 pp.*

International Library of Welfare and Philosophy

General Editors Noel Timms and David Watson

● **Plant, Raymond.** Community and Ideology. *104 pp.*

Primary Socialization, Language and Education

General Editor Basil Bernstein

Bernstein, Basil. Class, Codes and Control. *2 volumes.*
  1. *Theoretical Studies Towards a Sociology of Language. 254 pp.*
  2. *Applied Studies Towards a Sociology of Language. About 400 pp.*

Brandis, W., and **Bernstein, B.** Selection and Control. *176 pp.*

Brandis, Walter, and **Henderson, Dorothy.** Social Class, Language and Communication. *288 pp.*

Cook-Gumperz, Jenny. Social Control and Socialization. *A Study of Class Differences in the Language of Maternal Control. 290 pp.*

● **Gahagan, D. M.,** and **G. A.** Talk Reform. *Exploration in Language for Infant School Children. 160 pp.*

Robinson, W. P., and **Rackstraw, Susan D. A.** A Question of Answers. *2 volumes. 192 pp. and 180 pp.*

Turner, Geoffrey J., and **Mohan, Bernard A.** A Linguistic Description and Computer Programme for Children's Speech. *208 pp.*

Reports of the Institute of Community Studies

Cartwright, Ann. Human Relations and Hospital Care. *272 pp.*

● Parents and Family Planning Services. *306 pp.*
  Patients and their Doctors. *A Study of General Practice. 304 pp.*

● **Jackson, Brian.** Streaming: *an Education System in Miniature. 168 pp.*

Jackson, Brian, and **Marsden, Dennis.** Education and the Working Class: *Some General Themes raised by a Study of 88 Working-class Children in a Northern Industrial City. 268 pp. 2 folders.*

Marris, Peter. The Experience of Higher Education. *232 pp. 27 tables.*
  Loss and Change. *192 pp.*

Marris, Peter, and **Rein, Martin.** Dilemmas of Social Reform. *Poverty and Community Action in the United States. 256 pp.*

Marris, Peter, and **Somerset, Anthony.** African Businessmen. *A Study of Entrepreneurship and Development in Kenya. 256 pp.*

Mills, Richard. Young Outsiders: *a Study in Alternative Communities. 216 pp.*

Runciman, W. G. Relative Deprivation and Social Justice. *A Study of Attitudes to Social Inequality in Twentieth-Century England. 352 pp.*

Willmott, Peter. Adolescent Boys in East London. *230 pp.*

Willmott, Peter, and **Young, Michael.** Family and Class in a London Suburb. *202 pp. 47 tables.*

Young, Michael. Innovation and Research in Education. *192 pp.*

●**Young, Michael,** and **McGeeney, Patrick.** Learning Begins at Home. *A Study of a Junior School and its Parents. 128 pp.*

Young, Michael, and **Willmott, Peter.** Family and Kinship in East London. *Foreword by Richard M. Titmuss. 252 pp. 39 tables.*

The Symmetrical Family. *410 pp.*

Reports of the Institute for Social Studies in Medical Care

Cartwright, Ann, Hockey, Lisbeth, and **Anderson, John L.** Life Before Death. *310 pp.*

Dunnell, Karen, and **Cartwright, Ann.** Medicine Takers, Prescribers and Hoarders. *190 pp.*

Medicine, Illness and Society

General Editor W. M. Williams

Robinson, David. The Process of Becoming Ill. *142 pp.*

Stacey, Margaret, *et al.* Hospitals, Children and Their Families. *The Report of a Pilot Study. 202 pp.*

Monographs in Social Theory

General Editor Arthur Brittan

●**Barnes, B.** Scientific Knowledge and Sociological Theory. *About 200 pp.*

Bauman, Zygmunt. Culture as Praxis. *204 pp.*

● **Dixon, Keith.** Sociological Theory. *Pretence and Possibility. 142 pp.*

●**Smith, Anthony D.** The Concept of Social Change. *A Critique of the Functionalist Theory of Social Change. 208 pp.*

Routledge Social Science Journals

The British Journal of Sociology. *Edited by Terence P. Morris. Vol. 1, No. 1, March 1950 and Quarterly. Roy. 8vo. Back numbers available. An international journal with articles on all aspects of sociology.*

Economy and Society. *Vol. 1, No. 1. February 1972 and Quarterly. Metric Roy. 8vo. A journal for all social scientists covering sociology, philosophy, anthropology, economics and history. Back numbers available.*

Year Book of Social Policy in Britain, The. *Edited by Kathleen Jones. 1971. Published annually.*

Printed in Great Britain by Unwin Brothers Limited
The Gresham Press Old Woking Surrey
A member of the Staples Printing Group

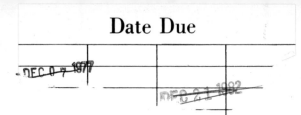

Date Due